Beyond the Gateway

Beyond the Gateway

Immigrants in a Changing America

Edited by Elżbieta M. Goździak
and Susan F. Martin

LEXINGTON BOOKS
Lanham • Boulder • New York • Toronto • Oxford

LEXINGTON BOOKS

Published in the United States of America
by Lexington Books
An imprint of The Rowman & Littlefield Publishing Group, Inc.
4501 Forbes Boulevard, Suite 200, Lanham, Maryland 20706

PO Box 317
Oxford
OX2 9RU, UK

British Library Cataloguing in Publication Information Available

Library of Congress Cataloging-in-Publication Data
Gozdziak, Elzbieta M., 1954–
    Beyond the gateway : immigrants in a changing America / Elzbieta M.
Gozdziak and   Susan F. Martin.
        p.   cm.
    Includes bibliographical references and index.
    ISBN 0-7391-0633-3 (cloth : alk. paper)—ISBN 0-7391-0636-8 (pbk. : alk.
paper)
    1. Immigrants—United States—Social conditions.   2. United
States—Emigration
    and immigration—Social aspects.   3. Assimilation (Sociology)   4. Social
    integration—United States.   5. Minorities—United States—Social
conditions.   6.
    United States—Ethnic relations.   I. Martin, Susan Forbes.   II. Title.
    JV6450.G69   2005
    304.8′73—dc22   2004025433

Printed in the United States of America

♾ ™ The paper used in this publication meets the minimum requirements of
American National Standard for Information Sciences—Permanence of Paper for
Printed Library Materials, ANSI/NISO Z39.48–1992.

Contents

Part I: Introduction

1 New Immigrant Communities and Integration   3
   Elżbieta M. Goździak

2 The Growth and Population Characteristics of
   Immigrants and Minorities in America's New
   Settlement States   19
   *Micah N. Bump, B. Lindsay Lowell, and Silje
   Pettersen*

Part II: Case Studies

3 New Immigrant Communities in the North Carolina
   Piedmont Triad: Integration Issues and Challenges   57
   Raleigh Bailey

4 Black and White and the Other: International
   Immigration and Change in Metropolitan Atlanta   87
   Art Hansen

5 Latinos, Africans, and Asians in the North Star State:
   Immigrant Communities in Minnesota   111
   Katherine Fennelly

6 From Temporary Picking to Permanent Plucking:
   Hispanic Newcomers, Integration, and Change in the
   Shenandoah Valley   137
   Micah N. Bump

7 At the Gates of the Kingdom: Latino Immigrants in
Utah, 1900 to 2003   177
Armando Solórzano

8 Newcomers in Rural America: Hispanic Immigrants in
Rogers, Arkansas   213
Andrew I. Schoenholtz

Part III: Best Practices

9 Promising Practices for Immigrant Integration
Elżbieta M. Goździak and Michael J. Melia   241

Part IV: Conclusion

10 Challenges for the Future   277
Elżbieta M. Goździak and Susan F. Martin

Index   285

About the Contributors   299

I

INTRODUCTION

1

New Immigrant Communities and Integration

Elżbieta M. Goździak

From the colonial period through the first decades of the twentieth century, European immigrants arriving in the United States followed well-established settlement patterns. Most immigrants settled in major port cities such as New York, Boston, and Chicago, but a smaller number headed west, especially after the Civil War. By the turn of the century most viable land was settled, leading immigrants to stay in the Eastern seaboard or upper Midwest to work in urban factories. Threads of continuity and discontinuity relate these historic waves to today's immigration.

By the 1980s, researchers noticed that a growing number of newcomers were moving to communities with little previous experience with immigrants.[1] Most immigrants continue to settle in the heart of few metropolitan areas, even though they have moved to "new" destinations such as central Los Angeles and Miami since 1965. Immigrants remain highly concentrated: 70 percent of immigrants in 2000 lived in just six states, 26 percent of them in California alone.[2] Yet the growth rate of immigrants in these six states has slowed considerably, from 60 percent in the 1970s to only 28 percent in the 1990s. New settlement areas outside these core immigration states, in contrast, grew by 45 percent in the 1980s and an astonishing 94 percent in the 1990s.[3]

As in the past, a few nationalities dominate, but Latinos and Asians have replaced Southern and Eastern Europeans as the predominant newcomer groups. The immigrant pioneers moving to new settlement areas tend to be Latino and to a lesser extent Asian. As a leading demographer noted, "some minorities are migrating to parts of the country where most residents have never heard Spanish or Chinese spoken, primarily suburbs, smaller metropolitan areas, and rural towns."[4] Latinos have moved primarily to Southern metropolitan areas and rural counties in Middle and Rocky Mountain states, while Asians have gravitated to the suburban metropolitan areas in new destination states.

Theorists have predicted that immigrants will continue to concentrate in the central cities of the six traditional immigration states and a few metropolitan areas. Immigrants' choices of residence, after all, are predicated less on wages than the presence of ethnic community-based support networks and enclave labor markets.[5] Of course, employers often start the process by directly recruiting foreign workers, occasionally with government assistance.

The roots of today's new settlement patterns are complex. In some cases, businesses actively recruited immigrants into new communities. During the 1980s, industries involved in the processing of beef, pork, chicken, and fish began to relocate from north central states to south central states to recruit nonunion, low-wage labor.[6] Establishing themselves in rural communities with small labor forces, processing companies have recruited immigrant workers from California and Texas, as well as directly from Mexico and Central America. Such communities as Rogers, Arkansas; Georgetown, Delaware; and Faribault, Minnesota now have sizable immigrant populations. Aggressive recruitment becomes unnecessary because immigrant networks attract newcomers.

Agriculture has also anchored many new settlement areas as growers in labor-intensive crops have cast a broader net for workers. The Latinization of agriculture has characterized the apple groves of Washington State, the mushroom sheds of New England, the grape and row crops of southern California, and the orange groves of southern Florida. A 1986 amnesty for nearly three million unauthorized workers created several settlement areas with distinct demographic and employment patterns.[7] Legal status created job stability if not income security, allowing families to reunite with relatives who had been living overseas and develop stronger roots in their new communities.

In other cases, government programs have dispersed newcomers to communities with growing economies and appropriate support networks. The Office of Refugee Resettlement (ORR), for example, provides grants to voluntary resettlement agencies to place newly arrived refugees in "preferred communities where there is a history of low welfare utilization and a favorable earned income potential relative to the cost of living."[8] ORR has funded projects including the relocation of unemployed Hmong refugees in the central valley of California to towns with lower unemployment rates and the resettlement of the Sudanese "Lost Boys" in areas with services for unaccompanied refugee minors. As a result of such initiatives, new immigrant communities have sprouted in such places as Fargo, North Dakota; Greensboro, North Carolina; and Lincoln, Nebraska.

While these new settlement areas have been the subject of significant public debate,[9] the effects of immigration on policy and programmatic responses in local communities have received little attention. Journalists[10] and community leaders[11] have begun to discuss approaches of different communities, but the need remains for systematic analysis and evaluation of best practices adopted in new settlement areas to address the influx of immigrants and their impact on the host society. The policies widely adopted by traditional gateway communities with long-standing immigrant populations and resources are not always transferable to new settlement areas. Many of the new immigrant communities have been experimenting with different models, searching for one that meets their needs.

INTEGRATION: A PERENNIAL CHALLENGE

Despite changes in settlement patterns, immigrants today struggle no less than their nineteenth-century predecessors with integration and the question of how to preserve their ethnic identity. Some authors have argued that the modern phenomena of multiculturalism and transnational communities diminish incentives to participate in their new communities, but immigrants today still confront the tension between defending the old and embracing the new. Particularly in new settlement areas with little previous exposure to immigrants, the issue also demands the attention of the host society, which must strike a balance between engaging newcomers and developing tolerance of differences. In this volume we conceptualize integration as sustained interaction between and among newcomers and host communities.

Although the term "integration" gained currency only recently in the policy community, it represents an evolution in scholarship more than any change in the immigrant experience. Most of the terms used by migration scholars over the last century to describe the immigrants' construction of new lives have been related to an outsider-insider dichotomy, conjuring a process of several degrees that doesn't necessarily end with inclusion.[12] Indeed, a vocabulary that included such terms as assimilation, acculturation, incorporation, and socioeconomic adjustment seemed "wedded to a normative vision of societies as culturally homogeneous, in which residents born in other places are exceptional rather than customary participants in economic, social, and cultural life."[13] Assimilation and acculturation, terms often used interchangeably, were first introduced to examine the cultural and social changes set off by immigrants' second journey: their incorporation—or integration—into mainstream American life.[14] The term assimilation, which implies a willful departure from the culture of the sending country, has fallen into disrepute of late.[15]

Popular conceptions of integration reflect its traditional place in the academy, where sociologists, demographers, and labor economists have long dominated the discourse and research agenda. As Mary Waters observes, immigration and immigrant integration have been at the core of American sociology since the early twentieth century, when the Chicago school of sociology studied immigrants' impact on American cities.[16] Sociologists today maintain interests in assimilation, residential segregation, occupational specialization, marginality, and ethnic and race relations. Not surprisingly, "immigration has long been a major topic in American history, given immigration's critical role in the making of the United States."[17] Historians have pursued comparative research on assimilation processes, the transplantation of immigrant cultures to America, and increasingly, the role of race in newcomers' adaptation.[18]

In contrast, anthropologists, psychologists, legal scholars and scholars of the health sciences have played a less visible role in the field. Anthropologists only recently adopted immigrant integration as a legitimate topic of study.[19] They have focused on transnational communities, emphasizing the migrants' links with their home societies, the continuities as well as changes in immigrants' cultural and social patterns, the role of immigrant networks, and the complexity of immigrant identities.[20] The same is true in the field of political science where, according to Zoldberg, immigration generated very little interest until recently.[21] Political scientists have demonstrated concern primarily with issues related to political incorporation and civic engagement of immigrants.

Due perhaps to the discipline's long-established place in the field, sociological approaches to assimilation are influencing scholars engaged in the study of immigrant incorporation, whatever their academic background.[22] As the foreign-born population in the United States has grown, so has its popularity as a research subject, with each of the social sciences applying its own tools to grasp the complexity of the integration experience. One newly popular theory, for example, is segmented assimilation, which offers a theoretical framework for understanding the process by which the new second generation becomes incorporated into the system of stratification in the host society. As researchers cross disciplinary boundaries, they draw on other fields and contribute to the emerging subfield of immigration.

COMPETING THEORIES

For much of the past century, the dominant analytical framework for immigrant integration was the great transatlantic European migration, which changed the face of the United States in the early 1900s. The political context dominated by two world wars reinforced the conception of integration as a linear process of movement away from the culture and social relations of the sending country. After World War I, pressure for Americanization equated assimilation with acculturation into an Anglo-American mold. In the years following World War II, imagery of a melting pot offered an idealistic vision of American society and identity. After a period of marginalization in residential, linguistic, and economic terms—particularly acute for the first generation of immigrants—the second or third generation would finally incorporate itself into the mainstream, leaving behind the social structures of the country and culture of origin.

The persistent theme in the assimilation and acculturation theories was that immigration sets in motion a process of change that is "directional, indeed unilinear, nonreversible, and continuous."[23] As Suarez-Orozco points out, the dominant narratives of immigrant assimilation were based on three assumptions: that a "clean break" from the country of origin was needed before the process of Americanization could begin; that immigrants would eventually join the mainstream dominated by a homogeneous middle-class society of European ancestry; and that this transition was inherently good for the immigrants.

For decades now, assimilation theory has come under intensive critique, dismissed by many as imposing ethnocentric and patronizing demands on minorities struggling to retain their cultural heritage.[24] In a 1945 study, Warner and Sole examined integration in New Haven,

Connecticut, and described immigrant groups as "unlearning" their inferior cultural traits in order to "successfully learn the new way of life necessary for full acceptance."[25] They also correlated the potential for speedy integration with a hierarchy of racial and cultural acceptability, ranging from English-speaking Protestants at the top to "Negroes and Negroid mixtures" at the bottom. The ethnocentricity could hardly be more evident in this discussion, typical of mid-century viewpoints.

Still, many scholars have attempted to redefine assimilation to salvage its usefulness for the study of new immigration patterns. Alba and Nee, for example, hold that the concept is useful to understand the integration of many immigrant groups, even if it cannot be regarded as a universal outcome of the American immigrant experience.[26] They reject assimilation as a state-imposed program aimed at eradicating minority cultures, but defend it as a social process that occurs spontaneously through interaction between minority and majority groups. Many sociologists have viewed assimilation as an inevitable and necessary process for permanent migrants, leading logically to the incorporation of immigrants and their descendants as new citizens.

In an early analysis of assimilation, Park and Burgess, members of the Chicago school of sociology, described "a process of interpenetration and fusion in which persons and groups acquire the memories, sentiments, and attitudes of other persons and groups and, by sharing their experience and history, are incorporated with them in a common cultural life."[27] This 1921 definition equates assimilation with a social process that brings ethnic minorities into the mainstream of American life. Park later advocated another definition that implied less cultural absorption by newcomers, describing social assimilation as a "process or processes by which people of diverse racial origins and different cultural heritages, occupying a common territory, achieve a cultural solidarity sufficient at least to sustain a national existence."[28] Later still he described it as an end stage in a race relations cycle of "contact, competition, accommodation, and eventual assimilation."[29]

The early sociological literature displayed no small amount of confusion over the concept of assimilation, worsened perhaps by its varied categorizations. Milton Gordon's *Assimilation in American Life*, published in 1964, systematically dissects the process into several steps of a linear model. One of the first steps is "structural assimilation," the acceptance of members of the group into the institutions of the host society. At that point other forms of assimilation will follow; prejudice and discrimination will decline, intermarriage will increase and the minority's separate identity will fade. This two-group framework, however, does not extend to relationships between members of different ethnic groups. It also omits important forms of assimilation including occupational mobility and economic integration.

Research in recent decades has called this theory into question, suggesting that immigrants and their children do not uniformly cease to identify with their origins. A theory of straight-line assimilation popularized by Gans and Standberg in the 1970s envisions a process unfolding in a sequence of generational stages. Each new generation, in their theory, represents on average a new stage of adjustment to the host society, moving toward more complete assimilation as they step away from their ethnic origins. As each generation faces a new set of issues in its relationship with the host society, its response to the challenges creates a distinctive pattern of integration. They point out that immigrants may nevertheless retain their ethnic identities in a "symbolic form," even as they abandon cultural traits associated with their countries of origin.

Scholars have increasingly recognized that immigrants adapting to American life follow a number of different paths. Some cultural traits were not abandoned at all by the immigrants, but incorporated into the mainstream culture. More recently, Gans has warned that the discussion of whether the descendants of the "old" European migration and members of the "new" mainly non-European migration are assimilating or retaining ties to their ethnic heritage was becoming polarized. "As a result, what is in reality a range of adaptations is sometimes being turned into a dichotomy, and a moral one, with the alleged assimilationists, and particularly 'straight-line theory,' becoming the villains in a researchers' morality play."[30]

As much as the characteristics of immigrants themselves, theories of immigrant reception and integration today consider the contours of the host society. Jeffrey G. Reitz identifies four dimensions of host societies that influence the course of integration: preexisting ethnic or race relations within the host population; differences in labor markets and related institutions; the impact of governmental policies and programs (including immigration policy, integration policies, and policies regulating social institutions); and globalization.[31]

MEASURES OF INTEGRATION

The United States is among the few postindustrial democracies in the world where immigration is at once history and destiny.[32] As a consequence, immigration scholarship and immigration policy debate are integral to the academic and public discourse. Every new immigration wave revives the perennial question: How do the "new" immigrants fare in comparison with the "old"?

Conventionally, cultural integration has been equated with immigrants' sense of belonging, measured by the quality of interaction between newcomers and established residents. Socioeconomic assimilation has been determined in terms of socioeconomic standing relative to the host society, measured by indicators such as education, occupation, and income. Alba and Golden have used data on intermarriage to measure the pace of assimilation. Incorporation, of course, is an extraordinarily complex process, shaped by factors including human and social capital and the characteristics of sending and receiving countries.

In the 1990s, a heated discussion emerged over the extent to which the integration of the post-1965 immigrants parallels the assimilation processes of immigrants who came from Southern and Eastern Europe between 1880 and 1920. Many expressed concerns that newcomers were not 'Americanizing' as thoroughly as a century ago, clinging to their own traditions in an age of multiculturalism and dual nationality. Others cited low naturalization rates, accusing new immigrants of plundering the United States for jobs without investing in its democratic experiment. Foner points out that fears of newcomers not forming allegiances to the United States are nothing new and any such differences across time are based on myth.[33] Even though naturalization rates today are low, particularly among Latin American and Caribbean immigrants, rates are still higher for many major new immigrant groups than they were for eastern and southern Europeans at the time of the last great wave.

Perceptions of immigrants as detached from their new host communities owes in part to the rise of transnational communities, whose members retain ties to the sending country through frequent travel, communication, remittances and other linkages. Even while sinking roots in their new countries, they remain powerful protagonists in the social, economic and political spheres at home. As Castles observes, the phenomenon of transnational communities is not new, despite the novelty of the terminology.[34] Migrants have long preserved economic, political and cultural links to their home societies even as they built new lives for themselves in the United States. Going back to ancient times, the diaspora concept has been used for peoples displaced by force, trading groups, and labor migrants. Then as now, transnational migrants confronted ambiguity in defining "home." The greatest difference today is immigrants are instantly transnationalized due to global integration, improved transportation and accessible real-time electronic communication.

As newcomers continue discovering ways to stay connected with their home countries, it is possible that transnational consciousness could become more widespread and even define migrant belonging in the future. At the level of government, many sending countries in the 1990s enacted dual nationality laws, allowing immigrants to become U.S. citizens without losing privileges in their native lands. Transnational identities take on a variety of forms, with theorists divided on the question of where loyalty lies for such communities. Some portray transmigrants as building hybrid identities across cultural boundaries. Others argue that despite the sophistication of their linkages, such migrants primarily feel solidarity with others of their own ethnicity in their homelands and elsewhere. Castles has argued that successful transnational strategies are likely to involve adaptation to multiple social settings as well as cross-cultural competence, rendering the notion of primary loyalty obsolete in a mobile world.

The growing multiculturalism of the United States has prompted concerns similar to those raised by transnational communities, namely that immigrants are losing incentives to integrate into the broader society. Not only do today's new arrivals find a nation more racially, ethnically, and culturally diverse; they frequently have little contact with the increasingly remote protestant middle class of European ancestry. The point of reference for many immigrants becomes instead the cultural sensibilities and social practices of the more established Latinos and Asians. For this reason, many researchers have focused on identity at the level of the global city rather than the nation-state, with local citizenship interpreted as a substitute for waning political influence at the national level. In many ways, the growing diversity indirectly supports processes of integration. The increasing percentage of people of color in the United States, for example, pressures employers and schools to accommodate a more heterogeneous population. In a cultural sense, ethnic neighborhoods and social structures also create a milieu supportive of ethnic distinctiveness.

Cultural diversity at the local level, however, does not guarantee harmony among ethnic groups. Certain groups, both new and established, have access to positions of status and power while others might be excluded entirely from the labor market. "Processes of differentiation based on class, race, gender and legal status lead to complex hierarchies of privilege in global cities."[35] Massey and Denton have written that the spatial distribution of groups is a reflection of their human capital, with life in highly segregated areas limiting economic opportunities in the wider society. Indicators such as education and occupational mobility reveal that even though a multicultural society can create pockets of ethnic homogeneity, incentives to connect with the wider society remain strong. Integration does not end in this context; it merely takes on different dimensions.

METHODOLOGY

In 2002, the Institute for the Study of International Migration at Georgetown University embarked on a multiyear project to study integration in areas without recent experience with foreign-born newcomers. A multidisciplinary team of researchers explored opportunities, problems, and solutions to the social and economic integration of immigrants in these areas and identified promising practices and creative strategies to facilitate integration. The goal of the project was to inform policymaking and provide examples for new immigrant communities of how others have adapted to similar challenges.

To identify the most fruitful locations for this study of new settlement areas, we conducted a mapping exercise to understand the geography of the rapid immigrant growth. New growth areas at the state and county level became apparent through a comparison of data on Hispanics and Asians from the U.S. Census in 1990 and 2000. The mapping of the new settlement areas was an important first step in choosing case studies for further analysis, but it could not provide clues to where best practices might be found. We used existing literature, particularly local newspaper accounts, and recommendations from knowledgeable informants at the state and local levels as well as members of our Advisory Board to further inform our site selection. We ultimately selected five case studies: Winchester, Virginia; the Triad, North Carolina; Atlanta and Chamblee, Georgia; Faribault, Minnesota; and Salt Lake City and Park City, Utah.

The next stage of our research included fieldwork in the selected sites, which involved a combination of ethnographic interviews, focus group discussions, and participant observation. Many public officials and representatives of local governments were interviewed. Other subjects included community leaders and activists, health care providers and public health officials, representatives of faith-based organizations, directors and caseworkers of different refugee resettlement programs, and representatives of civic groups.

The research team conducted week-long site visits to each location. The team included two researchers based at Georgetown University—an anthropologist and a Latin American studies specialist—as well as four "site researchers," seasoned social scientists conducting research on different immigrant and refugee communities in their respective states. These "site researchers" included two anthropologists, a public policy researcher, and an ethnic studies scholar. Two members of the research team were also immigrants themselves, from Poland and Mexico, respectively. The primary focus of this research was to identify best—or as one of the team members put it: "promising, good, not so bad"—practices adopted in the communities under study to facilitate the integration of newcomers and mitigate any negative impacts the influx of immigrants might have on local communities.

The findings of the study are presented in four parts. The next chapter, which completes the introductory section, presents detailed findings from the mapping exercise. It also draws on existing literature and analysis of secondary data to draw general conclusions about not only the movement but also the socioeconomic characteristics of immigrants to new settlement areas. An examination of local-level phenomena reveals that although the immigrant population might be relatively small in new settlement states, high rates of growth create daunting integration challenges.

The second part, based on our original research in five newcomer communities, represents the core of the volume. The case studies followed a flexible outline to capture the unique characteristics and issues emerging in each state. Indeed, the framework of the individual chapters was frequently driven by the nature of the focus area's most pressing obstacles.

A study of Greensboro, North Carolina, identified a Hispanic population that began growing rapidly during a boom in construction, food processing, and other industries in the 1990s, quickly becoming the area's predominant immigrant group. The pace of the growth and the need for bilingual services have posed many problems, which become all the more urgent because Hispanic laborers represent the core of many sectors of the North Carolina economy. In addition to the Hispanic immigrants, Greensboro is also home to a smaller but more diversified refugee population. The case study emphasized the role of

AmeriCorps members, local university students involved in community service, and the Quaker philosophy in facilitating positive relationships between newcomers and established residents.

The Atlanta area also witnessed a sudden increase in ethnic diversity over the last two decades as the Hispanic population grew and Asians arrived largely through the federal refugee resettlement program. In an area where most efforts at improving race relations targeted interaction between blacks and whites, tensions emerged with the introduction of newcomers. The case study, however, describes how the Atlanta suburb of Chamblee overcame some of the resentment by investing in a multicultural neighborhood as a cultural and economic resource for the wider community.

The case study of Faribault, Minnesota, encapsulates some of the challenges faced by immigrants seeking entry to a largely homogeneous population. Although the newcomer communities were smaller than those explored elsewhere in the volume, the heavy secondary migration by refugees and the increased settlement of agricultural workers received a disproportionate amount of attention. Immigrant groups in this case study played a major role in revitalizing dilapidated urban centers and bolstering the local economy. Yet they still contend with xenophobia and the accusations of established residents that they threaten local jobs.

In Winchester, Virginia, Hispanics began arriving in great numbers in the 1980s as corporate oligopolies emerged in the processing of beef, pork, and chicken. As Hispanics who once worked as migrant laborers began to settle in the area, the state failed to adjust its services to accommodate the new residents, leading to gaps in health insurance coverage among other areas. The case study emphasizes the development and evolution of an advocacy group created by outreach workers to better address the needs of the newcomer community. It offers a powerful example of a bottom-up approach to integration.

The final case study focuses on religion as a barrier to integration for non-Mormon immigrants to the state of Utah. The foreign-born population has grown dramatically in the state, with Latinos now comprising nearly 20 percent of Salt Lake City residents. Yet most Hispanic immigrants, who arrived in pursuit of jobs including many created by the 2002 Olympics, have not fared nearly as well as their Mormon counterparts. Issues highlighted by the case study include the exploitation of low-wage laborers and racial tensions.

The third section of the volume reviews and critically evaluates many of the best practices identified in the course of our fieldwork.

These included programs facilitating English-language acquisition, access to culturally sensitive and linguistically appropriate health care services, vocational training, and community development. In the hope that these practices might prove useful elsewhere, they are also presented in more detail in a companion volume, *New Immigrant Communities: A Handbook of Promising Practices Facilitating Immigrant Integration.*[36] The fourth and final section summarizes some of the obstacles that appeared in several case studies. It highlights the challenges to integration faced by policymakers, service providers, community leaders, and the community members themselves.

NOTES

1. B. Lindsay Lowell, "Regional and Local Effects of Immigration: The President's Comprehensive Triennial Report on Immigration" (Washington, DC: U.S. Government Printing Office, 1989).

2. Dianne A. Schmidley, "Profile of the Foreign-Born Population in the United States: 2000," U.S. Census Bureau, Current Population Reports, Series P23-206 (Washington, DC: U.S. Government Printing Office, 2001).

3. Jeffrey Passel and Wendy Zimmerman, "Are Immigrants Leaving California? Settlement Patterns of Immigrants in the Late 1990s," paper presented at the meeting of the Population Association of America, Los Angeles, CA, 2000.

4. William H. Frey, "The Diversity Myth" *American Demographics* 20, no. 6 (June 1998): 38–43.

5. Alejandro Portes and Rubén Rumbaut, *Immigrant America: A Portrait* (Los Angeles: University of California Press, 1996).

6. Michael J. Brodway and Terry Ward, "Recent Changes in the Structure and Location of the U.S. Meatpacking Industry," *Geography* 75, no. 1 (1990): 76–79.

7. B. Lindsay Lowell, "Circular Mobility, Migrant Communities, and Policy Restrictions: Unauthorized Flows from Mexico," in *Migration, Population Structure, and Redistribution Policies*, ed. C. Goldsheider (Boulder, CO.: Westview Press, 1992), 137–58.

8. ORR website www.acf.dhhs.gov/programs/orr (accessed March 8, 2004).

9. See James H. Johnson, Karen D. Johnson-Webb, and Walter C. Farrell Jr., "New Emerging Hispanic Communities in the United States: A Spatial Analysis of Settlement Patterns, In-Migration Fields, and Social Receptivity," in *Immigration and Opportunity: Race, Ethnicity, and Employment in the United States*, ed. Frank D. Bean and Stephanie Bell-Rose (New York: Russell Sage Foundation, 1999).

10. In the summer of 2002, the *Atlanta Journal-Constitution* ran a series of articles on newcomers settling in metropolitan Atlanta.

11. Iraqi, Bosnian, and Sudanese community leaders came together to discuss integration challenges of refugees from their countries during ORR-sponsored

conferences held in Detroit, Michigan; Washington, D.C.; and Baltimore, Maryland.

12. Rogers Brubaker, "The Return of Assimilation? Changing Perspectives on Immigration and Its Sequels in France, Germany, and the United States," *Ethnic and Racial Studies* 24 (2001): 531–48.

13. Brian Ray, "Immigrant Integration: Building to Opportunity," October 1, 2002, Migration Information Source, www.migrationinformation.org/Feature.

14. See, among others, Robert E. Park and Ernest W. Burgess, *Introduction to the Science of Sociology* (Chicago: University of Chicago Press, 1965); Milton M. Gordon, *Assimilation in American Life: The Role of Race, Religion, and National Origins* (New York: Oxford University Press, 1964); and Richard Alba and Victor Nee, "Rethinking Assimilation Theory for a New Era of Immigration," *International Migration Review* 31, no. 4 (winter 1997): 826–74.

15. Nathan Glazer, "Is Assimilation Dead?" *The Annals of the American Academy of Social and Political Sciences* 530 (1993): 122–36.

16. Mary Waters, "Sociology and the Study of Immigration," *American Behavioral Scientist* 42, no. 9 (June/July 1999): 1264–68.

17. Ruben G. Rumbaut, Nancy Foner, and Steven J. Gold, "Introduction: Immigration and Immigration Research in the United States," *American Behavioral Scientist* 42, no. 9 (June/July1999): 1258–64.

18. For a more detailed discussion of the social scientific study of immigration, including immigrant integration, see the special issue of the *American Behavioral Scientist* 42, no. 9 (June/July 1999).

19. The Committee on Refugee Issues (CORI) was established within the American Anthropological Association (AAA) in 1988, and it expanded its mandate to include immigrants only in 1996.

20. Nancy Foner, "Anthropology and the Study of Immigration," *The American Behavioral Scientist* 42, no. 9 (June/July 1999): 1268–71.

21. Aristide Zoldberg, "The Politics of Immigration Policy: An Externalist Perspective," *American Behavioral Scientist* 42, no. 9 (June/July 1999): 1276–79.

22. Rumbaut, Foner, and Gold, "Immigration and Immigration Research."

23. Marcelo M. Suárez-Orozco, "Everything You Ever Wanted to Know about Assimilation but Were Afraid to Ask," *Daedalus* 129, no. 4 (fall 2000): 1–30.

24. Alba and Nee, "Rethinking Assimilation Theory."

25. W. L. Warner and L. Sole, *The Social Systems of American Ethnic Groups* (New Haven, CT: Yale University Press, 1945), 285.

26. Alba and Nee, "Rethinking Assimilation Theory."

27. Robert E. Park and E. Burgess, *Introduction to the Science of Sociology* (1921; repr., Chicago: University of Chicago Press, 1969), 735.

28. Robert E. Park, "Assimilation, Social," in *Encyclopedia of Social Sciences*, ed. E. Seligman and A. Johnson (New York: Macmillian, 1930), 281.

29. Robert E. Park, *Race and Culture* (Glencoe, IL: Free Press, 1950).

30. Herbert J. Gans, "Toward a Reconciliation of 'Assimilation' and 'Pluralism': The Interplay of Acculturation and Ethnic Retention," *International Migration Review* 31, no. 4 (winter 1997): 875–92.

31. Jeffrey G. Reitz, "Host Societies and the Reception of Immigrants:

Research Themes, Emerging Theories and Methodological Issues," *International Migration Review* 36, no. 4 (2002): 1005–20.

32. Suárez-Orozco, "Everything You Ever Wanted to Know."

33. Nancy Foner, "Immigrant Commitment to America, Then and Now: Myths and Realities," *Citizenship Studies* 5, no. 1 (2001): 27–40.

34. Stephen Castles, "Migration and Community Formation under Conditions of Globalization," *International Migration Review* 36, no. 4 (winter 2002): 1143–69.

35. Castles, "Migration and Community Formation."

36. Elżbieta M. Goździak and Micah N. Bump, *New Immigrant Communities: A Handbook of Promising Practices Facilitating Immigrant Integration* (Lanham, MD: Lexington Books, forthcoming).

2

The Growth and Population Characteristics of Immigrants and Minorities in America's New Settlement States

Micah N. Bump, B. Lindsay Lowell, and Silje Pettersen

Immigrants came to the United States in record numbers during the 1990s. While the majority settled in traditional receiving states, many others moved to states that had seen few immigrants since the late nineteenth century. These "new settlement" destinations stretch from the southeast in Georgia and North Carolina, then across the Great Plains to Nevada and Minnesota. As noted by William Frey, a leading demographer of the geography of immigration, "some minorities are migrating to parts of the country where most residents have never heard Spanish or Chinese being spoken."[1] In another break with tradition, immigrants were also moving to suburbs, smaller metropolitan areas, and rural towns.

As in the past, immigrants and their children will remain the major force behind population growth. Their choice of new settlement states is redefining the American map. The U.S. Census Bureau forecasts that today's immigrant minority populations will grow more rapidly than native whites or African Americans. The foreign born, largely Latinos and Asians, are younger and have more children than natives. If current trends persist, the native white population will be a minority by 2050, although it is already quickly becoming a minority in many traditional receiving metro areas and states.[2] In the new settlement states, the growth of immigrant populations will likely create significant minority populations for the first time.

This chapter presents census data on the population growth and socioeconomic character of today's immigrant population in both traditional and new settlement states. At a state and county level, it maps the growth of the foreign born and the total Latino and Asian populations, two principal U.S. minority groups with large immigrant elements. The chapter then analyzes the characteristics of the foreign born, comparing them with the native population. Since the foreign born are a heterogeneous group, the Latino and Asian immigrant populations are considered separately for selected characteristics. We want to know whether immigrants in the new settlement areas look different from those in the traditional states. The comparisons focus on age, gender, English-language ability, years of formal education, labor force participation, home ownership, poverty rates, and industry of employment. The analysis of these variables highlights differences between the populations and underscores the key attributes of the newcomers, all of which have implications for the formulation of integration policies and programs at state and local levels.

DEFINING IMMIGRATIONS' TRADITIONAL, NEW, AND MODERATE GROWTH STATES

The foreign-born population in the United States grew by eleven million people, or 58 percent, during the 1990s. Census data show that as of the year 2000, the population of the United States included thirty-one million foreign born, representing 11 percent of the total population. As table 2.1 shows, all fifty states and the District of Columbia experienced an increase in their foreign-born populations.[3] This study explores this absolute growth in terms of states, classifying them as traditional, new, and moderate growth states.

Traditional states averaged 56 percent growth. The largest absolute increases of the foreign-born population occurred in the traditional states of California, Florida, Illinois, New Jersey, New York, and Texas. These traditional states recorded the highest absolute *numerical* growth in foreign-born population in the 1990s, but not the most rapid percentage growth. In fact, the growth rate of the foreign-born population in the traditional states slowed while the growth rate accelerated in the new settlement states. Although 87 percent of net foreign-born growth in the 1980s took place in the traditional states, only 60 percent of foreign-born growth occurred in those states in the 1990s.

New settlement states had growth of more than 100 percent. During the 1990s, the foreign born increasingly moved to states without a recent history of immigration. The 2000 census data indicate that states mainly in the south and west emerged as more popular destinations than traditional states for the foreign born. Table 2.1 shows that during the 1990s, nineteen "new settlement" states experienced extremely high rates of growth, defined here as net increases in their foreign-born populations of more than 100 percent. Figure 2.1 shows that these states span a wide band in the southeast, Midwest, and Rocky Mountain regions. The fastest growth of foreign-born population occurred in North Carolina, Georgia, and Nevada, which experienced growth rates of 274 percent, 233 percent, and 202 percent, respectively.

Moderate-growth states had growth of less than 100 percent. Outside of the traditional and new settlement areas, twenty-six states can be classified as having moderate rates of population growth. These "moderate growth" states have relatively small foreign-born populations and experienced immigrant growth rates of less than 100 percent during the 1990s. Despite their lower statewide growth rates, many local communities within the moderate-growth states witnessed significant increases in their foreign-born populations. They face many of the same integration challenges as the new settlement states. This is the case for Winchester, Virginia, a small community that experienced rapid immigration growth during the 1990s even though Virginia itself could not be classified a new settlement state.

Slower growth does not mean small numbers. Although their rate of growth slowed during the 1990s, traditional migration states still retain the bulk of the total foreign-born population. More than two-thirds—69 percent—of the foreign born resided in the traditional states in 2000. As can be seen in table 2.2, California alone held 28 percent of the entire foreign-born population, while New York held another 12 percent. In contrast, the rapidly growing new settlement states together had slightly more than 13 percent of the national foreign-born population at the end of the last decade. The remaining 18 percent lived in the twenty-six moderately growing states.

The foreign-born populations in the traditional states are so large

Table 2.1   **Ranking of States: Traditional, New Settlement, and Moderate Growth**

Traditional, New Settlement, and Moderate-Growth States	Total population: 2000	Total Foreign-Born Population: 2000	Total Foreign-Born Population: 1990	Absolute Change in Foreign-Born Population: 1990–2000	Percent Change in Foreign-Born Population: 1990–2000
Total USA	**281,421,906**	**31,107,889**	**19,767,316**	**11,340,573**	**57.4**
Traditional States					
California	33,871,648	8,864,255	6,458,825	2,405,430	37.2
Florida	15,982,378	2,670,828	1,662,601	1,008,227	60.6
Illinois	12,419,293	1,529,058	952,272	576,786	60.6
New Jersey	8,414,350	1,476,327	966,610	509,717	52.7
New York	18,976,457	3,868,133	2,851,861	1,016,272	35.6
Texas	20,851,820	2,899,642	1,524,436	1,375,206	90.2
Total	**110,515,946**	**21,308,243**	**14,416,605**	**6,891,638**	**56.2**
New Settlement States					
Alabama	4,447,100	87,772	43,533	44,239	101.6
Arizona	5,130,632	656,183	278,205	377,978	135.9
Arkansas	2,673,400	73,690	24,867	48,823	196.3
Colorado	4,301,261	369,903	142,434	227,469	159.7
Delaware	783,600	44,898	22,275	22,623	101.6
Georgia	8,186,453	577,273	173,126	404,147	233.4
Idaho	1,293,953	64,080	28,905	35,175	121.7
Iowa	2,926,324	91,085	43,316	47,769	110.3
Kansas	2,688,418	134,735	62,840	71,895	114.4
Kentucky	4,041,769	80,271	34,119	46,152	135.3
Minnesota	4,919,479	260,463	113,039	147,424	130.4
Nebraska	1,711,263	74,638	28,198	46,440	164.7
Nevada	1,998,257	316,593	104,828	211,765	202.0
North Carolina	4,049,313	430,000	115,077	314,923	273.7
Oklahoma	3,450,654	131,747	65,489	66,258	101.2
Oregon	3,421,399	289,702	139,307	150,395	108.0
South Carolina	4,012,012	115,978	49,964	66,014	132.1
Tennessee	5,689,283	159,004	59,114	99,890	169.0
Utah	2,233,169	158,664	58,600	100,064	170.8
Total	**71,957,739**	**4,116,679**	**1,587,236**	**2,529,443**	**159.1**
Moderate-Growth States					
Alaska	626,932	37,170	24,814	12,356	49.8
Connecticut	3,405,565	369,967	279,383	90,584	32.4
District of Columbia	572,059	73,561	58,887	14,674	24.9
Hawaii	1,211,537	212,229	162,704	49,525	30.4
Indiana	6,080,485	186,534	94,263	92,271	97.9
Louisiana	4,468,976	115,885	87,407	28,478	32.6
Maine	1,274,923	36,691	36,296	395	1.1

Table 2.1   (Continued)

Traditional, New Settlement, and Moderate-Growth States	Total population: 2000	Total Foreign-Born Population: 2000	Total Foreign-Born Population: 1990	Absolute Change in Foreign-Born Population: 1990–2000	Percent Change in Foreign-Born Population: 1990–2000
Maryland	5,296,486	518,315	313,494	204,821	65.3
Massachusetts	6,349,097	772,983	573,733	199,250	34.7
Michigan	9,938,444	523,589	355,393	168,196	47.3
Mississippi	2,844,658	39,908	20,383	19,525	95.8
Missouri	5,595,211	151,196	83,633	67,563	80.8
Montana	902,195	16,396	13,779	2,617	19.0
New Hampshire	1,235,786	54,154	41,193	12,961	31.5
New Mexico	1,819,046	149,606	80,514	69,092	85.8
North Dakota	642,200	12,114	9,388	2,726	29.0
Ohio	11,353,140	339,279	259,673	79,606	30.7
Pennsylvania	12,281,054	508,291	369,316	138,975	37.6
Rhode Island	1,048,319	119,277	95,088	24,189	25.4
South Dakota	754,844	13,495	7,731	5,764	74.6
Vermont	608,827	23,245	17,544	5,701	32.5
Virginia	7,078,515	570,279	311,809	258,470	82.9
Washington	5,894,121	614,457	322,144	292,313	90.7
West Virginia	1,808,344	19,390	15,712	3,678	23.4
Wisconsin	5,363,675	193,751	121,547	72,204	59.4
Wyoming	493,782	11,205	7,647	3,558	46.5
Total	**98,948,221**	**5,682,967**	**3,763,475**	**1,919,492**	**55.9**

Source: U.S. Census 1990 and U.S. Census 2000

that immigrants make up more of the total (native and immigrant) populations than they do in other states (see table 2.2). More than one-quarter of all Californians are foreign born while about one-fifth of all New Yorkers are foreign born. As a whole, the foreign-born population comprises 19.1 percent of the total population in the traditional states, more than three times the density of immigrants in other states. Immigrants also comprise a significant share of some of the moderate-growth states like Hawaii, whose population is approximately 18 percent foreign born. This observation casts doubt on the notion that immigrants have a larger presence in the high-growth new settlement states than elsewhere. What is truly remarkable about the new settlement states is the rapid pace of immigration in just the 1990s. Where communities were often homogenously white, or perhaps white and African American, such communities now include new and growing minority populations.

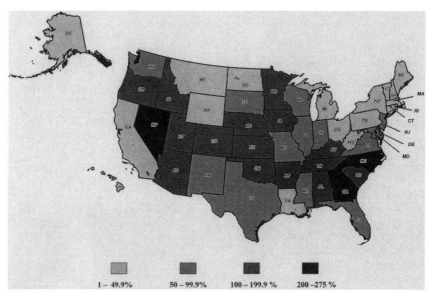

Figure 2.1   Percent Growth of Immigrant Population, 1990 to 2000
Source: U.S. Census 1990 and 2000

THE NEW MAP FOR LATINOS
AND ASIAN MINORITIES

The new minorities are "non-Anglos" who are generally either Latino or Asian. These umbrella terms can hide great differences among individuals of varied ancestries or countries of birth, but U.S. statistics are generally available only for major race/ethnic groups and they do convey a rough sense of commonalities. The distribution of these minority groups also varies widely from state to state. Given this project's focus on immigration, nativity (place of birth) assumes primary importance, but the total composition of minority groups is also an important part of the evolving mosaic of traditional, new settlement, and moderate-growth regions.

Most American immigrants are Latino or Asian. Foreign-born Latinos and, to a lesser degree, foreign-born Asians have comprised the vast majority of the foreign-born population, regardless of its growth rate. Nearly 80 percent of the immigrants living in the United States are either of Latin American or Asian origin. Latino immigrants, as can be seen in figure 2.2, made up about 52 percent of the foreign-born population in the year 2000. Mexicans alone, who represent more

Table 2.2   Percent of State and National Population by Nativity and State, 2000

Traditional, New Settlement, and Moderate-Growth States	Percent of State Population			Percent of National Population		
	Native Born	Foreign Born	Total	Native Born	Foreign Born	Total
Total USA	**89.0**	**11.0**	**100**	**100**	**100**	**100**
Traditional States						
California	74.0	26.0	100	10.0	28.4	12.0
Florida	83.5	16.5	100	5.3	8.5	5.7
Illinois	87.7	12.3	100	4.3	4.9	4.4
New Jersey	82.4	17.6	100	2.8	4.8	3.0
New York	80.0	20.0	100	6.1	12.3	6.7
Texas	86.2	13.8	100	7.2	9.3	7.4
Total	**80.9**	**19.1**	**100**	**35.7**	**68.3**	**39.3**
New Settlement States						
Alabama	98.0	2.0	100	1.7	0.3	1.6
Arizona	87.3	12.7	100	1.8	2.1	1.8
Arkansas	97.2	2.8	100	1.0	0.2	1.0
Colorado	91.1	8.9	100	1.6	1.2	1.5
Delaware	94.7	5.3	100	0.3	0.1	0.3
Georgia	93.0	7.0	100	3.0	1.8	2.9
Idaho	95.0	5.0	100	0.5	0.2	0.5
Iowa	97.1	2.9	100	1.1	0.3	1.0
Kansas	94.8	5.2	100	1.0	0.4	1.0
Kentucky	98.0	2.0	100	1.6	0.3	1.4
Minnesota	94.7	5.3	100	1.9	0.8	1.7
Nebraska	95.6	4.4	100	0.7	0.2	0.6
Nevada	84.7	15.3	100	0.7	1.0	0.7
North Carolina	94.6	5.4	100	3.0	1.4	2.9
Oklahoma	96.1	3.9	100	1.3	0.4	1.2
Oregon	91.3	8.7	100	1.2	1.0	1.2
South Carolina	97.1	2.9	100	1.6	0.4	1.4
Tennessee	97.0	3.0	100	2.2	0.5	2.0
Utah	92.9	7.1	100	0.8	0.5	0.8
Total	**94.3**	**5.7**	**100**	**27.1**	**13.3**	**25.6**
Moderate-Growth States						
Alaska	94.6	5.4	100	0.2	0.1	0.2
Connecticut	89.0	11.0	100	1.2	1.2	1.2
District of Columbia	87.7	12.3	100	0.2	0.2	0.2
Hawaii	82.3	17.7	100	0.4	0.7	0.4
Indiana	96.8	3.2	100	2.3	0.6	2.2
Louisiana	97.5	2.5	100	1.7	0.4	1.6
Maine	97.0	3.0	100	0.5	0.1	0.5
Maryland	90.0	10.0	100	1.9	1.7	1.9

Table 2.2   (Continued)

Traditional, New Settlement, and Moderate-Growth States	Percent of State Population			Percent of National Population		
	Native Born	Foreign Born	Total	Native Born	Foreign Born	Total
Massachusetts	87.8	12.2	100	2.2	2.5	2.3
Michigan	94.7	5.3	100	3.8	1.7	3.5
Mississippi	98.6	1.4	100	1.1	0.1	1.0
Missouri	97.3	2.7	100	2.2	0.5	2.0
Montana	98.4	1.6	100	0.4	0.0	0.3
New Hampshire	95.7	4.3	100	0.5	0.2	0.4
New Mexico	91.9	8.1	100	0.7	0.5	0.6
North Dakota	98.3	1.7	100	0.3	0.0	0.2
Ohio	97.0	3.0	100	4.4	1.1	4.0
Pennsylvania	96.0	4.0	100	4.7	1.6	4.4
Rhode Island	88.0	12.0	100	0.4	0.4	0.4
South Dakota	98.1	1.9	100	0.3	0.0	0.3
Vermont	95.8	4.2	100	0.2	0.1	0.2
Virginia	91.7	8.3	100	2.6	1.9	2.5
Washington	89.6	10.4	100	2.1	2.0	2.1
West Virginia	99.0	1.0	100	0.7	0.1	0.6
Wisconsin	96.4	3.6	100	2.1	0.6	1.9
Wyoming	97.9	2.1	100	0.2	0.0	0.2
Total	**94.2**	**5.8**	**100**	**37.2**	**18.4**	**35.2**

Source: U.S. Census microdata

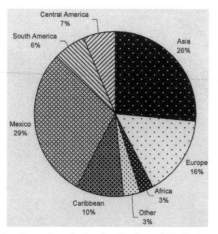

Figure 2.2   U.S. Foreign-Born Population by Region of Birth: 2000

Source: U.S. Census 1990 and U.S. Census 20000

than 55 percent of all Latino immigrants, were approximately 30 percent of the total foreign-born population. Among the remaining foreign-born population 26 percent were born in Asia, 16 percent were born in Europe, 3 percent were born in Africa, and 3 percent were born elsewhere.

In 2000, there were 16,086,974 foreign-born Latinos in the United States. Slightly more than three-fourths of them resided in the traditional states. Approximately 13 percent of the foreign-born Latinos lived in the new settlement states and the remaining 10 percent in the moderate-growth states. Latino foreign-born residents accounted for 49 percent of the total foreign-born population in the new settlement states. This percentage rises to 57 percent in the top-five new settlement states of Arizona, Georgia, North Carolina, Colorado, and Nevada.

By comparison, there were 8,226,254 foreign-born Asians in the United States in 2000, with more than two-thirds of them living in the traditional states. The percentage of foreign-born Asians living outside the traditional states is higher than that of foreign-born Latinos: Washington, Virginia, Michigan, and Massachusetts all have a high number of Asian immigrants. Seventy-five percent of foreign-born Asians live in these and the traditional states. In 2000, 11.8 percent of the total Asian foreign born lived in the new settlement states, comprising one-quarter of the total foreign born in those states.

Natives are prevalent in states with historical flows but few newcomers. So while most immigrants in America today are either Latino or Asian, these groups are themselves made up of new foreign-born populations. Indeed, the share of foreign born in these minority populations is closely related to the strength and timing of their immigration history. Latinos, Mexicans in particular, have a long history of migration to the United States, while most Asian immigrants were effectively banned until the 1960s. So perhaps it is not surprising that while more than two-thirds of Asians are foreign born, only four out of every ten Latinos were born outside the United States (see table 2.3).

The foreign born make up a similar share of the minority population in traditional states and new settlement states. Latino immigrants comprise 42 percent of the total Latino population in both categories. The percentage of Asians in traditional states who are foreign born, as expected, is much higher at 70 percent, which is equal to the average of Asians in new settlement states. Yet both Latinos and Asians are less likely to be foreign born in the moderate-growth states that have

Table 2.3   Percent of Principal Minority Groups by Nativity and State, 2000

Traditional, New Settlement, and Moderate-Growth States	Asian			Latino			White non-Hispanic		
	Foreign Born	Native Born	Asian Total	Foreign Born	Native Born	Latino Total	Foreign Born	Native Born	White Total
Total USA	**67.3**	**32.7**	**100**	**40.1**	**59.9**	**100**	**3.7**	**96.3**	**100**
Traditional States									
California	66.5	33.5	100	43.5	56.5	100	8.2	91.8	100
Florida	71.7	28.3	100	55.9	44.1	100	5.2	94.8	100
Illinois	71.6	28.4	100	45.5	54.5	100	5.5	94.5	100
New Jersey	74.8	25.2	100	44.9	55.1	100	8.3	91.7	100
New York	75.5	24.5	100	39.7	60.3	100	9.3	90.7	100
Texas	72.5	27.5	100	31.7	68.3	100	2.4	97.6	100
Total	**69.6**	**30.4**	**100**	**41.5**	**58.5**	**100**	**6.6**	**93.4**	**100**
New Settlement States									
Alabama	69.4	30.6	100	48.4	51.6	100	0.8	99.2	100
Arizona	65.5	34.5	100	35.6	64.4	100	3.6	96.4	100
Arkansas	60.0	40.0	100	46.9	53.1	100	0.6	99.4	100
Colorado	62.2	37.8	100	28.9	71.1	100	3.0	97.0	100
Delaware	71.9	28.1	100	35.4	64.6	100	2.3	97.7	100
Georgia	74.9	25.1	100	59.5	40.5	100	2.0	98.0	100
Idaho	56.2	43.8	100	38.1	61.9	100	1.5	98.5	100
Iowa	82.0	18.0	100	34.2	65.8	100	1.1	98.9	100
Kansas	76.4	23.6	100	39.4	60.6	100	1.2	98.8	100
Kentucky	70.1	29.9	100	40.1	59.9	100	0.8	99.2	100
Minnesota	76.9	23.1	100	43.5	56.5	100	1.4	98.6	100
Nebraska	82.9	17.1	100	38.5	61.5	100	1.3	98.7	100
Nevada	65.4	34.6	100	47.6	52.4	100	3.9	96.1	100
North Carolina	71.2	28.8	100	60.8	39.2	100	1.7	98.3	100
Oklahoma	75.2	24.8	100	38.2	61.8	100	1.0	99.0	100
Oregon	67.7	32.3	100	46.6	53.4	100	3.1	96.9	100
South Carolina	72.2	27.8	100	48.3	51.7	100	1.3	98.7	100
Tennessee	69.0	31.0	100	52.5	47.5	100	1.1	98.9	100
Utah	55.1	44.9	100	43.1	56.9	100	2.2	97.8	100
Total	**70.0**	**30.0**	**100**	**42.1**	**57.9**	**100**	**1.7**	**98.3**	**100**
Moderate-Growth States									
Alaska	59.8	40.2	100	21.8	78.2	100	1.8	98.2	100
Connecticut	75.9	24.1	100	23.2	76.8	100	7.1	92.9	100
District of Columbia	64.3	35.7	100	60.6	39.4	100	10.7	89.3	100
Hawaii	28.2	71.8	100	7.1	92.9	100	4.9	95.1	100
Indiana	75.9	24.1	100	36.6	63.4	100	1.2	98.8	100
Louisiana	64.7	35.3	100	36.9	63.1	100	1.1	98.9	100
Maine	67.3	32.7	100	15.1	84.9	100	2.4	97.6	100
Maryland	74.5	25.5	100	54.2	45.8	100	4.0	96.0	100

Table 2.3   (Continued)

Traditional, New Settlement, and Moderate-Growth States	Asian			Latino			White non-Hispanic		
	Foreign Born	Native Born	Asian Total	Foreign Born	Native Born	Latino Total	Foreign Born	Native Born	White Total
Massachusetts	71.7	28.3	100	31.8	68.2	100	6.9	93.1	100
Michigan	75.0	25.0	100	25.3	74.7	100	3.6	96.4	100
Mississippi	69.0	31.0	100	30.6	69.4	100	0.6	99.4	100
Missouri	69.2	30.8	100	34.0	66.0	100	1.2	98.8	100
Montana	41.9	58.1	100	8.7	91.3	100	1.4	98.6	100
New Hampshire	67.6	32.4	100	34.6	65.4	100	2.6	97.4	100
New Mexico	63.5	36.5	100	14.2	85.8	100	3.0	97.0	100
North Dakota	60.0	40.0	100	6.7	93.3	100	0.9	99.1	100
Ohio	74.1	25.9	100	18.5	81.5	100	1.8	98.2	100
Pennsylvania	72.8	27.2	100	16.7	83.3	100	2.2	97.8	100
Rhode Island	70.8	29.2	100	46.1	53.9	100	6.2	93.8	100
South Dakota	60.2	39.8	100	25.0	75.0	100	0.9	99.1	100
Vermont	75.2	24.8	100	16.9	83.1	100	3.1	96.9	100
Virginia	73.4	26.6	100	53.8	46.2	100	3.0	97.0	100
Washington	63.8	36.2	100	38.8	61.2	100	4.0	96.0	100
West Virginia	62.5	37.5	100	20.2	79.8	100	0.4	99.6	100
Wisconsin	74.9	25.1	100	35.7	64.3	100	1.3	98.7	100
Wyoming	44.5	55.5	100	15.1	84.9	100	1.0	99.0	100
Total	**60.2**	**39.8**	**100**	**29.4**	**70.6**	**100**	**2.8**	**97.2**	**100**

Source: U.S. Census 2000 microdata

not received strong infusions of newcomers in recent decades—29 percent of the Latinos and 60 percent of the Asians are foreign born.

The share of the native or foreign-born minority can also vary sharply among states within a region. An unusually high 82 to 83 percent of Asians in Nebraska and Iowa are foreign born, perhaps because these states drew heavily on refugee populations to work in the relocated meatpacking industry. In contrast, states in the intermountain West have relatively high shares of native-born Asians reflecting, perhaps, a long history of Western settlement and relative tolerance (see Idaho, Utah, and Nevada, despite the latter's rapid recent growth). But the greatest variation in nativity is found in the moderate growth states. The most striking example of length of settlement—coupled with little recent immigration—is that of Hawaii, where 72 percent of Asians are native born. Asians in the western states of Montana and Wyoming also are more likely to be native than foreign born. Elsewhere, Asians are mostly immigrants.

The Latino minority grew fastest in new settlement states. Because the largest minority populations include so many immigrants it should come as no surprise that a map of minority population growth appears very similar to the map of immigrant growth presented above (compare figure 2.1 to the discussion here). This can be seen starting with a look at the rate of growth during the 1990s of the Latino population, including both its native and foreign-born components. Figure 2.3 shows a map of the rate of growth of the Latino population in the fifty states—53 percent of Latino population growth, or 8.37 million people, appeared in the traditional states, which had 25,833,973 Latinos in 2000. Still, 73 percent of Latinos lived in traditional states in 2000, down from 78 percent in 1990.

The Latino population grew by nearly 183 percent in the new settlement states during the 1990s, outpacing the growth rate in traditional immigrant states. Census data indicate that sixteen of the nineteen new settlement states and six of the moderate growth states, had an increase in Latinos of more than 100 percent during the 1990s. North Carolina, for instance, experienced an increase of 394 percent, from 76,726 Latinos in 1990 to almost 400,000 Latinos in 2000. Georgia witnessed an increase of 300 percent, reporting 435,227 Latinos in 2000.

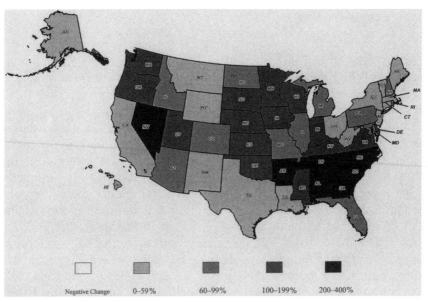

Figure 2.3   Percent Growth of the Latino Population, 1990 to 2000

Source: U.S. Census 1990 and U.S. Census 2000

The Asian minority population remains concentrated in traditional states. The Asian population grew by a little more than two million in the traditional states, but this was a historically significant figure that maintained Asian concentration. The share of Asians in traditional states only declined from 63 to 62 percent during the 1990s. This suggests that Asians were more likely than Latinos to stay or settle in the traditional states during the 1990s. Correspondingly, with an overall growth rate of 77.3 percent, the Asian minority population grew less rapidly than Latinos in new settlement states. Sixteen of the new settlement states saw their Asian populations grow more than 50 percent. Just three new settlement states, Nevada, Georgia, and North Carolina, experienced Asian growth rates above 100 percent, at 159, 134, and 126 percent, respectively.

Figure 2.4 shows that twelve of the moderate-growth states also had Asian population growth rates above 50 percent, but none was higher than 100 percent. The percent change of the Asian population in the new settlement states was approximately 15 percent higher than that of the traditional states. Although Latinos are scattered more widely than Asians, an increase in both populations in the new settlement

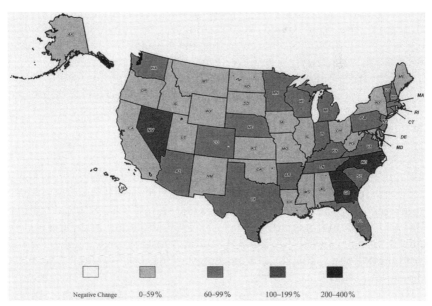

Figure 2.4   Proportionate Growth of the Asian Population, 1990 to 2000

Source: U.S. Census 1990 and U.S. Census 2000

areas and moderate-growth states paralleled the traditional states' loss in their share of Latino and Asian populations.

These patterns of minority population growth and loss are even more marked at the county level because state maps do not reveal the full range of diversity. Appendix 2.1 presents a discussion for selected counties and their 1990s population growth for all immigrants and for the Latino and Asian minorities. While the appendix maps tell much the same story as the one just outlined here, they reveal an extra dimension of diversity that, if pushed further, suggests ever more complexity at smaller geographic levels. So while an analytic focus on states gives us the broad picture, local actors should not be surprised to see that their stories are only vaguely represented.

SOURCES OF FOREIGN-BORN GROWTH: SECONDARY MIGRANTS OR NEW ARRIVALS?

Observers throughout the 1990s debated whether the redistribution of immigrants around the country was driven by internal or international migration. Many experts believed that immigrants were leaving traditional states to find new homes in the new settlement areas. After all, it was evident that natives were leaving such traditional states as California; perhaps immigrants were joining the search for new places.[4] The other natural possibility was that the foreign born in new settlement areas were arriving directly from abroad.

Whichever explanation holds true promises intriguing insights into the forces behind new geographic patterns. Demographers point out that the United States has always been a highly mobile country due to the migration of the native population, and now increasingly, its foreign-born population. The new settlement states were attractive during the 1990s because of their growing economies, lower cost of living, and quality-of-life factors relating to climate, safety, and environment. But if the foreign born are "just off the boat" they will have less experience than relocating immigrants who have already lived in the United States. This could mean differences in English ability and capacity to integrate. Answers to this demographic question may shed light on special challenges that local communities face in responding to new migration patterns.

New settlement immigrants arrive from abroad. Table 2.4 shows 2000 census data for place of residence five years earlier, data that only recently became available to address this migration question. Pre-

Table 2.4 Percent of Population that Migrated across State or National Boundaries Five Years Ago, 2000

Traditional, New Settlement, and Moderate- Growth States	Residence Five Years				
	Traditional State	New Settlement State	Moderate- Growth State	Abroad	Total
Total	**48.3**	**8.1**	**11.8**	**31.8**	**100**
Foreign					
Traditional	67.4	1.3	2.2	29.1	100
New Settlement	15.1	42.0	4.6	38.3	100
Moderate Growth	10.1	2.7	51.2	36.0	100
Native					
Traditional	86.7	4.5	6.6	2.2	100
New Settlement	8.8	81.3	8.5	1.5	100
Moderate Growth	6.7	5.3	86.4	1.7	100

Source: U.S. Census 2000 microdata

dictably, most native-born migrants did not reside abroad in the five years prior to 2000, but rather moved to their state of residence from another state. The foreign born, on the other hand, tend to be new arrivals in their current state of residence in 2000 after having been resident abroad as of 1995. In short, the pattern of immigrant movement into new settlement states appears to be primarily a phenomenon of new arrival and not one of redistribution away from traditional states.

Beyond these obvious differences, both native and foreign-born migrants tend to migrate from states within the regional typology constructed in this chapter. That is to say, most cross-state migrants in the traditional states come from another traditional state, just as most migrants in new settlement and moderate growth states come from other new settlement and moderate growth states. This data indicates that immigrants did not leave traditional states in mass during the 1990s to settle in the new settlement states.

However, new settlement states have gained some immigrants from traditional states. In the five years prior to 2000, 15 percent of the total foreign-born population in the new settlement states migrated from a traditional state.[5] At the same time, immigrants in new settlement states are more likely to have come from abroad during the last decade than immigrants in traditional states. This suggests that immigrants in traditional states are less likely to be newcomers from abroad than those in new settlement states.

Another way to analyze the source of immigration flows is to examine the data on foreign born year of entry. For example, 42 percent of the foreign-born population as of the year 2000 entered the country between 1990 and 2000.[6] Yet this percentage is more than 10 percent higher in the new settlement states, where 54 percent of the foreign-born population entered during the 1990s. The Latino foreign-born population in the new settlement states tends to have arrived more recently than its Asian counterpart. Overall, 63 percent of the foreign-born Latinos residing in new settlement states moved there during the 1990s. The percentage of foreign-born Asians in new settlement states who entered the United States between 1990 and 2000 was smaller but still significant at 49 percent. Thus, the year of immigration data suggest the same conclusion as the data on place of last residence: most immigrants in new settlement states are new arrivals from abroad and not redistributed internal migrants.

COMPARING SOCIOECONOMIC CHARACTERISTICS
OF THE FOREIGN AND NATIVE BORN

Because the immigrants in new settlement states are more likely to be arrivals from abroad, often in the five years leading up to the 2000 census, they may have distinctive socioeconomic characteristics that set them apart from more established immigrants. For example, they may be more likely to be young males. After all, migrants to new regions are more often young males while longer-resident internal migrants might tend to be entire family units. This casual speculation generally holds true, as will be shown below, but there are otherwise few socioeconomic differences between immigrants in traditional, new settlement, and moderate growth states.

Immigrants in new settlement states are young. The foreign born were slightly more than a year younger than the natives on average for the nation as a whole. Furthermore, the age of natives varies less than that of the foreign born across states. The national average age of thirty-nine years for the native-born resident does not change more than 0.2 years across the traditional, new, and moderate-growth states. The age of the foreign-born population, however, varies substantially, especially in the new settlement states where immigrants are about three years younger than the foreign-born population in the traditional and moderate-growth states. This fits with the expectation that immigrants in new settlement states are a more mobile population.

Immigrant males outnumber females in new settlement states. Immigrant women slightly outnumber men, with 99.5 males for every 100 females. But table 2.5 shows that this ratio varies across traditional, new settlement, and moderate-growth states, supporting the supposition that immigrants in the new settlement states are younger and more recent arrivals. Males have a greater tendency to be migratory pioneers. In the traditional states there are 98 males for every 100 females, a male deficit that is typical of settled migrant populations. The same is true in the moderate growth states, where there were 94 males for every 100 females. In the new settlement states, however, there are 112 males for every 100 females.

English ability does not vary greatly between settlement states. Knowledge of the English language is an important indicator of integration. English-language ability generally increases with the length of stay in the United States. But statistics in table 7 show no tendency for newcomers in the new settlement states to be any less fluent than immigrants in the traditional states. Interestingly, immigrants in the moderate-growth states are more likely to speak English well than those in the traditional and new settlement states. In fact, immigrants in moderate-growth states are also somewhat better situated socioeconomically than immigrants elsewhere (see below).

Linguistic isolation varies somewhat between states. The census measure of linguistic isolation captures individuals in households where no adult speaks English at home. As with English ability, the rate of linguistic isolation does not vary greatly among different regions. But table 5 shows that the new settlement states, at 33 percent, had the highest rate of linguistic isolation. This figure was slightly lower in traditional states, where 30 percent of the foreign-born population indicated that they were linguistically isolated. Only 25 percent of the foreign born in moderate-growth states live in linguistically isolated households. It appears that individuals in the new settlement states have English skills comparable to those in traditional states, yet their more recently formed *households* are on average less linguistically able than those immigrants elsewhere.

Immigrants have less education than natives in all states. The native-born population in the United States has an average of 13.1 years of formal education, exactly one year more than the foreign-born population. Table 6 shows that this difference is less pronounced in the moderate-growth states where the foreign born averaged 12.7 years of

Table 2.5 Selected Demographic and Language Characteristics by State, 2000

Traditional, New Settlement, and Moderate-Growth States	Average Years of Age		Foreign Born		
	Foreign Born	Native Born	Male to Female Population	Speaks English Well or Better	Linguistically Isolated
Total USA	**37.9**	**39.4**	**99.5**	**75.3**	**28.4**
Traditional States					
California	37.8	38.8	99	66.0	31.1
Florida	40.0	40.1	93	72.1	28.1
Illinois	38.0	39.2	108	69.4	33.1
New Jersey	39.3	39.9	98	76.6	25.0
New York	39.4	39.3	91	75.5	26.7
Texas	36.6	38.6	106	60.4	36.3
Total	**38.3**	**39.2**	**98**	**68.7**	**30.4**
New Settlement States					
Alabama	36.8	39.6	107	75.5	25.8
Arizona	36.3	39.3	104	64.4	34.4
Arkansas	35.0	39.7	115	67.8	37.6
Colorado	35.8	39.2	112	66.5	33.9
Delaware	38.4	39.5	104	76.9	28.1
Georgia	34.8	38.7	125	68.7	33.3
Idaho	36.0	39.0	115	67.2	39.5
Iowa	35.5	39.7	103	71.5	37.5
Kansas	34.8	39.4	113	68.8	33.3
Kentucky	37.0	39.4	105	78.0	25.5
Minnesota	35.5	39.4	98	74.3	29.1
Nebraska	35.6	39.1	106	68.0	37.0
Nevada	37.3	40.3	98	70.6	34.7
North Carolina	34.5	39.5	128	66.7	36.2
Oklahoma	36.0	39.4	106	70.9	26.9
Oregon	36.4	40.0	111	69.4	35.1
South Carolina	36.8	39.6	113	73.0	31.9
Tennessee	36.1	39.7	126	73.0	24.8
Utah	35.1	36.5	116	71.3	32.3
Total	**35.8**	**39.3**	**112**	**69.1**	**33.1**
Moderate-Growth States					
Alaska	39.1	39.1	78	78.6	36.4
Connecticut	39.6	40.0	91	81.6	25.1
District of Columbia	36.4	38.0	93	75.7	26.5
Hawaii	41.4	38.9	72	77.2	21.9
Indiana	36.1	39.4	118	75.6	26.2
Louisiana	38.8	39.0	90	85.6	23.7

Table 2.5   (Continued)

Traditional, New Settlement, and Moderate-Growth States	Average Years of Age		Foreign Born		
	Foreign Born	Native Born	Male to Female Population	Speaks English Well or Better	Linguistically Isolated
Maine	43.2	40.8	66	95.7	7.3
Maryland	38.9	40.0	92	82.3	22.0
Massachusetts	38.7	39.4	93	79.2	25.4
Michigan	39.1	39.5	101	82.8	19.8
Mississippi	36.0	38.8	98	81.6	22.9
Missouri	37.6	39.5	89	79.2	27.6
Montana	44.3	40.2	83	91.4	15.3
New Hampshire	41.0	40.1	83	85.5	19.4
New Mexico	39.3	39.5	93	64.5	31.5
North Dakota	36.9	38.7	61	79.0	27.1
Ohio	39.1	39.5	93	85.4	21.1
Pennsylvania	39.3	40.1	93	83.9	22.4
Rhode Island	38.8	39.4	94	73.6	28.9
South Dakota	40.5	39.3	82	88.3	23.1
Vermont	40.2	40.1	85	89.3	26.5
Virginia	37.9	39.7	96	79.2	24.3
Washington	37.4	39.6	95	75.0	30.6
West Virginia	42.2	40.1	93	89.8	10.8
Wisconsin	37.1	39.4	107	72.1	30.5
Wyoming	39.4	39.9	122	86.4	36.7
Total	**38.6**	**39.6**	**94**	**79.8**	**24.6**

Source: U.S. Census 2000 microdata

formal education, only 0.4 years less than their native-born counterparts. The education disparity was slightly more pronounced in the traditional and new settlement states, where natives averaged 13.2 and 13.0 years of education, respectively, or 1.9 and 1.7 years more than the foreign born in these states.

Immigrants have a lower labor force participation rate than natives. The labor force participation rate measures the percentage of employed and unemployed workers in the population sixteen years and older. Nationally, the foreign-born labor force participation rate is 71 percent, compared to 79 percent for the native population. As illustrated by table 6, all three groups of settlement states exhibit a discrepancy in labor force participation rates. The greatest difference occurs in the traditional states, where the foreign-born labor force participa-

Table 2.6   Selected Educational and Economic Characteristics by Nativity and State, 2000

Traditional, New Settlement, and Moderate-Growth States	Average Years of Education		Labor Force Participation Rate		Home Ownership Rate		150% of Official Poverty Line	
	Native Born	Foreign Born	Native Born	Foreign Born	Native Born	Foreign Born	Native Born	Foreign Born
Total USA	**13.1**	**12.1**	**78.0**	**70.5**	**72.1**	**54.5**	**22.2**	**29.9**
Traditional States								
California	13.4	10.8	76.8	66.5	62.1	47.9	23.0	33.8
Florida	13.0	12.0	74.7	69.6	73.3	61.4	22.1	29.4
Illinois	13.3	11.6	78.4	70.1	73.4	59.3	19.5	23.3
New Jersey	13.5	12.8	78.6	72.9	73.8	51.0	15.3	20.0
New York	13.4	12.1	75.6	68.7	62.1	39.4	23.5	29.6
Texas	12.9	10.0	75.9	64.8	69.1	53.4	26.1	41.8
Total	**13.2**	**11.3**	**76.4**	**67.7**	**67.5**	**49.9**	**22.6**	**31.9**
New Settlement States								
Alabama	12.6	12.6	71.8	68.9	75.7	51.2	28.3	33.3
Arizona	13.1	10.3	75.3	63.6	72.0	55.8	22.7	39.3
Arkansas	12.4	10.6	73.1	68.7	71.3	50.2	28.9	45.5
Colorado	13.7	11.1	81.4	65.8	72.3	54.0	17.2	31.5
Delaware	13.1	13.4	79.5	76.2	76.5	53.5	16.8	29.5
Georgia	12.9	11.6	76.2	72.5	71.2	47.0	23.6	28.7
Idaho	13.0	10.1	77.6	71.3	75.3	49.2	24.2	49.9
Iowa	13.1	11.0	83.6	74.7	77.2	56.6	19.2	28.5
Kansas	13.3	11.6	81.0	68.5	73.8	54.3	20.1	33.1
Kentucky	12.4	13.4	71.9	69.7	74.1	41.2	27.9	34.6
Minnesota	13.5	11.9	84.8	70.7	81.4	54.9	15.2	31.4
Nebraska	13.4	11.1	84.7	64.7	73.0	51.0	19.5	33.7
Nevada	129	10.7	77.0	68.4	65.8	55.0	18.2	25.7
North Carolina	12.9	11.2	77.6	73.4	73.0	42.4	22.4	33.1
Oklahoma	12.8	11.1	74.5	66.4	71.4	51.5	27.6	39.7
Oregon	13.3	11.0	79.3	72.2	68.3	51.9	20.7	34.6
South Carolina	12.7	12.2	74.7	73.6	75.1	53.0	26.6	33.6
Tennessee	12.6	12.4	74.7	72.7	73.8	46.8	24.8	29.7
Utah	13.3	11.5	79.0	69.6	77.3	58.2	17.2	41.1
Total	**13.0**	**11.3**	**77.2**	**69.5**	**73.6**	**51.4**	**22.7**	**33.6**
Moderate-Growth States								
Alaska	13.2	12.0	80.3	68.0	66.4	567	17.9	25.2
Connecticut	13.6	12.7	81.2	74.5	73.0	56.8	14.9	19.4
District of Columbia	14.0	12.6	74.4	78.1	45.4	36.2	33.3	26.8
Hawaii	13.5	12.0	80.7	71.9	60.4	56.5	19.1	24.1
Indiana	12.8	12.5	79.0	72.7	75.9	54.5	19.1	28.1

Table 2.6   (Continued)

Traditional, New Settlement, and Moderate-Growth States	Average Years of Education		Labor Force Participation Rate		Home Ownership Rate		150% of Official Poverty Line	
	Native Born	Foreign Born	Native Born	Foreign Born	Native Born	Foreign Born	Native Born	Foreign Born
Louisiana	12.4	12.9	71.0	67.6	71.2	55.7	32.4	31.5
Maine	13.2	12.7	79.1	72.8	76.6	68.0	21.6	20.6
Maryland	13.5	13.6	80.2	74.5	72.9	58.0	15.9	17.8
Massachusetts	13.8	12.7	81.4	73.7	70.3	48.7	17.4	23.5
Michigan	13.0	13.1	77.0	69.6	78.1	65.3	19.4	23.5
Mississippi	12.4	12.2	71.2	69.0	74.1	51.2	35.1	40.6
Missouri	12.9	12.8	77.8	72.3	74.4	55.6	22.4	30.3
Montana	13.1	12.7	77.0	64.7	72.5	66.9	26.7	29.8
New Hampshire	13.4	13.3	82.7	69.6	75.4	57.9	13.8	22.8
New Mexico	13.0	9.8	73.9	62.3	74.4	64.5	30.8	50.5
North Dakota	13.2	14.0	84.2	56.1	72.9	48.7	23.4	21.9
Ohio	12.9	13.8	77.9	72.6	73.4	60.4	20.4	22.0
Pennsylvania	13.1	13.6	77.1	70.9	76.5	60.7	21.5	25.5
Rhode Island	13.4	11.1	80.1	70.3	68.0	49.1	21.6	31.1
South Dakota	13.0	12.2	82.5	71.4	72.5	68.3	26.3	27.2
Vermont	13.4	13.7	83.1	78.4	74.4	64.2	18.9	19.3
Virginia	13.3	12.9	78.3	74.1	72.2	54.3	19.3	19.5
Washington	13.4	12.0	79.0	73.4	69.9	54.2	18.5	31.1
West Virginia	12.3	14.5	67.0	69.5	77.7	72.3	31.3	28.5
Wisconsin	13.2	11.8	83.1	72.0	74.0	49.8	17.4	31.7
Wyoming	13.1	11.8	78.7	78.9	74.5	53.4	22.4	19.7
Total	**13.1**	**12.7**	**78.0**	**72.4**	**73.7**	**56.2**	**21.1**	**25.0**

Source: U.S. Census 2000 microdata
Note: Education for adults ages 25 and older, labor force ages 16 and over, and eligible population other characteristics.

tion rate is 9 percent lower than that of the natives. With a difference of 8 percent, the disparity is slightly smaller in the new settlement states. The gap is smallest in moderate-growth states, with a difference of 6 percent in labor force participation rates between natives and immigrants. The lower average participation rate of immigrants is largely due to the category's inclusion of males and females. While male immigrants tend to participate as much as native males, female immigrants generally have participation rates lower than native women.

The foreign born are less likely to own a home. Homeownership rates are substantially lower among the foreign born than among natives. Table 6 shows the national homeownership rate for the native population is 72 percent, compared to 55 percent for the foreign born. The size of the gap varies little in the traditional and moderate-growth states, but the disparity is striking in the new settlement states, where the native homeownership rate of 74 percent is about 22 percent greater than the foreign-born rate. This likely reflects the shorter-than-average length of residency for immigrants in new settlement states. Over time it is possible that the foreign born in new settlement states will begin to purchase their own homes.

Immigrants are more likely to live in poverty than natives. Table 2.6 also shows the percentage of the population living below 150 percent of the poverty line—in other words, individuals who live in households with a total income less than 1.5 times the government-defined poverty cutoff point. Given that immigrants have less education and experience in the U.S. labor force, it is not surprising that immigrants are more likely than natives to live in poverty. The foreign born in new settlement states are more likely to live in poverty than their counterparts in both traditional states and moderate-growth states.

The foreign born are less likely to work in a professional industry. Nationally, natives are more likely to work in professional industries than immigrants. Table 2.7 shows that 26 percent of all natives work in professional industries, compared to only 21 percent of immigrants. The gap is smaller in moderate growth states, however, where the rate of the foreign born in professional industries, 26 percent, is approximately 0.5 percent less than that of the natives. Table 2.7 shows that while the foreign born are less likely to work in professional industries, they are more likely to work in retail trade, construction, agriculture, and nondurable goods. The distribution of the foreign-born population among these industries varies by state.

The foreign born in new settlement states are substantially more likely to work in primary industries and nondurable manufacturing than immigrants in either traditional or moderate growth states. Construction, another cyclical industry, is also a large employer of the foreign born in new settlement states. In contrast, the foreign born in new settlement states are much less likely to work in professional industries, especially compared to immigrants in the moderate growth states.

CONCLUSION

This analysis of 1990 and 2000 census data reveals that the U.S. foreign-born, Latino, and Asian populations increased significantly dur-

Table 2.7   **Percent of Natives and Immigrants Who Work in Major Industries, 2000**

Industry and Nativity of Labor	Traditional States	New Settlement States	Moderate-Growth States	National Total
Foreign				
Agriculture, forestry, fishing, and mining	4.3	5.5	3.0	4.2
Construction	7.6	11.4	5.9	7.8
Durable goods	8.5	9.3	10.3	8.9
Nondurable goods	8.5	10.6	7.7	8.6
Transportation, communications	4.5	3.1	3.3	4.1
Wholesale trade	4.0	2.8	2.5	3.5
Retail trade	18.9	18.8	19.1	18.9
Finance, insurance, and real estate	5.3	3.4	5.0	5.0
Business and repair services	7.9	6.6	6.9	7.5
Personal services, including	5.7	6.1	5.4	5.7
Entertainment and recreation	2.1	2.7	1.7	2.1
Professional and related	20.2	16.9	25.5	20.7
Public administration	2.6	2.6	3.8	2.8
	100.0	**100.0**	**100.0**	**100.0**
Native				
Agriculture, forestry, fishing, and mining	2.1	3.0	2.5	2.5
Construction	6.3	7.3	6.6	6.7
Durable goods	6.3	8.4	9.8	8.2
Nondurable goods	4.7	6.9	5.9	5.8
Transportation, communications	5.4	5.2	4.5	5.0
Wholesale trade	3.3	3.1	3.0	3.1
Retail	18.0	18.4	18.4	18.3
Finance, insurance, and real estate	7.1	5.8	5.7	6.2
Business and repair services	7.4	6.2	6.0	6.5
Personal services, including	2.7	3.0	2.8	2.8
Entertainment and recreation	3.4	2.6	2.5	2.8
Professional and related	26.9	24.0	25.9	25.7
Public administration	6.4	6.0	6.4	6.3
	100.0	**100.0**	**100.0**	**100.0**

Source: U.S. Census 2000 microdata

ing the 1990s. These groups have grown over the last decade in states and regions with little prior exposure to foreign-born populations. The new settlers do not appear to be from California or other established states. Rather, they come from nearby states, likely a consequence of shared regional economic conditions and migrant streams. To some degree, the new settlers come from abroad. These data cannot answer whether the strength of international migration to new settler areas has anything to do with U.S. policies on the border, or instead, with the emergence of new industries in these states. In comparison with the traditional and moderate-growth states, the foreign-born population in the new settlement states tends to be younger with a proportionately higher number of recently arrived males. But otherwise and somewhat surprisingly, new settlers differ little socioeconomically from immigrants in established states. The greatest socioeconomic differences tend to be not between immigrants in new and established areas, but rather between these states and the moderate-growth states.

The U.S. Census Bureau forecasts more rapid growth of today's immigrant-minority populations than expected for native whites or African Americans. As long as the number of newly arriving immigrants persists, the total population living in the United States will likely double before the end of this coming century. By the year 2050, the native white population will be in the minority nationally, although it is already rapidly becoming the minority in many traditional receiving metros and states. Even the new settlement states are likely to see the number of their immigrant minorities continue to grow and, for the first time, will have significant minority populations. In response to the new settlement, national, state, and local officials must promote the active implementation of effective policies that facilitate social, economic and civic integration and mitigate social tensions. In new settlement areas, state and local officials often have few resources and experience to call upon when faced with new populations. Current research on new settlement areas recognizes these shortcomings and urges policymakers to support federal, state, and local support of policies and programs to orient both newcomers and receiving communities, educate newcomers, and encourage civic participation.

The case studies that follow provide both quantitative and qualitative information on immigrant integration in the Atlanta metropolitan area in Georgia; Salt Lake and Park City, Utah; Minneapolis/St. Paul and Faribault, Minnesota; the Triad cities of Greensboro, Winston-Salem, and Highpoint, North Carolina; and Winchester, Virginia. Four of the five sites are located in new settlement states. Winchester is located in a moderate-growth state but the foreign-born and Latino populations experienced significant growth in local areas during the 1990s. The sites were selected to represent some variation in geographic location, type of migration, urban-rural differences, and integration programs and practices. It is clear that the substantial and rapid growth in the foreign-born and ethnic populations in the new settlement areas pose both challenges and opportunities to the communities.

While they bring ethnic and cultural diversity, communities must find ways to allocate resources and implement institutional reforms to help both newcomers and established residents adapt.

NOTES

1. William H. Frey, "The Diversity Myth," *American Demographics* 20, no. 6 (June 1998): 38–43.

2. U.S. Census Bureau, "Census Bureau Projects Doubling of Nation's Population by 2100," January 13, 2000, available at www.census.gov/Press-Release/www/2000/cb00-05.html; U.S. Census Bureau, "The National Population Projections Program," table: (NP-T5) Projections of the Resident Population by Race, Latino Origin, and Nativity, Middle Series: 1999–2100.

3. Hawaii's Asian population decreased by 10 percent.

4. William H. Frey, "Census 2000 Reveals New Native-Born and Foreign-Born Shifts across U.S.," Population Studies Center Research Report No. 02-520, August 2002, available at www.frey-demographer.org/reports/rr02-520.pdf.

5. For more information on the contribution of secondary migrants to the foreign-born growth of new settlement areas, see U.S. Census Bureau, "Domestic Migration across Regions, Division, and States: 1995 to 2000," August 2003.

6. Frey, "Census 2000."

Appendix 2.1
Minority Population Growth at the County Level

The state-level and regional data on the foreign born are valuable for their aggregate indication of the regions where one may find new immigrant clusters and where there may be a need to develop state-wide integration policies and programs. This information is important for state politicians, policymakers, and local leaders, including ethnic community leaders, to set up local programs and initiatives and to access resources for the newcomers. County-level demographic analysis is important to identify the counties, communities, and substate regions where demographic change has occurred during the 1990s. A county-level analysis of seventeen new settlement states (Colorado and Arizona excluded) and five moderate growth states (Indiana, South Dakota, Virginia, Washington, and Wisconsin) with more than 100 percent increase in Latinos and a notable increase in Asians indicates interesting patterns of settlement and remarkable growth at a micro level.

Among the 1,695 counties studied here, the average growth of Latinos in the last decade was 315 percent, while the average growth of Asians was 122 percent.[1] Twelve percent or nineteen counties had experienced more than a 500 percent increase in Latinos, and forty-nine counties (3 percent) had seen an increase of 1,000 percent or more in the last ten years. A ten-year growth rate of 1,000 percent indicates that the county on average doubled its Latino population every year in the ten-year period. This finding is remarkable. Figure A.2 shows that the most notable growth areas are found in North Caro-

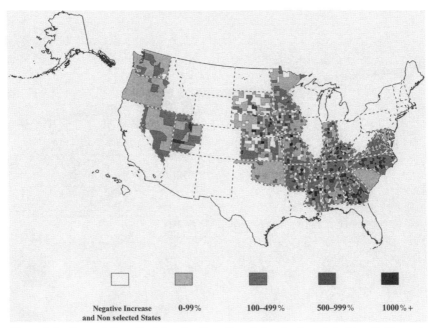

Figure A.1 Percent Growth of Foreign-Born Population by County in New Settlement States, 1990 to 2000

Source: U.S. Census 1990 and U.S. Census 2000

lina, parts of South Carolina, Georgia, Alabama, Arkansas, Kentucky, and in the border area between Nebraska, Iowa, and South Dakota. All these areas have experienced particularly large increases in Latinos in the last decade, with Latinos comprising as much as 20 percent of the total population in certain areas in 2000.

In North Carolina, the Latino and Asian population growth areas are located in the counties surrounding the city of Charlotte (Mecklenburg County), stretching north toward the area around the city of Winston-Salem (Forsyth County), and west as far as Yancey and Mitchell counties. In addition, North Carolina has seen significant growth of Latinos and Asians in the counties surrounding the city of Fayetteville (Cumberland County), stretching into South Carolina and Dillon County. In all these counties, the Latino population grew by more than 500 percent while the Asian population grew by more than 100 percent. For instance, Randolph County, south of Winston-Salem, saw its Latino population increase by more than 1,000 percent, while the Asian population grew 138 percent. By 2000, there were 8,646 Latinos in the county, about 7 percent of the total population, and 851 Asians.

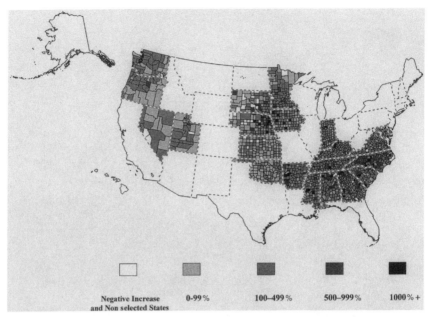

Negative Increase   0-99%   100–499%   500–999%   1000%+
and Non selected States

Figure A.2   Percent Growth of Latino Population by County in New Settlement States, 1990 to 2000

Source: U.S. Census 1990 and U.S. Census 2000

It is interesting to note that the Asian and Latino growth in North Carolina has taken place both in metropolitan areas such as Charlotte and Winston-Salem, and in the nearby rural counties. This has resulted in a sizable Latino population in rural counties around Fayetteville, such as Duplin and Lee, where Latinos constitute between 10 and 19 percent of the total population, 7,426 and 5,715 Latinos, respectively.

Georgia has seen a significant growth of Latinos and Asians east of Atlanta (Cobb County) in Gwinnett, and Rockdale; north toward the primarily rural counties of Forsyth, Dawson, Gordon, Gilmer, Whitfield, and Murray; and west toward Chattooga, Floyd, and Polk, "spilling over" to DeKalb, Marshall, and the counties north of Birmingham in Alabama. As in North Carolina, the growth in Latinos has occurred mostly in the suburbs and rural counties, in this case near Atlanta, although Cobb County itself had experienced a remarkable increase of 400 percent since 1990 and reached 46,964 Latinos in 2000. As a result of the growth, a sizable share (5 to 9 percent) of the population in many of the rural counties north of Atlanta is Latino. Rural Whitfield County stands out with 22 percent of its population, or 18,419 people, being Latino in 2000, the result of a 694 percent growth the last decade.

Large increases have also been seen in Candler County (539 percent), just south of the city of Swainsboro, and northern counties stretching into South Carolina and the counties east of the South Carolina state capital Columbia. Similar growth is seen between Macon and Atkinson counties in southern Georgia. In Atkinson and Candler counties, Latinos constitute more than 5 percent of the total population, though the other growth counties in this area still have relatively small Latino populations.

Interestingly, the Asian populations have grown in many of the counties that have seen a growth in Latinos, but more so in counties bordering those with growing Latino populations. For instance, Greene (city of Greensboro) and Hancock counties have experienced more than 1,000 percent increase in Asians, but moderate to no increase in Latinos. In nearby Warren and McDuffie counties, the Latino population has grown much more than the Asian population.

As mentioned above, Alabama has experienced a dramatic increase in Latinos in the last decade, particularly in the northern counties between the metropolitan areas of Huntsville-Decatur and Birmingham. In this area, the predominantly rural counties of DeKalb, Marshall, Blount, and Franklin have seen their Latino populations grow between 850 and 2,193 percent. In 2000, Marshall County hosted 4,656 Latinos, 6 percent of the total population in that county. In the three other growth counties highlighted here, the Latino population comprised 5 to 7 percent of the total population in 2000.

In Arkansas, a belt of urban counties in the north more than quadrupled their Latino populations in ten years, to 12,932 in Washington County (city of Springdale and Fayetteville), 13,469 in Benton County (city of Rogers), and 7,710 in Sebastian County (city of Fort Smith). In these counties, the Latino population comprises 7 to 9 percent of the total population. However, the most significant growth has occurred in the nearby rural counties, where the share of the Latino population in many cases is larger than that of the urban areas. For instance, primarily rural Carroll County in the north had grown by more than 1,000 percent to 2,471 Latinos in 2000, 10 percent of the total population. Similarly, rural Yell County between Sebastian County and the metropolitan area around Little Rock saw the Latino population grow to 2,691, or 13 percent of the total population in 2000. Further south, near Texarkana city, a remarkable 20 percent of rural Sevier County is Latino, an increase of 392 percent to 3,107 people in 2000. In several

nearby rural counties such as Howard, Pike, and Hempstead, the Latino population has increased even more, but has not yet reached the
high numbers of Sevier County.

In Kentucky, a notable increase in the Latino population occurred in
the northern part of the state, between the metropolitan areas of Louisville and Lexington-Fayette, and south of Cincinnati, Ohio. Urban
counties such as Jefferson (city of Louisville), Boone, and Fayette
have all at least tripled their Latino populations the last decade, with
Jefferson reaching more than 12,000 Latinos in 2000. Several of the
rural and urban counties located between the metropolitan areas experienced significant Latino population growth in the 1990s, resulting in
a 3 to 5 percent share of the total population in these counties. Rural
Shelby County saw its Latino population increase by 1,572 percent to
1,505 people in 2000, a 5 percent share of the county population. Far-
ther south, urban Warren County has increased its Latino population
by 475 percent to 2,466 Latinos and a 3 percent share in the county.
Warren County is located north of the metropolitan area of Nashville,
Tennessee.

The Asian population has increased in many of the same counties,
but even more so in counties where the Latino growth has been less
significant, such as Bracken County in the north, and Russell County
in the south. Based on these observations, it seems both the urban centers and the surrounding rural areas in Kentucky have attracted many
newcomers in the last decade.

The large growth of Latinos in Nashville and Davidson Counties in
Tennessee expands to the southern counties of Kentucky. By 2000,
Davidson County had increased its Latino population by almost 500
percent since 1990, to 26,091 people. The Asian population had
almost doubled its population, to 13,678 or 2 percent of the population
in the county. Many counties around Nashville, particularly in the
south, have seen a similar growth, resulting in a Latino share of the
county population of up to 7 percent. For example, the urban counties
Williamson and Rutherford, just south of Nashville, doubled their Latino and Asian populations in the 1990s. Primarily rural Bedford
County increased its Latino population by almost 1,800 percent over
the same period, to 2,811 Latinos or 7 percent of the total county population. A similar increase was seen east of Bedford, in rural Warren
County.

A remarkable increase in Latinos was also seen in Hamblen County
in eastern Tennessee, and in Marion County in the south. Both counties are located near metropolitan areas, but are considered primarily

rural counties. Hamblen County, southwest of the cities Bristol, Kingsport, and Johnson City, increased its Latino population by 1,785 percent to comprise 6 percent of the total population in 2000 (3,299 Latinos). Marion County, just west of Chattanooga city, increased its Latino population by over 600 percent, to 2,264 people in ten years.

Counties in the border area between Nebraska, Iowa, and South Dakota have seen an increase of Latinos and Asians from 500 to more than 1,000 percent. The area stretches from the rural counties north of Sioux City in Iowa, to rural and suburban counties west and south of South Sioux City in Nebraska, toward the cities of Stanton, West Point, and Columbus. In Dakota (South Sioux City) and rural Colfax counties, Latinos make up more than 20 percent of the total population. Dakota County has increased its Latino population by 350 percent to just over 20,000 Latinos in 2000, while Colfax has increased its Latino population by more than 1,000 percent to just over 10,000 people in ten years. In several nearby primarily rural counties such as Platte, Cuming, and Dixon, Latinos constitute between 5 and 9 percent of the total population, but the growth since 1990 averages more than 4,000 percent, a total increase of close to 50,000 Latinos in the area.

NOTE

1. Authors' calculations from 2000 Census American FactFinder data.

Appendix 2.2
Percent of Total 2000 Foreign-Born
Population from Latin America and Asia

Traditional, New Settlement, and Moderate-Growth States	Total Foreign-Born Population: 2000	Percent of Total Foreign-Born Population from Latin America	Percent of Total Foreign-Born Population from Asia
Total USA	**31,107,889.0**	**51.7**	**26.4**
Traditional States			
California	8,864,255.0	55.6	32.9
Florida	2,670,828.0	72.8	8.7
Illinois	1,529,058.0	47.8	23.5
New Jersey	1,476,327.0	43.0	27.8
New York	3,868,133.0	48.9	23.7
Texas	2,899,642.0	74.9	16.1
Total	**21,308,243.0**	**57.2**	**22.1**
New Settlement States			
Alabama	87,772.0	40.5	29.9
Arizona	656,183.0	71.5	11.8
Arkansas	73,690.0	58.8	21.5
Colorado	369,903.0	55.6	19.6
Delaware	44,898.0	39.0	30.1
Georgia	577,273.0	52.0	25.2
Idaho	64,080.0	59.8	12.6
Iowa	91.085.0	36.0	33.1
Kansas	134,735.0	54.7	28.2

Kentucky	80,271.0	31.9	33.4
Minnesota	260,463.0	24.0	40.4
Nebraska	74,638.0	53.6	25.7
Nevada	316,593.0	61.4	22.9
North Carolina	430,000.0	55.8	21.7
Oklahoma	131,747.0	50.6	30.2
Oregon	289,702.0	44.6	27.3
South Carolina	115,978.0	42.8	25.4
Tennessee	159,004.0	39.9	31.8
Utah	158,664.0	55.4	17.9
Total	**4,116,679.0**	**48.8**	**25.7**
Moderate-Growth States			
Alaska	37,170.0	17.9	50.6
Connecticut	369,967.0	34.7	19.0
District of Columbia	73,561.0	50.4	17.0
Hawaii	212,229.0	3.2	83.3
Indiana	186,534.0	41.5	26.6
Louisiana	115,885.0	40.2	37.5
Maine	36,691.0	6.0	18.9
Maryland	518,315.0	34.0	35.0
Massachusetts	772,983.0	30.0	26.1
Michigan	523,589.0	16.9	40.0
Mississippi	39,908.0	36.5	36.2
Missouri	151,196.0	25.8	34.9
Montana	16,396.0	9.5	20.2
New Hampshire	54,154.0	14.3	24.9
New Mexico	149,606.0	76.8	9.6
North Dakota	12,114.0	11.3	23.1
Ohio	339,279.0	13.9	35.4
Pennsylvania	508,291.0	19.6	36.0
Rhode Island	119,277.0	36.8	16.4
South Dakota	13,495.0	18.5	30.1
Vermont	23,245.0	5.2	19.2
Virginia	570,279.0	33.3	41.3
Washington	614,457.0	28.3	39.0
West Virginia	19,390.0	12.4	43.2
Wisconsin	193,751.0	33.9	32.4
Wyoming	11,205.0	40.3	19.4
Total	**5,682,967.0**	**26.6**	**31.4**

Source: U.S. Census 1990 and U.S. Census 2000

Appendix 2.3
Percent of the Foreign-Born Population
Entered 1990 to 2000

Traditional, New Settlement, and Moderate- Growth States	Percent of Total Foreign-Born, Entered 1990 to March 2000	Percent of Latin American Foreign-Born, Entered 1990 to March 2000	Percent of Asian Foreign-Born, Entered 1990 to March 2000
Total USA	**42.4**	**44.8**	**42.9**
Traditional States			
California	36.9	37.8	37.1
New York	40.4	39.8	46.8
Texas	46.1	46.1	46.5
Florida	38.6	40.6	41.7
Illinois	45.0	47.5	45.0
New Jersey	41.6	46.5	46.3
Total	**41.4**	**43.1**	**43.9**
New Settlement States			
Alabama	53.0	66.5	47.8
Arizona	48.4	52.6	44.4
Arkansas	55.3	65.1	46.1
Colorado	54.4	63.1	46.7
Delaware	47.2	59.3	48.8
Georgia	59.7	67.6	51.5
Idaho	47.7	52.7	46.9
Iowa	57.5	59.6	54.8
Kansas	55.1	61.5	50.6
Kentucky	58.8	73.0	56.9

Minnesota	54.5	66.3	46.2
Nebraska	57.8	59.5	63.5
Nevada	44.0	50.9	37.4
North Carolina	62.4	74.5	48.8
Oklahoma	53.0	59.5	50.9
Oregon	50.0	60.0	45.2
South Carolina	52.4	70.9	43.1
Tennessee	57.7	70.3	52.3
Utah	57.2	67.0	52.8
Total	**54.0**	**63.2**	**49.2**
Moderate-Growth States			
Alaska	39.7	39.1	40.4
Connecticut	39.0	49.9	49.4
District of Columbia	51.0	47.2	54.5
Hawaii	34.1	35.0	32.9
Indiana	52.2	62.7	53.4
Louisiana	37.0	33.2	40.1
Maine	28.3	33.3	42.8
Maryland	44.1	45.2	41.6
Massachusetts	40.4	49.5	47.4
Michigan	44.9	56.8	52.4
Mississippi	49.6	64.0	44.8
Missouri	52.4	60.2	51.9
Montana	29.0	32.5	44.1
New Hampshire	37.3	50.4	53.2
New Mexico	39.1	39.7	43.4
North Dakota	52.3	40.1	57.3
Ohio	42.2	51.0	50.7
Pennsylvania	41.1	47.8	47.9
Rhode Island	34.8	51.3	37.7
South Dakota	55.0	42.1	58.8
Vermont	35.3	37.4	57.7
Virginia	47.2	53.2	44.0
Washington	46.6	54.6	43.4
West Virginia	35.7	42.0	41.2
Wisconsin	46.8	61.9	48.3
Wyoming	37.8	46.1	41.7
Total	**42.0**	**47.2**	**47.0**

Source: U.S. Census 1990 and U.S. Census 2000

II

CASE STUDIES

3

New Immigrant Communities in the North Carolina
Piedmont Triad: Integration Issues and Challenges

Raleigh Bailey

In the early 1990s, North Carolina began to witness a dramatic influx of immigrants. The foreign-born population increased by 273.6 percent between 1990 and 2000, growing from 115,077 to 430,000 residents. More than 60 percent of the state's foreign-born population arrived in this period. The primary influx was Hispanic/Latino,[1] especially from Mexico, but immigrants from other parts of the world also contributed to the population growth. Two major forces brought the recent immigrants to North Carolina: (1) a robust labor market that attracted primarily unskilled Latino immigrants, and (2) a federally funded program that settled refugees in selected parts of the state. Integration of these two groups of newcomers, therefore, was facilitated by two overlapping systems: (1) employers and the workplace in the case of the mostly Latino immigrants who arrived in the 1990s, and (2) a social service system developed for refugees in the 1980s. While the systems served different populations, they had a similar impact on integration of newcomers to North Carolina.

PAST WAVES OF IMMIGRANTS AND THEIR RELIGIOUS ROOTS

The most recent newcomers are not the first group to seek a better life in North Carolina. The state's history of welcoming immigrants dates to the mid-1700s, when Quakers settled in Guilford County, bringing an ethos of moderation, peacemaking, and equality. The Quakers, also known as Friends, are credited with supporting the underground railroad that smuggled runaway slaves to freedom in the North. German Lutherans and Calvinists, Moravian Protestants, and Scotch-Irish Presbyterians also began arriving in the eighteenth century, seeking religious freedom and economic opportunity. By the mid-1800s, Irish immigrants began arriving in significant numbers, introducing the state's first sizable Roman Catholic population. The industrial revolution facilitated an influx of prominent Jewish families into central North Carolina, including the Cones and the Sternbergers, two textile giants who brought a spirit of philanthropy, justice, and altruism that influenced the region for generations.

Religion shaped the integration of the diverse groups. But unlike the Utah case study discussed in chapter 7, in which the Mormon Church exerted dominant influence, the immigrant experience in North Carolina has been shaped by the legacies of multiple value systems. Evangelical Protestantism reinforced an ethnoreligious identity and promoted a Protestant ethic: neighborliness, family and community responsibility, suspicion of big governments, and self-reliance. Many African slaves converted to Protestant Christianity, which became a base for their own community development and rebellion against oppression. In addition to the Moravians, Lutherans, and Quakers, other Protestant denominations grew and flourished in the region. Baptist, Methodist, independent fundamentalist, and Pentecostal churches have been part of the fiber of the Piedmont community. The religious values of these early European immigrant populations, along with other historical traditions of the South including the civil rights movement, would influence the state's response to refugees and other newcomers in the late twentieth century.

RECENT IMMIGRANT GROWTH IN NORTH CAROLINA

Two areas in North Carolina with large concentrations of recent immigrants are known locally as the Triad and the Triangle. The Piedmont Triad of North Carolina,[2] the focus of this chapter, is just east of the Southern Appalachian Mountains. "Triad" (see figure 3.1) refers to the region's three principle cities: Winston-Salem, which is in Forsyth County; and Greensboro and High Point, which are in Guilford

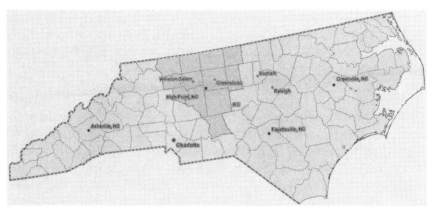

Figure 3.1   The Piedmont Triad of North Carolina

County. Greensboro is the third most populous city in the state, with 223,891 residents; Winston-Salem is the fifth, at 185,776; and High Point is the eighth, at 85,839. Alamance County, immediately east of Guilford, showed the highest Latino increase in the state in the last census, at 1,124 percent.

The Triangle, an hour east of the Triad, claims Raleigh, Durham, and Chapel Hill as its primary cities. With the state capital (Raleigh) and an internationally renowned research area nurtured by local universities and corporations (the Research Triangle), the Triangle has a more diverse economy and greater affluence than the Triad. Beyond its own large population of Latino newcomers, the region has also attracted many highly skilled foreign-born professionals. In contrast to the Triad, fewer refugees have been resettled in the Triangle.

Other urban areas that have attracted diverse immigrant populations include Charlotte, located about two hours southwest of the Triad, and Asheville, about three hours west of the Triad. The Latino population has spread into urban and rural areas of the Piedmont, the central region of the state. The Hmong tribal peoples from Laos, who came to the United States mostly as refugees, constitute another special population in the state. More than ten thousand have come to North Carolina as secondary migrants, attracted to the small towns and rural hills of the Western Piedmont.

The Triad emerged as a favored location for newcomers following the emergence of refugee service agencies in the area. Lutheran Family Services (LFS), an affiliate of the Lutheran Immigration and Refugee Services (LIRS), established its headquarters as a refugee resettlement program for North and South Carolina in Greensboro in 1979. By the 1990s, other voluntary agencies launched refugee resettlement programs in Guilford County. World Relief established a statewide refugee office in High Point; Jewish Family Services (JFS) set up a refugee resettlement project in Greensboro through its partner agency, Hebrew Immigrant Aid Society (HIAS); and Church World Service (CWS) contracted with LFS in Greensboro to serve as its state office. Although these national voluntary agencies had authority in various parts of the state, the convenience of their offices and staff being based in Guilford County made the Triad a prime location for incoming refugees. As refugee communities took root in the Triad, they became magnets for newcomers with the same cultural heritage.

The major influx of African refugees to the United States began in the 1990s, growing by 188 percent to 20,639 people in ten years, according to the U.S. Census. African immigrants and refugees living in Guilford County, in the heart of the Triad, totaled ten thousand people in 2000, according to the African Services Coalition.[3] These included newcomers from Sudan, Somalia, Niger, Nigeria, Ghana, and other sub-Saharan countries. In 1992, a group of some four hundred Montagnards, representing about thirty indigenous tribes from the Highlands of South Vietnam, was resettled in North Carolina, mostly in the Triad. An earlier group of two hundred Montagnards arrived in the area in 1986, followed by family members who came through reunification programs.

NORTH CAROLINA, NUMBER ONE
HISPANIC IN-MIGRATION STATE

In 2000, North Carolina was cited as the number one in-migration state for Hispanics. The state had 378,963 Hispanic residents, representing 4.71 percent of the state population and indicating a 449 percent increase in the Hispanic population since the 1990 Census.[4] The Triad was cited as the third-fastest growing Hispanic settlement in the United States. Additionally, six of the ten fastest-growing Latino communities can be found in North Carolina.[5] As shown by table 3.1, the Triad counties of Alamance, Davidson, and Forsyth have seen the highest growth of the Latino population, 1,124, 905, and 898 percent, respectively. In Alamance County, the Latino population grew to 8,835 residents, representing 6.8 percent of the county population.

Advocates and service providers estimate the growth of the Hispanic

Table 3.1   Hispanic Population in Selected Triad Counties, 2000 Census

	Alamance	Davidson	Forsyth	Guilford	North Carolina Total
2000 pop.	130,800	147,246	306,067	421,048	8,052,313
2000 H.pop	8,835	4,765	19,517	15,985	378,963
2000 H. %	6.75%	3.24%	6.4%	3.8%	4.71%
1990 pop.	108,213	126,667	265,878	347,420	6,628,653
1990 H.pop	722	474	1,961	2,525	69,020
1990 H.%	00.67	00.37	00.75	00.73	1.04
1990–2000% H. Increase	1124%	905%	898%	533%	449%

population in the region has been even larger than indicated by census data. As early as 1993, the Hispanic League of the Piedmont Triad (HLPT) and *Casa Guadalupe* claimed there were about 25,000 Hispanics living permanently in the Triad. In the summer of 2002, Faith-Action, a nonprofit organization in Greensboro that generates demographic data by extrapolating from the number of Hispanic births at local hospitals, estimated that there were 530,328 Hispanics in North Carolina, including 12,607 in Alamance County, 6,284 in Davidson, 32,000 in Forsyth, and 25,927 in Guilford.[6]

According to a report released by the Immigration and Naturalization Service (INS) in January 2003, North Carolina witnessed one of the largest increases in unauthorized residents between 1990 and 2000, with more than 100,000 undocumented residents settling in the state.[7] Despite increased border control since September 11, 2001, unauthorized migrants have continued to cross the border through skill, determination, and payments to coyotes who smuggle immigrants into the United States from Mexico. Undocumented workers can find work in the cash economy or "under the table." Forged documents are easy to buy. Frequently, the business and legal communities do not challenge questionable documents because the North Carolina economy—from farms to manufacturing to the service industry—depends on the labor of undocumented workers.

As an agricultural state, North Carolina has long depended on migrant labor. It is the second-largest migrant labor state in the East, second only to Florida, and the fifth-largest migrant-labor state in the nation, with a labor force that is 90 percent Hispanic.[8] Close to one hundred thousand migrant laborers spend part of each year in North

Carolina,[9] but until recently most returned home after the harvest or moved north to pick a different crop. The long-standing presence of migrant workers in North Carolina is evidenced by the remnants of migrant children educational programs and migrant health programs. Currently, Alamance is the only county in the Triad that reports migrant children in its school system. Programs that directed migrant workers to farmers needing seasonal labor have dwindled in the Triad, another sign that immigrants found work outside agriculture in the flourishing economy and settled permanently. Though still a key component of the state economy, Latino migrant farm labor has fallen off in the Triad with increased industrial development.

Indeed, the burgeoning industrial economy in the Triad pushed unemployment down to about 3 percent by 1993. Construction, roadwork, manufacturing, and mills all were seeking cheap labor. The resident refugees were unable to fill all the demanding, low-paying positions, creating opportunities for Latinos to find permanent work and break out of the migrant labor stream. For many migrant agricultural workers, it was a dramatic step forward—they found a place to live and a relatively stable income. Circular migration has not stopped completely, however. Many Latinos with a permanent residence in the Triad still return home annually to see their families. Unauthorized border crossings are still commonplace and relatively simple though hazardous, making travel between the old hometowns and the new settlements possible.

Although the newcomers find jobs in a variety of industries, many still work in agriculture. While the Piedmont economy has shifted largely toward manufacturing, even relatively urban counties like Guilford and Forsyth have numerous small tobacco plots that still depend on seasonal farm labor for planting and harvesting. Far from the plantations of Southern mythology, these are small family plots that provide supplemental income to part-time farmers. Other traditional North Carolina crops that depend on seasonal labor include cotton and soybeans in the eastern part of the state and apples and Christmas trees in the mountains. While the majority of Latino immigrants that settled in the Triad now work in manufacturing, construction, and the service sector, the state's agricultural industry continues to rely on Latino labor.

The Latino newcomers who settled recently in North Carolina have little in common with earlier Cuban refugees and South American immigrants. A few hundred Cuban refugees arrived in the Triad through a refugee resettlement program that started in 1980, but most of them eventually moved to Florida. A small and well-educated community of mostly second- and third-generation Cubans, however, maintains a strong identity in the area. The 2000 Census reported 577 Cuban Americans in Guilford County. The Triad has also been home to an affluent Latino population from various South American countries and Puerto Rico. Many of them came for business or to pursue higher education and remained permanently, but their numbers have never been significant.

Most of the recent Latino immigrants to North Carolina have neither refugee status nor are they highly skilled professionals. Many Central Americans may have temporary protective status (TPS), while others may be here as legal permanent residents (LPRs) or under various worker contracts or specialized visas. Many of the young children are U.S. citizens, though their parents may have temporary status or no documents. They are also ethnically diverse. The 2000 Census reported 10,317 (65 percent) of the Guilford Hispanic population came from Mexico. An additional 3,817 (or 24 percent) are designated as "other," but presumably come from Central America, especially El Salvador, Guatemala, and Nicaragua. The Census also reported 1,274 (or 8 percent) Puerto Ricans.

The Latino population is predominantly working class, young, and male. The Census probably underreports the number of Latino immigrants from Mexico because they are more likely to lack documentation, live in rental apartments, and have low income. Many Latinos tend to settle near people with roots in the same village or town. Greensboro, for example, is believed to have a large population from Guanajuato in Mexico, while Winston-Salem has developed a small indigenous Mayan community. While people draw obvious comfort and support from informal ethnic networks and Latino stores and restaurants are on the rise, there is currently only one formal Latino ethnic community-based organization in the Triad.

NEW NORTH CAROLINIANS WITH ROOTS IN AFRICA, ASIA, AND EASTERN EUROPE

African Newcomers

When Africans first came to North Carolina in the 1600s, they were brought forcibly through the slave trade. In the late twentieth century, African immigrants settled in the state as refugees and asylees. Initially, the African immigrants, undifferentiated from African Americans in statistical databases, received little public attention.[10] The African immigrant populations at the two historically black universities in the Triad, North Carolina Agricultural and Technical State University in Greensboro and Winston-Salem State University, remained invisible to the mainstream community. The situation changed in the 1980s and 1990s as the American public became aware of the violent conflicts in Africa.

The major African refugee and immigrant influx began in the 1990s and by 2000 there were ten thousand Africans in Guilford County alone. While other counties in the Triad did not see nearly as large numbers of Africans, Wake County and the city of Raleigh as well as Mecklenburg County and the city of Charlotte reported increased settlement of African newcomers. The first African refugees resettled in North Carolina in the 1980s came from Ethiopia and settled mostly in the Triangle area. Although not very large, the Ethiopian community included many well-educated individuals who made a graceful transition into professional careers and the business world.

A small Somali community was established in the Triad in 1994 when members of the Benadir tribe were resettled as refugees in Greensboro. Unlike the nomadic tribes dominated by various warlords involved in the war in Somalia, the Benadir come from a sedentary merchant clan and are relatively well educated. These devout Muslims with strict codes of conduct caused some ripples in the workplace and schools, and clashed with some of their church sponsors. Issues that needed peaceful resolution included requests for school and work-site prayer rooms and dress code changes to accommodate *hijab* (traditional long dresses and scarves worn by Somali women). Parents demanded that culturally appropriate food be served in school lunchrooms and objected to coeducation and some of the subject matter taught in public schools. Health workers struggled with the time-honored practice of female genital cutting (also called female genital mutilation [FGM] by Western opponents of the practice). Large families with seven or eight children were not uncommon. Some newcomers had strong beliefs that women should not work outside the home, even though multiple incomes were needed to ensure economic self-sufficiency. Resettlement agencies and community advocates worked hard to resolve these cultural differences. The Somali community persevered and now has a stable population of a few hundred people.

The first Sudanese refugees were resettled in Greensboro in the mid-1990s and were soon joined by Sudanese immigrants, including many who came to the United States on diversity visas. Most were Muslims fleeing war in the Sudan. By 2000, there were about 2,200 Sudanese in Guilford County, many drawn by news of job opportunities and the tolerant attitudes of the host community. Since most did not have refugee status, they lacked access to public services but a progressive Sudanese community-based organization soon developed an informal support system. This network included medical professionals from the Sudan who were unable to obtain medical credentials in the United States but willingly provided medical advice and traditional medicines. By 2002, the Sudanese population dropped to about 1,700. Some attribute this population decrease to lack of job opportunities, while others suspect that many Sudanese, encouraged by peace prospects in the Sudan and disillusioned with life in the United States after September 11, have returned to their homeland.

Small numbers of refugees and asylum seekers from war-torn countries in Central and West Africa, including Rwanda, Burundi, Congo, and Liberia, have also been successfully resettled in North Carolina. They totaled only a few hundred, but their success attracted secondary migrants from larger northern cities where jobs were scarce and tolerance was low. More recently, a small group of approximately 100 Sudanese youth from the Kakuma camp in Kenya arrived in the spring and summer of 2001 with much public support and enthusiasm.

Refugees from Southeast Asia

The history of Southeast Asian refugee settlements in North Carolina began in the late 1970s and early 1980s when the first groups of Vietnamese and Cambodians were resettled by local faith-based organizations. North Carolina was not only a major refugee resettlement site, but also home to various demonstration projects, including the Favorable Alternative Sites Project (FASP), initiated in 1982.

By 1985 the Cambodian population in Guilford County had grown to more than 500 residents. A secondary migration cluster, attracted by ample factory jobs, developed in Davidson County. The Cambodian community in Davidson County eventually grew to about one thousand people. The Khmer Aid Group of the Triad, the first Cambodian Mutual Assistance Association (MAA) in the area, was incorporated in 1985 with the help of an ethnic community development grant from the federal Office of Refugee Resettlement (ORR). A year later, the Cambodian community, assisted by LFS and supported by a grant from a local foundation, established a Buddhist Temple in Greensboro to provide culturally appropriate mental health services to the many traumatized Cambodians. The temple proved an invaluable resource for community organization and cultural heritage preservation. The result was a viable ethnic and religious enclave that attracted other Buddhists, including Laotians. LFS recruited Laotian secondary migrants from states through a federal grant aimed at helping refugees find jobs. The Laotian community now exceeds 1,000 people, has multiple small businesses and communities of faith, competing MAAs, and a youth group committed to education and leadership development. The Cambodian population in the Triad currently totals approximately 1,500 people.

The monk who came to serve at the Greensboro Buddhist Center in 1989 spoke Khmer, Lao, Thai, and English. A gifted community organizer, he developed several community support organizations serving the multiethnic Southeast Asian community. The Thai Buddhist monk also became a popular spokesperson for the refugees and developed a strong rapport with the general public. A second Khmer Buddhist Temple was soon established in the nearby Davidson County.

The integration processes of the new Cambodian and Laotian populations offer a study in contrasts. The two groups share a common religious heritage, refugee experiences, and comparable size and arrival times, but the Laotian community has fared much better in business ventures, job advancement, and interaction with the mainstream community. In one example, the Lao youth have organized a youth group that is independent of their parents' MAA and the Buddhist Temple, while the Cambodian youth are not organized outside of the Temple. The obvious difference between the two populations is their socioeconomic and educational background. The Cambodian refugees were primarily rice farmers; the Khmer Rouge had killed most of the educated and middle class. The Laotian community includes many former military officers and representatives of the small middle class with ties to the United States established in prewar Laos. The differences in education and aspirations resulted in the creation of two different types of ethnic enclaves.

Another Laotian population, the Hmong, has a large presence in the state but few residents in the Triad. The Hmong have strong cultural traditions and a clan-based kinship system that bind them closely together, but their language and religion set them apart from their lowland Lao neighbors. Although the Hmong and lowland Lao have organized some joint community groups, they maintain separate identities in most parts of the state. Most of the ten thousand Hmong residing in North Carolina came as secondary migrants from other states and live in the Western Piedmont, around the cities of Hickory and Morganton. The few living in the Triad were recruited for factory and mill jobs in the late 1980s and mid 1990s. In 2002, ten Hmong college students were enrolled at the University of North Carolina at Greensboro.

In 1986, Greensboro attracted national press coverage when it welcomed a new refugee population, the Montagnards. The ethnonym "Montagnards" (French for mountain people) encompasses about thirty different indigenous tribes from the Highlands of South Vietnam with their own tribal languages and customs. Most of the two hundred Montagnards who arrived in North Carolina were resettled in Greensboro, but others went to Charlotte and Raleigh. LFS served as the lead resettlement agency in partnership with the local Catholic Social Services. By 1987, Montagnard leaders had established their own MAA, the Montagnard Dega Association (MDA). The MDA helped Montagnards organize over the next decade, but the fragile coalition of tribes, former military leaders, and populations scattered across three major centers in the state also stirred controversy. Many of the refugees, still hostile toward the Vietnamese government, resented that the MDA did not actively organize the Montagnard resistance movement in the United States.

A second group of some four hundred Montagnards arrived in 1992, soon after the United Nations found them on the Cambodian border. The former resistance fighters believed they were still at war with the Vietnamese government in alliance with the U.S. Army's Special Forces. Additional Montagnards were resettled in the Triad throughout the 1990s as family reunification cases, former reeducation camp prisoners, or others of special interest to the United States. In late 2002 and early 2003, some 1,000 Montagnards arrived in North Carolina, with close to half of them being resettled in the Triad.

Given their status as war heroes, the Montagnards attracted integration assistance from businesses, veteran groups, and a variety of nonprofit organizations. Since the Montagnards fought alongside U.S. Special Forces in Vietnam, the Special Forces Association at Fort Bragg in Fayetteville, North Carolina, and other veterans groups volunteered to assist with the resettlement process. As devout Christians, many Montagnards also received integration assistance from local churches. The evangelical Christian "freedom fighters" were welcomed and put to work in entry-level jobs in factories across the area.

In 1987, LFS and the Greensboro Chamber of Commerce were awarded a White House Citation for their joint resettlement efforts, enhancing the city's reputation for moderate progressivism.

As of early 2003, however, all was not well in the Montagnard community. Tensions were high as eligibility for refugee assistance neared expiration and some had yet to find stable employment. Newly arrived Montagnards were also distraught over the families they left behind. Refugee advocates pressured the United Nations and veterans urged the U.S. government to apply economic pressure on Vietnam, but it remained unclear how willing the Vietnamese government was to facilitate family reunification.

Newcomers from Eastern Europe and the former Soviet Union

Refugees from Eastern Europe and the former Soviet Union have come to North Carolina since the start of the formal refugee resettlement program authorized by the Refugee Act of 1980. Many of those who were originally resettled in the state, however, moved to large cities in the Midwest and on the East Coast with established immigrant communities from East and Central Europe. While the Triad did not become a major resettlement area for Eastern Europeans, the Bosnian refugee community in Greensboro grew to a couple thousand people in the 1990s. Although the Bosnians have not attempted to build a community-based organization, they managed to integrate fairly quickly. The community is composed of distinct groups—Serbs, Croats, and Bosnian Muslims as well as people of mixed heritage—that remain divided over national, ethnic, religious, and political sentiments. But Bosnian refugees have fared well in the state because of their industrial employment experience, relatively high levels of education, and presumably their skin color.

Other pockets of Eastern European refugees can be found across the state.[11] A Russian and Ukrainian refugee community has grown to approximately two hundred in Greensboro through the efforts of Jewish Family Services. The community has remained small and struggled to integrate because many of the refugees are older and retired. Some with professional and technical skills are unwilling to accept entry-level and unskilled jobs. Among the most recent newcomers from Eastern Europe are one hundred Albanian Kosovars, who arrived in the Triad in recent years. They have the benefit of a self-help network that an Albanian LFS staff member has built across the Carolinas and southern Virginia.

INTEGRATION OF NEW NORTH CAROLINIANS:
SUCCESSES AND CHALLENGES

Immigrants figure prominently in North Carolina's past, present, and future. Helping newcomers to develop a sense of belonging, take responsibility for the quality of life in their neighborhoods, and seize opportunities for success are key challenges for state and local leaders. The first official response to the growing Latino community in the Triad dates to 1987, when LFS expanded its refugee services in Guilford County to include legal assistance to Latinos seeking to change their immigration status. The Special Agricultural Workers (SAWs) legalization program, passed in 1986 as part of the Immigration Control and Reform Act (IRCA), authorized temporary resident status and eventual permanent status for up to 350,000 agricultural workers. Originally established with funds from the federal government, the program grew as a result of agency support and service fees. The client population expanded beyond the initial Latino target group as other immigrants became aware of the law.

In 1990, Catholic Social Services opened an office in Winston-Salem, *Casa Guadalupe*, to address primarily legal needs of Latino immigrants. In 1991, another nonprofit was organized by a group of Latino professionals and business people to raise public appreciation of Hispanic/Latino culture. The Hispanic League of the Piedmont Triad (HLPT) organized an annual Latino cultural festival in downtown Winston-Salem with corporate sponsors and media attention. Sponsors included R. J. Reynolds Tobacco Company and Haines Mills, which both depend heavily on Latino labor. By the mid-1990s, the festival was attracting thousands of people, both Latinos and Anglos. The Hispanic League did not provide services and had only minimal Mexican representation on its board of directors, but it effectively raised public awareness of the Latino population's rich cultural contributions.

By the early 1990s, three churches in Kernersville, a town on the Forsyth-Guilford border, were offering special programs for the Latino population. A Catholic church offered a special mass and outreach ministry, while an evangelical church led by a Latino pastor organized clothing drives and provided referral services. A Baptist church with a Spanish-speaking pastor, a former missionary in Central America, developed a health and dental clinic that attracted Latinos from across the Triad. By the mid-1990s mainstream Baptist and Methodist congregations were developing Latino outreach ministries across the Triad and much of the state. Storefront churches sprang up to serve the evangelical Latino population. Catholic churches were struggling to meet the spiritual and material needs of the historically Catholic Latino population. Catholic Social Services expanded its *Casa Guadalupe* office to Greensboro in 1998 and opened a Hispanic Center in High Point in 2002.

Meanwhile, federal welfare reforms were throwing up obstacles to the immigrant integration process. The most dramatic obstacle was the Personal Responsibility and Work Opportunity Reconciliation Act (PRWORA) of 1996, which changed the eligibility of noncitizens for public assistance. Eligibility for major federal benefits—such as food stamps, Supplemental Security Income (SSI), Temporary Assistance for Needy Families (TANF), the Women, Infants, and Children program (WIC), and Medicaid—was linked to immigration status and the date of arrival in the United States (prior to August 22, 1996). The act confused immigrant service providers, who struggled to keep up with changing welfare policies and procedures.

To facilitate integration of newcomers, some service providers took a systematic approach. Catholic Social Services and the Forsyth County Health Department, for example, initiated a demographic study of the Latino population funded by the Kate B. Reynolds Foundation in Winston Salem. A report entitled "Social, Economic, and Demographic Profile of the Hispanic Population of Forsyth County of North Carolina" was published in 1997 and became a basis for community planning and programming. The study estimated the Hispanic population in Forsyth County at 11,996 residents, not counting migrant farm workers. The 1990 Census figure was 2,106. The study indicated that the average age of the Latino population was twenty-three, with the majority of the residents between twenty-one and thirty-four years of age. Of this population, 71 percent had arrived in Forsyth County in the three years preceding the study, 61 percent of the adult population was male, and 96 percent of the men were employed. 76 percent of female immigrants were in the labor force. An impressive 97 percent reported feeling welcomed by the community.

The study sparked additional research and the formation of the Hispanic Services Coalition, composed of various service providers and ethnic community representatives. The group met monthly and developed a strategic plan called the *1999 Hispanic Community Plan*, which called for conducting further research, identifying service gaps, and developing a strategic response. While the research facilitated immigrant integration in Forsyth County, other counties were not conducting parallel studies. Most immigrant integration policies and programs have been developed locally within isolated arenas such as the labor market, schools, or the health care system.

Labor Market and the Workplace

Immigrants did not have trouble finding employment in the Triad's strong labor market. Manufacturing, construction, farming, and the service sector have integrated many newcomers into local workplaces. Poultry plants scattered across the Piedmont employ many Latino immigrants. Interestingly, some of the earlier Hmong refugees who settled in Montgomery County, in the south of the Triad, became chicken farmers in the mid-1980s and now supply poultry for the processing plants. Many undocumented Latinos find initial employment in Mexican restaurants and *tacquerias*, where they often work long hours with few benefits. The workers advance in the labor force as they find other job contacts, mainly through Latino networks, and purchase false documents from underground entrepreneurs.

Demand for immigrant workers in the state soared in the 1990s. Many employers actively recruited immigrants, even those with limited English-language abilities, because of their reputation as hard workers. In Guilford County, for instance, some factories and businesses aggressively sought Montagnard employees, citing their military background, strong work ethic, and Christian convictions as desirable characteristics. Unfortunately, while the Montagnards were considered model employees, few have been promoted beyond the assembly line because of English and educational limitations, and their own temerity with mainstream society.

In the mid-1990s, a trade union attempted to organize workers at a local Kmart distribution center to increase their wages and improve working conditions. Some 100 Montagnards were among the hundreds of workers at the center, many of them African American. By and large, the Montagnards did not respond to the union efforts, partially out of fear regarding the picketing. The Vietnamese refugees were unsure what was illegal and what constituted good citizenship. Few formal bridges of communication existed between the Montagnard and U.S.-born workers. Eventually a settlement that favored the workers was reached following demonstrations and civil disobedience supported by black churches and their leaders. The Montagnards were not yet ready to use their political and economic influence to shape labor conditions, but they benefited from the efforts of progressive black community leaders.

As the local economy slowed in 2001, the Triad was no longer an economic magnet for immigrants seeking work. Secondary migration from other states declined and there was speculation about declining migration from Mexico. Textile mills were closing and moving abroad. As the tobacco industry slumped, state agricultural services sought alternative crops for the small farms scattered around the Piedmont. Immigrants were still finding work, but most of the jobs were low-paying positions in high-risk industries that established residents were not pursuing even in a weak economy. By early 2003, the unemployment rate in the Triad exceeded 6 percent. The recession not only hurt immigrant employment, it also exacerbated tensions between immigrants and established residents who were competing for the same jobs. Misconceptions about immigrant eligibility for public benefits and tax responsibilities intensified misunderstandings. The tensions were more pronounced in rural areas and small towns, where the job market was tighter and the economy less diverse.

Ethnic businesses employ many newcomers, but do not foster integration because they have little contact with the host society. Latino bakeries, meat markets, and clothing stores flank Vietnamese grocery stores, travel agencies, and nail shops. Palestinian, Somali, and Sudanese stores each cater to different ethnic communities. Sudanese entrepreneurs own two of the four taxi companies in Guilford County and are more likely to have mainstream clientele than other ethnic businesses. Strip malls of immigrant-owned stores representing many cultures have developed along main thoroughfares, but go unrecognized by mainstream residents. Ethnic restaurants often do reach out to the mainstream community, but many native New Carolinians would be surprised that immigrants from Vietnam, Laos, and Cambodia work in the kitchens of popular Thai, Japanese, and Chinese restaurants.

Public Schools

Challenges to the school system did not surface until the late 1990s, when the children of Latino immigrant workers arrived or were born in North Carolina in great numbers. Siler City, about forty miles south of Greensboro, reported in 1997 that close to 50 percent of the kindergarten children were native Spanish speakers.[12] The North Carolina public school system does not have a designated English for Speakers of Other Languages (ESOL) curriculum and does not require ESOL certification to teach English to Limited English Proficient (LEP) students. While there are many committed and qualified teachers in the local school system, most ESOL teachers in the Triad have transferred from other fields. Without an educational infrastructure to advocate for improved standards, internal advocacy comes primarily from committed ESOL instructors, teachers who struggle to reach their foreign-born students, and administrators who do not want their schools to be penalized for poor standardized test results.

A chronic problem in North Carolina public schools and other new settlement states examined in this book is the disenfranchisement of immigrant youth. School enrollment of Hispanics drops sharply at age sixteen, when the state no longer requires attendance. That Hispanic youth leave school as soon as legally able indicates they do not feel engaged in the learning process. The influx of Hispanics has been so sudden that few members of the ethnic community have had time to advance their educations and establish themselves as bilingual role models. Educators have sought ways to address the drop in enrollment but without significant success. Less is known about dropout rates among other immigrant populations. It is possible that ethnic leadership intervention, congregational involvement, and influential mentors have reduced dropout rates among refugee youth. Congregational sponsors will sometimes champion a young person who is doing well in school and wants to attend college. Another likely scenario is that children's success in school is related to the educational level of their parents. Anecdotal evidence suggests that children of Montagnard and Cambodian farmers are less likely to finish school than those of Bosnian technicians or African educators.

Immigrant children in Guilford County face many obstacles to educational advancement. In the summer of 2002, the county school system eliminated designated magnet schools and related programs for ESOL students. Children were assigned to neighborhood schools with minimal ESOL resources. Cynics believed that the decision was made to artificially raise school test scores because "special populations" of fewer than 20 students enrolled in an American school for less than two years can be excluded from test score calculations.

In response to an outcry among immigrant advocates and educators, an immigrant advocacy group in Guilford County began researching the situation. The Multicultural Advisory Council (MAC) interviewed parents and teachers of LEP children and consulted the federal Office of Civil Rights to ascertain whether children's civil rights were violated. The school administration invited a national team of consultants to review the school system's approach to LEP learners and their families. The Council of Great Cities Schools (an organization of eighty of the largest school districts in the nation) sent a team of consultants to Greensboro in fall 2002 to review the situation. Their assessment and recommendations for serving LEP students, "Beyond Proficiency: Creating a State-of-the-Art Multilingual Program," was being reviewed by the Guilford County School System at the time of the study.[13] Among their recommendations is a call to ensure immigrant community representation and input in the school decision-making processes.

Another critical issue facing North Carolina is immigrant youth access to higher education. The state has a progressive and relatively inexpensive higher education system, but only legal residents can be admitted to the state's colleges and universities. Federal and state laws allow undocumented youth to attend public elementary and high schools, but exclude them from access to higher education except as international students at exorbitant tuition rates. As the first generation of Latino youth graduates from high school, many of them are undocumented although they have lived in the state for years. The Dream Act, a bill introduced by Senator Orrin Hatch of Utah, would allow undocumented students who have a de facto residency in a state to enroll in public universities at in-state tuition rates. A parallel, state-level bill was under consideration in North Carolina. Immigrant advocacy organizations in North Carolina are lobbying for passage of these bills, which would provide educated leaders for the second generation of Latinos.

Education, especially English-language skills, is an important measure of successful integration for all immigrants, including adults. Various strategies have been used in the Triad to provide English-language training to adult immigrants but progress is slow. Free ESOL classes are available through the community college system, which is closely aligned with the state's economic planning and job training strategies. Officials recognize the value of an English-speaking workforce. Community colleges receive reimbursement from the state if they can prove a sustained participation of at least ten students in a class. Undocumented immigrants are not excluded from ESOL classes, though they cannot register for academic credit or certification courses in the community college system.

Some churches and libraries offer their own English tutoring programs. The Glenwood Library in Greensboro maintains a computer-based ESOL program and a family literacy program that involves parents and children in cooperative English-language programs. Employers sometimes provide onsite ESOL classes to enhance worker safety and increase production goals. But for the many newcomers who have little formal education, progress is slow. As low-income people who work long hours, they do not have the time or energy to benefit from ESOL classes and typically get by with help from their families.

Health Care System

The impact of immigrants on the health care system is similar to the impact on local schools. When the immigrants were primarily single young men, the impact on local hospitals and health departments was minimal. As women of childbearing age and children joined male newcomers, the effects were greater. Local health departments open to anyone in the Triad are used predominantly by Latino clients. Challenges facing local health professionals include limited access to linguistically appropriate services and the immigrants' lack of familiarity with the Western health care system and practices.

In terms of access to health care, refugees are in a better situation than other immigrants. While refugees are eligible for Refugee Medical Assistance (RMA) in their first eight months after arrival, immigrants in low-income, entry-level jobs and those working in the cash economy do not have health insurance. Most newcomers in Guilford County seek medical care at institutions that are obligated to provide health care to anyone in need: the county health department, clinics for low-income patients, and public and nonprofit hospitals. As of this writing, however, health agencies were denying medical services to some immigrants because of new federally mandated documentation requirements. Patients have been required to show their income tax returns as an eligibility requirement. Advocates are encouraging immigrants without social security numbers to obtain taxpayer identification numbers and are negotiating with providers to accept them for identification purposes.

Hospitals eager to reduce emergency room costs have sought ways to treat nonemergencies outside of the hospital system. A local foundation supported the Center for New North Carolinians at the University of North Carolina at Greensboro (UNCG) to provide Lay Health Advisers (LHAs) to various immigrant communities in the county. Building on the immigrant network developed in Guilford County by the AmeriCorps ACCESS Project, the Immigrant Health ACCESS Project hired and trained health advisers from targeted communities. The advisers were charged with channeling immigrants into the health care system, providing interpretation and transportation as necessary, conducting health education activities, and advising providers on immigrant health and cultural traditions. The advisers initially included Latino, Somali, Sudanese, Montagnard, and Laotian representatives. Additional communities were served by community consultants and AmeriCorps members.

Limited access to services is not the only challenge faced by North Carolina's health care system. Many immigrants may be unfamiliar with Western concepts such as germ theory, contagious diseases, and drug therapies. Instead of preventive medicine, many prefer to use traditional healers, herbal medicines, and religious rituals and prayer, avoiding established health care systems except in emergencies. North Carolina law enforcement officials and health care providers report concern about medicines sold over the counter at small *tiendas*.[14] These stores sell medications available in Mexico over the counter that would require a doctor's prescription in the United States. Many Latinos self-medicate but keep their health providers unaware of these practices. Similar practices occur in African and Southeast Asian communities.

Language barriers seem insurmountable at times. Some health care providers rely on ethnic community members for interpretation. While there are many dedicated interpreters in North Carolina, they typically have no professional training and lack basic medical vocabulary. Some interpreters charge exorbitant fees to families that should have access to free linguistically appropriate health services in accordance with Title VI of the Civil Rights Act of 1964.[15] The Federal Office of Civil Rights threatens investigations and has challenged at least one local health department for being out of compliance, but most violations go unpunished.

The health care system has struggled to hire enough bilingual staff. Personnel policies for many state and county agencies require college degrees, but there is a shortage of bilingual candidates with appropriate credentials. An initiative by the State Office of Minority Health in cooperation with the Area Health Education Center (AHEC) has offered continuing education Spanish-language training to health professionals. However, busy medical professionals are not interested in learning Spanish. The Center for New North Carolinians offers a certificate in health and human services interpretation for bilingual persons who successfully complete the center's training program, but its resources are insufficient to train enough health interpreters. Those interpreters also have no assurance of employment by health providers who do not want the financial responsibility.

Legal Systems

Law enforcement agencies face extensive challenges in dealing with immigrants, particularly working-class Latinos. Traffic violations are a particular source of frustration. Latino immigrants may have been driving cars for many years but are unfamiliar with U.S. traffic laws and regulations. Faulty equipment, lack of car insurance, expired license tags and inspection stickers, and driving while intoxicated are common problems. Language and cultural barriers frequently exacerbate what might be minor violations. Police departments in the Triad actively seek bilingual officers. The Greensboro Police Department recently began sending some non Spanish-speaking officers to language and culture training programs in Costa Rica.

Allegations of police harassment of immigrants emerge periodically but with no greater incidence than other localities with large immigrant populations. The state Highway Patrol has been accused of targeting Spanish-speaking drivers on interstates, but this has not been a significant issue in the Triad. Only the Davidson County sheriff, who has a reputation for picking fights with groups including the opposition political party, has admitted singling out Hispanics for traffic violations and other offenses. For several years the city of High Point has had a well-respected police chief of Mexican heritage who has addressed the civil rights of immigrants and promoted understanding of their culture on various civic committees.

The North Carolina Department of Motor Vehicles has received several complaints of specific license examiners discriminating against immigrants, but the state has a reasonably progressive licensing system. Written exams are available in various languages, but the applicant also has to be able to understand English commands from the driving instructor in order to take the driving test. The Department of Motor Vehicles has accepted the Income Tax Identification Number (ITIN) in lieu of a social security number when applying for a driver's license. While this policy has come under attack in the state legislature, advocacy groups argue that testing and licensing immigrants helps to ensure everybody's safety. Efforts to screen out undocumented applicants result in more unlicensed and unregulated drivers on the roads. Additional advocacy efforts have made translated drivers' manuals available in the various languages spoken in the state.

In North Carolina's court system, where language barriers and igno-
rance of the law are common obstacles, many immigrants have also
been exploited by scam artists. Many Mexicans use the Spanish word
notario to indicate an attorney. Unscrupulous entrepreneurs have marketed themselves as *notarios* even though they typically have no legal
status in court and are in fact notaries, not attorneys. The unsuspecting
litigant pays hundreds of dollars for a service that has nothing to do
with legal representation and could even harm the litigant. The Latino
Lawyers Committee of the North Carolina Bar Association has been
fighting this practice in the state and has instituted some restrictions
on its use.[16]

Though the law requires interpretation services for LEP clients, they
are not always provided. A statewide foundation provided support to
train and license Spanish-speaking court interpreters a few years ago,
but not many people completed the rigorous program. Courts and individuals continue to contract with interpreters who do not have the
skills or professional code of ethics to provide this critical service.

HELPING THE NEWCOMERS

Religious Institutions

Religious institutions have a long history of welcoming immigrants to
the Triad. From the arrival of the state's first settlers, religious schools
and faith communities have facilitated the integration of newcomers.
Most religious scriptures commend believers to champion refugees,
the needy, and the afflicted. Influential religious groups such as the
Jews and the Quakers have emphasized acceptance as a primary value.
In this tradition, faith-based organizations have been the main channels of community support for refugees and other immigrants.
Lutheran Immigration and Refugee Services (LIRS), Church World
Service (CWS), Catholic Charities, World Relief, and Hebrew Immigrant Aid Society (HIAS) all have resettlement offices in the Triad.
Refugee populations with a strong Christian identity, such as the Montagnards and the Sudanese "Lost Boys,"[17] have received exceptional
support from mainstream churches and the broader public. The same
cannot be said about Muslim groups, such as immigrants from northern Sudan.

Many refugee and immigrant communities establish their own
places of worship to preserve their culture and religious traditions. In
the past twenty years, newcomers to the Triad have established Bud-

dhist, Cao Dai, and Hindu temples, Catholic and evangelical Christian churches, and mosques. Emerging immigrant faith communities serve to focus immigrant concerns and mobilize community development.

Mainstream religious organizations support these initiatives insofar as they are compatible with their values. Methodist and Presbyterian congregations share their worship space with Montagnards, while mainstream Baptist churches host Chinese- and Arabic-speaking congregations. Black Baptist churches have accommodated evangelical Africans. Some Protestant and Catholic churches have developed special native-language services and ministries for immigrants as part of their mission. Support has been particularly strong for Christian and Jewish immigrants. The primarily Christian population of the Triad has not helped Buddhist and Muslim congregations as much, but there are some examples of mainstream support.

Several religious organizations have taken an integrated approach to worship. St. Mary's Catholic Church in Greensboro, a historically black church, has masses in multiple languages and a multicultural pastoral staff. Its congregation includes immigrants from Southeast Asia, Latin America, and Africa. Our Lady of Grace Catholic Church in Greensboro recently acquired a Spanish-speaking priest, initiated a mass in Spanish, and provided space for the *Casa Guadalupe* program of Catholic Social Services.

Support can also take the form of culturally appropriate services. Catholic Social Ministries of the Diocese of Raleigh fostered the first immigrant service project in Alamance County through a program called *Centro la Comunidad,* which opened in 1999 in Burlington. In Durham, an ecumenical group including Catholic Social Ministries created *Centro Hispano* in 1994, a program that has since grown into a thriving and independent Hispanic community-based organization.

These developments are similar to the schools developed by Quakers, Moravians, Lutherans, Baptists, Methodists, Catholics, and Jews to educate their young in accordance with their spiritual beliefs and practices. The American black community depended on faith-based organizations to maintain their unique identity and build community strength in the struggle for civil rights, cultural identity, and political power. Mainstream religious communities such as the Methodists and the Lutherans occasionally helped to develop black schools to serve community needs.

Commerce chambers, human relations commissions, and similar organizations have also fostered religious cooperation. The Piedmont Interfaith Council, for example, has organized a youth choir composed primarily of immigrants and an annual interfaith Thanksgiving service. The FaithAction International House was organized in the late 1990s to build unity between immigrant and minority communities. While Greensboro has sought interfaith cooperation, the community has been unable to develop an interfaith clergy association other than an influential forum sustained by black ministers. The Pulpit Forum organizes community events, speaks out on policy issues, and mobilizes the community around issues of equal rights.

The overwhelmingly Catholic Latino community has looked primarily to the Catholic Church to meet its religious needs, but storefront Spanish-speaking evangelical churches are now commonplace. Mainstream Protestant churches, white and black, are also developing outreach programs for Latinos. Although the Catholic Church provides several Spanish-speaking priests and masses, the authoritarian structure of the Church modifies the independence of the ethnic community organizations. The Church nevertheless provides the Latino community with structural support and programs for leadership development.

Role of Ethnic Community

Multiple community-based ethnic organizations are emerging in the Triad. They include faith-based and secular organizations that emerged through grassroots efforts or with the help of mainstream organizations. They provide culturally appropriate services, foster ethnic leadership development, and serve as a bridge to mainstream organizations. Yet there are hardly any community-based organizations in the state serving Latinos, the single largest newcomer group in North Carolina. One exception, *Centro de Accion Latino*, resulted from the efforts of several advocates who set out in 1997 to create a nondenominational, nonprofit grassroots organization. Initially staffed by AmeriCorps members, the group slowly expanded its mission and began exploring collaborative relationships with the Catholic Social Services in Guilford County.

In contrast to the Latino community, refugees in the Triad benefit from a developed network of ethnic community-based organizations. Most Southeast Asian organizations are faith based. The Vietnamese, in particular, tend to affiliate with their places of worship, including Catholic and Protestant churches and Buddhist temples. There is no Vietnamese civic organization in the state. Efforts to organize an ethnic community have been met with indifference, due perhaps to the considerable religious and socioeconomic diversity of the Vietnamese community. The Montagnards, on the other hand, have established both church-based organizations and Mutual Assistance Associations (MAAs).

Organizations serving ethnic Africans in North Carolina include churches, mosques, national origin and tribal groups, and a pan-African organization, the African Services Coalition (ASC). The African Services Coalition, with ideological roots in the pan-African movement that was active in Greensboro in the early 1970s, grew out of the AmeriCorps ACCESS Project initiative and was formed in 1996. The organization, whose staff includes African immigrants, supports a job placement program for African refugees, provides referral services and organizes cultural and educational events. Local black clergy have lent support to ASC and its mission of cultural bridge building.

Community Relations

Mainstream institutions have gradually modified their diversity initiatives in response to the region's changing demographics. The Greensboro Chamber of Commerce, which has a long history of moderating race relations, began including immigrant and Native American communities in a leadership initiative in the late 1990s. The training program, called "Other Voices," brings diverse community representatives together to address issues including racism. While the immigrants thought the program worthwhile, they criticized exercises that lumped together Asian, Latino, and Native American immigrants together in a new category of "other," separating them from black and white participants. The chamber was trying to be inclusive, but had not found a conceptual model that reflected the range of diversity in the local community.

The Chamber of Commerce also had difficulty recruiting members of the immigrant community to participate in a diversity committee on small business issues. Immigrant business owners did not consider the chamber a resource, and linguistic and cultural barriers made it difficult for them to participate in mainstream events. While the chamber seeks other ways to include immigrants, the most successful initiatives have instructed mainstream business owners on immigration issues involving their employees and marketing strategies to target new immigrant communities.

The Greensboro Police Department has sought to improve relations with immigrant groups by hiring bilingual employees, but it currently has only half a dozen officers who are bilingual in Spanish and one who speaks Vietnamese. No tension is evident between the police and Greensboro's immigrant communities, but there is a struggle to communicate. Drinking and driving, lack of auto insurance, domestic violence, and reluctance to report crimes constitute ongoing challenges for the police.

Greensboro's Human Relations Department seems better equipped to relate to immigrant communities. The department has Spanish-speaking staff and is proactive in outreach, advocacy, and bridge building between immigrant and host communities. The Human Relations Commission and the National Conference for Community Justice (NCCJ) have recently added Latino and Muslim immigrant representatives. The city provides some educational materials in Spanish and has agreed to post pertinent information in Arabic and Vietnamese on their website as well.

PROSPECTS FOR THE FUTURE

The tragic events of September 11, 2001 have not affected immigrant integration in the Triad as severely as originally feared. Despite reports around the country of a backlash against immigrants, particularly Muslim Arabs and Middle Easterners, local reaction was moderate and even sparked development of new bridges of interfaith communication. Mainstream faith groups organized community visits to the Greensboro Islamic Center and Muslims were invited to speak at various community events and serve on civic committees. About fifty volunteers from local congregations offered to escort Muslim women who were reluctant to go shopping by themselves after the terrorist attacks, although the service was not utilized. At an event in front of the Greensboro City Hall, religious leaders affirmed the city's unity as a multicultural community.

Refugee resettlement halted immediately after the attacks, disappointing refugees in North Carolina who were awaiting reunification with family members from Africa. Many federally funded programs offering English classes, job placement, and health screening closed their doors, but an additional Montagnard refugee resettlement effort launched in the summer of 2002 kept the resettlement agencies open. Zealous advocates from veteran organizations and religious communities have kept the Montagnard refugee advocacy movement strong in Greensboro, Charlotte, and Raleigh.

Not surprisingly, September 11 affected the local Latino population the least. The business community has been particularly vocal in its advocacy of Latino integration in North Carolina. A cluster of service providers, Latino business community representatives, and faith-based organizations helped mobilize a Hispanic Services Coalition addressing integration issues. High Point, home of the International Home Furnishing Market, began to voice concerns about successful Hispanic integration not only to address needs of newcomers but also to project a positive image for its international clients. Chambers of Commerce have sponsored workshops for employers on how to recruit and maintain essential workers, with presentations by attorneys, the Mexican consulate, and the INS office in Charlotte.

The African American community, its churches, and the civil rights movement serve as a model for mobilizing an ethnic community finding its way in the integration process. African American community leaders recognize that Latinos are the largest minority nationally, if not locally. Minority groups have a history of competing for limited resources rather than addressing common limitations, but local African American leaders have begun seeking out areas for cooperation and noting repeated patterns of discrimination, such as racial profiling. While there is some resentment and prejudice toward newcomers, there is integration in working class neighborhoods and on the job, where neighborly traditions transcend cultural barriers. African American churches often define their outreach constituency by neighborhood more than ethnicity, and look for ways to include immigrants in their ministries.

African immigrants pose special challenges and opportunities for the African American community. The white community tends to group African immigrants with American blacks based on race and ancestry, but there are major cultural, historic, and legal differences. Relations can be tense, but leaders from both communities have sought ways to cooperate in advocating for equal rights. African immigrant groups in Greensboro are regularly invited to provide cultural programs for African American organizations and programs. The two groups, like the working-class whites, share similar struggles in the face of poverty, low wages, and the current economic decline.

In summary, prospects for immigrant integration in North Carolina are promising. The state has demonstrated the ability to accommodate non-European groups in the past twenty-five years. Just as the integration of African Americans after hundreds of years of segregation was not without a struggle, advocates of modern immigrants predict that today's newcomers will eventually overcome obstacles. Different immigrant and refugee communities will integrate at different rates. Some will cling to their ethnic enclaves, while others will quickly become part of mainstream society. The pace of integration is influenced by variables including the size of the community, length of time in the United States, educational background, leadership experiences, the degree of acceptance by the mainstream community, and the range of cultural differences.

NOTES

1. The terms "Hispanic" and "Latino" are sometimes used interchangeably. Some advocates strongly prefer one term or the other for varied political or cultural reasons. "Hispanic" alludes to the heritage from Spain while "Latino" alludes to the heritage from Latin America. The U.S. Census has popularized the term Hispanic but some people believe that this term does not do justice to the African and indigenous influences of Latin America. The terms Latino and Hispanic will be used interchangeably in this chapter as related to sources, but without judgment regarding the appropriateness of either term. In practice, most people identify themselves by country of origin.

2. The Triad is a governmental district designating a cluster of counties in north central North Carolina. Greensboro and High Point are in Guilford County, and Winston-Salem is in Forsyth County. Adjoining counties are Surry, Stokes, Rockingham, Caswell, Yadkin, Alamance, Davidson, Randolph, and Montgomery.

3. African Services Coalition is a community-based nonprofit that serves the African immigrant communities in the Piedmont. The board is composed of representatives from different immigrant communities.

4. North Carolina Governor's Office for Latino/Hispanic Affairs, North Carolina Cooperative Extension Service and El Pueblo, "Demographics," *Ayudate 2002*, www.ayudate.org/ayudate/CountyDemographics.html (accessed January 20 2003).

5. Paul Muschick, "Guilford Leaders to Bring Lessons Back from Mexico," *News & Record*, March 22, 2002, 1A.

6. Mark Sills, "2002 Annual Report on the Hispanic/Latino Population in All 100 North Carolina Counties," *FaithAction International House*, 2002.

7. Piedmont Triad Council of Governments, "Census 2000 Data," www.ptcog .org/ (accessed December 28, 2001).

8. Jack G. Dale, Susan Andreatta, and Elizabeth Freeman, "Language and the Migrant Worker Experience in Rural North Carolina Communities," in *Latino Workers in the Contemporary South*, ed. Arthur Murphy, Colleen Blanchard, and Jennifer Hill (Athens: University of Georgia Press, 2001), 93–94.

9. Fasih U. Ahmed, "Social, Economic, and Demographic Profile of the Hispanic Population of Forsyth County, North Carolina," prepared for Catholic Social Services, Winston-Salem, NC, and the Forsyth County Department of Public Health," 1997, i–iii. A follow-up report was prepared by Jerry Arias, Miriam Her-

nandez, Margaret Moore, and Advisory Council and Members of the Hispanic Services Coalition, "1999 Hispanic Community Plan: Forsyth County, North Carolina," Neighbors in Ministry Hispanic Services Coalition, 1999.

10. In standard reporting systems where respondents indicate ethnicity, "African American" is offered as an option. African immigrants typically selected this option.

11. Asheville, three hours west of the Triad in the Appalachian Mountains, has developed a Russian and Ukrainian refugee community of several thousand members. Most came as secondary migrants during the 1990s, attracted by a core group from a couple of large ethnic evangelical churches targeting the Eastern European community. It posed initial challenges because there were no refugee resettlement agencies with established offices in the area. However, Russians and Ukrainians continue to migrate to the community, both in initial refugee resettlement and as secondary migrants. World Relief Refugee Services and Catholic Social Services have also opened offices in the area to serve these populations.

12. By early 2003 the kindergarten population in Siler City was over 60 percent Latino, according to the local Family Resource Center.

13. Terry B. Grier, "Guilford County Schools," Council of the Great City Schools' Final Report of the Strategic Support Team's Review of ESOL Services in Guilford County Schools, 2003, www.guilford.k12.nc.us/instruction/esol/final_esol_cogcs.pdf (accessed February 20, 2003).

14. The Associated Press, "Tiendas Selling Imported Medicine," *News & Record*, February 10, 2003, p. B-3.

15. This provision received new attention in the summer of 2000, when the Clinton administration issued a directive emphasizing that immigrants were covered in the act.

16. This initiative was championed by the chair of the committee, Ed Pons (recently deceased), who was deputy county manager in Guilford County and of Mexican descent.

17. The name "Lost Boys" refers to a generation of Sudanese boys driven from their tribal villages by a civil war between north and south Sudan. Some twelve thousand boys walked first to Ethiopia, then back to Sudan, before reaching the Kakuma refugee camp in Kenya in the early 1990s. The United States agreed to resettle about 3,600 Lost Boys in 2000.

4

Black and White and the Other: International Immigration and Change in Metropolitan Atlanta

Art Hansen

International immigration during the 1990s transformed the state of Georgia, particularly the Atlanta area. A social and political arena that used to host only two significant subpopulations—black and white Americans—became a more diverse mixture with the arrival of the "other," Hispanics, Asians, Europeans, and Africans. By 2000, one-tenth of metro residents were foreign born, the majority having immigrated to the United States during the 1990s. In proportion to the state population, Hispanics[1] more than tripled and Asians almost doubled over the decade (see table 4.1).

The Atlanta Metropolitan Area (AMA),[2] an entity composed of the city and several surrounding counties, is the destination for most of the international immigrants who come to Georgia. The growth of the foreign-born population in recent decades has come amid even more dramatic changes for the metro area. Between 1980 and 2000, the metropolitan economic system expanded geographically to include twenty counties and the overall population more than doubled from 1.6 million to 4.1 million people. Half of the state's population (50.2 percent) lives in the metro area.[3] Immigration and transportation created the city of Atlanta, and the area's position as a transportation hub, its reputation as a dynamic business center, and the availability of jobs are major reasons why the metropolitan area has continued to grow in size and population.

Art Hansen

Table 4.1   Racial and Ethnic Composition of the Population of the United States and Georgia, 1950 to 2000

| | United States | | | | | |
	1950	*1960*	*1970*	*1980*	*1990*	*2000*
White	89.5%	88.6%	87.5%	83.1%	80.3%	75.1%
Black	10.0%	10.5%	11.1%	11.7%	12.1%	12.3%
Asian	0.2%	0.5%	0.7%	1.5%	2.9%	3.6%
Other Races*	NA	NA	NA	3.0%	3.9%	7.9%
Hispanic**	NA	NA	NA	6.4%	9.0%	12.5%

| | Georgia | | | | | |
	1950	*1960*	*1970*	*1980*	*1990*	*2000*
White	69.1%	71.4%	73.9%	72.3%	71.0%	65.1%
Black	30.9%	28.5%	25.9%	26.8%	27.0%	28.7%
Asian	NA	0.1%	0.1%	0.4%	1.2%	2.1%
Other Races*	NA	NA	NA	0.3%	0.7%	3.8%
Hispanic**	NA	NA	NA	1.1%	1.7%	5.3%

Notes: The Asian category also includes Pacific Islanders, who are a statistically insignificant minority in Georgia. NA means that the data are not available. *Other Races in 2000 includes two subcategories: the earlier "some other race" plus the new "two or more races." The number of people selecting to identify themselves in the other races category increased significantly in the 2000 census for two reasons. First, there was an increase in people of other racial categories. Second, the 2000 census allowed respondents for the first time to select multiple-race self-reported identities. **Hispanic appears in the census for the first time in 1980, which is why the data for earlier years are not available (NA). The Hispanic or Latin category is listed in the census apart from the "racial" breakdown and reflects people who are also counted in one of the racial categories. This is why the racial categories (without including Hispanics) total 100%. *Source:* U.S. Census Bureau; Hobbs and Stoops 2000.

The population within the metro area has also shifted considerably in recent decades. Racial tensions, the aftermath of the civil rights movement, and desegregation (with only partial integration) all contributed to internal movement. Perhaps the most visible example was "white flight," the growth of the predominantly white population outside of the city after 1970. Atlanta itself lost population during this period and became overwhelmingly African American.

Although this chapter focuses on international immigrants, the integration of black and white Americans remains a work in progress. A prevailing ethos that focuses on business and prosperity has counterbalanced the racial tensions in Atlanta, perhaps best captured by its motto that it is the "City Too Busy to Hate." Racial issues have significantly influenced the area, of course, but the pace of business effectively diminished the racial violence that erupted in other cities.

The city has launched several successful campaigns over the decades to attract more corporations to Atlanta, fueling the growth of employment opportunities. Business and civic leaders have also described Atlanta as an international city since 1970, cultivating linkages that help explain the rise in international migration. As a result the concept of integration has expanded to include people with a variety of backgrounds and concerns about undocumented immigrants, particularly since the major influx of Mexicans that began near 1980.

The visibility of the international population varies. The city's leading newspaper frequently spotlights immigrants and refugees, but many of the international immigrants blend into their corporate, commercial, and university workplaces without attracting much public attention. Many Atlanta-area churches advertise meeting places for foreign-language congregations, and many public schools enroll large numbers of international students with limited English proficiency. State and municipal agencies have recognized the need for translators and interpreters to service their multilingual clientele.

The international presence is especially notable in DeKalb County, the most ethnically diverse metropolitan county. International immigrants, their restaurants and their stores are concentrated in pockets scattered through the county. One example is the "International Village," a miles-long strip of Buford Highway in the small cities of Chamblee and Doraville that showcases a striking mixture of Asian and Hispanic shopping centers, stores, restaurants, and service agencies. The case of Chamblee, described later in the chapter, illustrates how one city has managed to capitalize on the opportunities presented by international migration.

GEORGIA'S CHANGING POPULATION

Early in the twentieth century, Georgia's population was largely rural, divided almost evenly between black and white with very few foreigners, and growing slower than the rest of the country. In the last hundred years, rapid population growth, international immigration, and urbanization have changed the state dramatically. Between 1980 and 2000, the state grew twice as fast as the national average, increasing 50 percent to 8.2 million people. This growth reflects one of the most significant demographic trends of the last century, the dispersion of the population to the western and southern United States.[4]

International immigrants represent a significant part of this growth. The proportion of foreign-born residents in the state almost tripled during the 1990s, from 2.7 percent to 7.1 percent of the population.

The 2000 Census showed that one in every twenty-five people in Georgia was an international immigrant who had entered the country since 1990. In this regard, the state fits a national pattern. Historically, most of the country's foreign born lived in the Northeast and Midwest (86.3 percent in 1900), but regional distribution changed so that by 1990 about one-quarter of the foreign born lived in the South (23.2 percent). In Georgia, the "other" had arrived and was becoming more visible.

The growing presence of people who lack facility with the English language has created significant integration challenges for Georgia. The proportion of people who speak a language other than English at home in the state has more than doubled to 9.9 percent.[5] One in every twenty Georgians did not speak English very well in 2000. The rapid increase in people lacking English proficiency has a significant impact on society, especially public schools, which are perhaps the most important vehicle for the integration of immigrant children.

Urbanization was another dramatic change in Georgia over the last century. Half the population of the once rural state now lives in a single metropolitan area, and fully 69.2 percent lived in one urban area or another in 2000. Rural-urban migration swept the entire country, but the South had been the most rural region. Only 8 percent of Georgians lived in urban areas in 1910.

Rapid population growth, urbanization, and international immigration add new dimensions to the sociopolitical dynamics of a state where gender and race issues remain close to the surface. This chapter focuses on the addition of international immigrants. The most important nontraditional populations that can be identified from the census data are the foreign born, Hispanics, Asians, and those who speak other languages or have difficulties with English. The international population has grown faster than the state overall. To summarize the data presented to this point, this was the demographic picture of Georgia in 2000:

1. One in every fourteen Georgians is foreign born, and 60 percent of these immigrated to the United States after 1990. These rates almost tripled in the 1990s.
2. One in every nineteen Georgians is Hispanic. This has more than tripled.
3. One in every forty-eight is Asian. This has almost doubled.
4. One in every twenty-six reported another or a mixed racial/ethnic identity. This jumped by a factor of five in the 1990s.
5. One in every ten speaks another language at home, and one in

every twenty does not speak English very well. These rates more than doubled.

Population growth and the growing presence and importance of the "other" are not uniform across Georgia. The Atlanta Metropolitan Area has been the destination for most of the international and domestic immigrants to the state. The creation of the AMA only fifty years ago acknowledged the rapid growth of the regional socioeconomic system around the core city of Atlanta.

THE CITY OF ATLANTA

The civil rights struggle drove many dramatic changes in Atlanta in the second half of the last century. The city had strong black leadership, including the ministers Martin Luther King Sr. and Martin Luther King Jr. A strong white leader was newspaper editor Ralph McGill, who won a Pulitzer Prize for his columns in the *Atlanta Constitution* about racial problems and the need for integration in the 1950s.[6]

Even when whites dominated politics and economics in Atlanta, blacks were a significant minority, comprising more than one-third of the city's residents in 1950. Atlanta was recognized by many as the capital of black America. African American businesses downtown along Auburn Avenue comprised one of the largest concentrations of black wealth in America by the 1920s, and in 1929 seven historically black colleges and universities on adjacent campuses near downtown joined forces to create the Atlanta University Center.

Predominantly white until the early 1960s, the city changed as the state began adjusting to desegregation and the efforts of blacks to attain equal civil rights. While blacks were still immigrating to the city, whites began to leave for the suburbs. By 1970 blacks were the majority (51.3 percent) in the city, and the first black mayor, Maynard Jackson, was elected in 1973.

White flight surged during the 1970s when the city lost 42.7 percent of its white population (see table 4.2). Immigration of blacks and much smaller numbers of international immigrants did not make up for the exodus, and the city lost population between 1970 and 1990. The trend began to reverse itself only during the 1990s when traffic congestion induced more people to move closer to their jobs in the city.

These changes in the city's racial composition coincided with the

Table 4.2a   Composition, Growth, and Decline of the City of Atlanta, 1950 to 2000

	1950	1960	1970	1980	1990	2000
White	63.4%	61.7%	48.4%	32.4%	31.1%	33.2%
Black	36.6%	38.3%	51.3%	66.6%	67.1%	61.4%
Other*	Insig.	Insig.	0.3%	1.0%	1.9%	5.4%
Hispanic**	NA	NA	NA	NA	1.9%	4.5%
Total	331,210	487,455	496,973	425,022	394,017	416,474

Table 4.2b   Population Growth and Decline of the City by Race and Culture,
1950 to 2000

	1950–1960	1960–1970	1970–1980	1980–1990	1990–2000	2000
White	+ 43.2%	− 20.0%	− 42.7%	−11.3%	+ 13.1%	138,352
Black	+ 53.9%	+ 36.8%	+ 10.9%	− 6.6%	− 3.2%	255,689
Other*	+129.7%	+298.6%	+198.2%	+75.5%	+202.0%	22,433
Hispanic**	NA	NA	NA	NA	+148.8%	18,720
Total	+ 47.2%	+ 2.0%	− 14.5%	− 7.3%	+ 5.7%	416,474

Notes: Other* was an undifferentiated category until the 1990 census. There was significant growth in this category, but an insignificant number of people (less than 0.1% of the population) self-reported themselves in this category in the 1950 and 1960 censuses. By 1980 this had risen to 1.0%. Hispanic** appears in the Atlanta census for the first time in 1990. The Hispanic or Latin category is listed in the Atlanta census apart from the "racial" breakdown and reflects people who are also counted in one of the racial categories. The total is a sum of the racial categories and does not recognize the Hispanic or Latin category.
Source: U.S. Census Bureau

development of new global linkages. International flights from the airport began with a daily flight to Mexico in 1971, and Atlanta began an "International City" campaign. In 1980, Cable News Network (CNN) began transmitting from Atlanta, and international businesses gained a much higher profile. By 1985 one million international passengers passed through the airport every year. The number of international passengers swelled to 5.7 million in 2002 as twelve international airlines made use of the airport.[7]

By the mid-1990s the metro area also hosted more than forty consulates, more than two hundred ethnic or national origin-based social and religious organizations, at least ten foreign-language newspapers, and many immigrant-owned stores.[8] Most international immigrants to the state have settled in the metropolitan area but outside the city. In Atlanta proper, 95 percent of the residents were either black or white in 2000. One of every 15 people in the city was foreign born, two-thirds of those having entered the country since 1990. Fewer than 2 percent were Asian and one in every twenty-two residents was Hispanic. One in every nine spoke a language other than English at home, and one in every twenty did not speak English very well.

THE ATLANTA METROPOLITAN AREA 2000

The city of Atlanta fits almost entirely into southern Fulton County with a small portion extending east into DeKalb County.[9] The Atlanta Metropolitan Area (AMA) was established in 1950 as a statistical area with the city at its demographic and socioeconomic core. The area encompasses three counties: Fulton in the center, bracketed by DeKalb to the east and Cobb County to the west. The AMA boundaries recognized that surrounding populations were socially and economically integrated with the core city. At the time these three counties were home to 19.5 percent of the state's population.

Through the 1950s, the city grew on pace with the metro area. The growth rates then diverged dramatically, with the city shrinking as the AMA quadrupled in population (see table 4.3) and incorporated more counties. Hundreds of thousands of people immigrated into the metro area, but did not move into the city, which experienced a net loss of population. One exception was immigration to the area by blacks, who generally moved to the city rather than outlying areas between 1950 and 1970.

The growth of the metropolitan population has been fueled in part by the addition of more counties to the AMA. Two counties were included in 1960, giving the metro area claim to a quarter of Georgia's residents. Fifteen more counties were included in 1980. By 2000, a total of twenty counties were economically integrated with the metropolitan area, covering one-eighth of the state's geographical area and containing more than four million people, half the state population.

Another factor in the area's rapid population increase has been the growth of the five counties at the core of the metro area since 1960. In the four decades leading up to 2000, these counties tripled in size to 2.9 million people, representing more than a third of the state's population.

International immigration has constituted a significant part of this growth, especially over the past twenty years. Of Georgia's foreign born, 73.3 percent lived in the AMA in 2000, including the vast majority of recent arrivals. By 2000 more than 420,000 international immigrants lived in the metropolitan area. The international presence was striking:

Table 4.3   Population of Atlanta Metropolitan Area by County, 1950 to 2000 (in Thousands)

County	Years Included in Metropolitan Area	1950	1960	1970	1980	1990	2000
Clayton	1960–2000	—	46.4	98.0	150.4	182.1	236.5
Cobb	1950–2000	61.8	114.2	196.8	297.7	447.7	607.8
DeKalb	1950–2000	136.4	256.8	415.4	483.0	545.8	665.9
Fulton	1950–2000	473.6	556.3	607.6	589.9	649.0	816.0
Gwinnett	1960–2000	—	43.5	72.3	166.9	352.9	588.4
Subtotals for 3–5 Original Counties 3–5 Country Population (in thousands)		671.8	1,017.2	1,390.2	1,687.9	2,177.5	2,914.6
Percentage of State Population		19.5%	25.8%	30.3%	30.9%	33.6%	35.6%
Barrow	1990–2000	—	—	—	—	29.7	46.1
Bartow	2000	—	—	—	—	—	76.0
Butts	1980–1990	—	—	—	13.7	15.3	—
Carroll	2000	—	—	—	—	—	87.3
Cherokee	1980–2000	—	—	—	51.7	90.2	141.9
Coweta	1990–2000	—	—	—	—	53.9	89.2
Douglas	1980–2000	—	—	—	54.6	71.1	92.2
Fayette	1980–2000	—	—	—	29.0	62.4	91.3
Forsyth	1980–2000	—	—	—	28.0	44.0	98.4
Henry	1980–2000	—	—	—	36.3	58.7	119.3
Newton	1980–2000	—	—	—	34.5	41.8	62.0
Paulding	1980–2000	—	—	—	26.1	41.6	81.7
Pickens	2000	—	—	—	—	—	23.0
Rockdale	1980–2000	—	—	—	36.7	54.1	70.1
Spalding	1990–2000	—	—	—	—	54.5	58.4
Walton	1980–2000	—	—	—	31.2	38.6	60.7
Totals for Metropolitan Area Number of Counties in Metropolitan Area		3	5	5	15	18	20
Metropolitan Population (in thousands)		671.8	1,017.2	1,390.2	2,030.0	2,833.5	4,112.2
Percentage of State Population		19.5%	25.8%	30.3%	37.2%	43.7%	50.2%
State Population (in thousands)		3,444.6	3,943.1	4,589.6	5,463.1	6,478.2	8,186.5

Notes: The name of the county is followed by the years it has been considered to be part of the metropolitan (statistical) area. The U.S. Office of Management and Budget (OMB) decides which counties will be considered part of a metro area. In the 1980 census the OMB greatly expanded the AMA from five to fifteen counties. The number rose to eighteen for 1990 and twenty for 2000. Note that Butts County was part of the area for two decades but was dropped for 2000.
Sources: American FactFinder, U.S. Census Bureau

1. One in every ten people in the metro area was foreign born in 2000. This proportion more than doubled in ten years.
2. One in sixteen entered the country during the 1990s.
3. Almost one in seven spoke another language at home.
4. One in fifteen was Hispanic. This has more than tripled.
5. One in thirty was Asian. This has almost doubled.

These international immigrants to Atlanta come from every continent. More than half (51.3 percent) come from the Americas,[10] and more than one-quarter (27.2 percent) from Asia. Smaller percentages come from Europe, Africa, and Oceania.

Mexico, the origin of a quarter of the Atlanta area's international immigrants, is clearly the dominant source country. More immigrants come from Mexico than all of Asia combined. Other significant source countries in the Americas include Jamaica, Canada, Colombia, El Salvador, and Guatemala. The top-four source countries in Asia are India, Vietnam, Korea, and China. Vietnam is unique among this group because it is the source of refugees, whereas immigrants from other countries typically are economically motivated. The United Kingdom and Germany are the major European originating countries, but Bosnia and Herzegovina are the source of significant numbers of refugees. Nigeria is the major African originating country. Rather than settling evenly across Georgia's 159 counties, international immigrants have gravitated toward two counties in the metropolitan area that have offered job opportunities and access to mass transit.

Limited access to public transportation in the metro area is a legacy of the city's racial divide. The Metropolitan Atlanta Rapid Transit Authority (MARTA) was established in 1971 to improve access to downtown businesses. Although the metropolitan area included five counties by 1970, the transit authority was only allowed to operate in the city of Atlanta and the two core counties of Fulton and DeKalb. Apparently, just as streets and bus lines were designed to block expansion of blacks into white neighborhoods, residents in other counties did not want public transportation to help minorities access their communities.[11] This restriction has influenced the settlement and integration of refugees and other international immigrants who arrived in Georgia without access to private transportation.

New immigrants and others without cars have generally settled inside the perimeter created by Interstate 285, the highway encircling the city. The highway, constructed in the 1970s to allow interstate traffic to bypass downtown Atlanta, encloses the city, part of Fulton and

DeKalb Counties, the airport and small sections of adjacent counties. Public transportation is generally limited to the territory within this perimeter, making it a prime destination for new immigrants.

INTERNATIONAL IMMIGRANTS IN DEKALB COUNTY

DeKalb County has become the most diverse county in metro Atlanta with the highest proportion of international immigrants.[12] The second-largest county in the state with more than 665,000 people, it grew 22 percent during the 1990s. Almost one-sixth of the county's population is foreign born, and almost one-tenth entered the United States during the 1990s. These figures are 50 percent greater than the rates for the metropolitan area as a whole and more than double the statewide rates. More than one-sixth of county residents speak a language other than English in their homes, and one-tenth do not speak English very well, double the statewide rate.

Most of DeKalb County consists of densely settled, unincorporated areas. Decatur, the county seat, is the largest of the county's eight small cities with around eighteen thousand residents, but most of them live in the unincorporated areas inside the perimeter. In black and white terms, DeKalb resembles the city more than the white counties outside the perimeter. More than half of the county population is black, which is less than in the city but nearly double the metro average. More than one-third of the people in DeKalb are white, slightly more than in the city but about half the metro average. Almost 8 percent of the county population is Hispanic with half as many Asians, higher than in the city or the metro average.

This diversity is not evenly distributed. The proportions of black, white, Hispanic, and Asian differ from one city and neighborhood to another. The small city of Chamblee is a clear example. Described in more detail later in this chapter, Chamblee has a much higher proportion of Hispanics, Asians, and other races and a much lower proportion of blacks than the county average.

Another lens on the distribution of international immigrants is the enrollment of international students in public schools. In the 2001–2002 school year, 12.8 percent of the students in DeKalb County's public schools were categorized as international. The uneven geographical distribution of international immigrants shows clearly in the county's eighty-three public elementary schools, which have an average enrollment of 581 students. The enrollment of international students exceeds one hundred in nineteen of these schools, where the international students range from 21 percent to a high of 85 percent of the total student population. In seven of these elementary schools, international students are in the majority. Elsewhere, twenty-four schools have fewer than ten international students each and in fifteen others international students comprise 1 percent or less of the student population. These rates clearly identify neighborhoods with higher proportions of international immigrants.

Only 6 percent of the 11,920 international students speak English at home. In the Georgia school system, the others are labeled "language minority" students. The most common language spoken at home by these students is Spanish (42.2 percent). Other languages, spoken primarily by refugee children, include Vietnamese (7.6 percent), Somali (5.1 percent), and Amharic and Tigrinia from Ethiopia (5 percent).

Beyond their concentrations in some areas, several other factors influence the degree to which newcomers blend into Atlanta society. Significant differences in language, culture, and socioeconomic position between immigrants and established residents generally draw attention to the immigrants' foreignness. One key factor is the media, which influences but does not determine residents' perceptions of the new arrivals. Refugees arriving in Atlanta generally receive positive attention. Immigrants coming for work or family reunification are often ignored outside of infrequent human interest stories. Undocumented immigrants are sometimes portrayed as criminal aliens, but are more often described as an important and necessary source of labor.

REFUGEES IN GEORGIA

Before 1980, U.S. policy toward refugees was driven by Cold War politics. The government accepted people fleeing communist regimes in order to embarrass those governments and encourage others to leave. With the Refugee Act of 1980, the country accepted the UN definition of refugees. Since then the federal government and the fifty states have established procedures to manage refugee admissions and facilitate the resettlement and integration of refugees arriving in this country.

Georgia established its state-level program to administer refugee resettlement in 1981, the year the state began recording refugee arrivals. The arrival and place of residence of refugees was documented with more rigor compared to other immigrants because the refugees arrived with government assistance and needed to register to receive special resettlement benefits.

Statistics about refugee arrivals illustrate trends, but do not provide a complete picture of current residents. Only the primary migration to the United States was well documented. An unknown number of refugees left their first location, and secondary migration was recorded only if they applied in the new location for refugee benefits they did not access in the first location. The same opportunities that brought immigrants to the state undoubtedly attracted refugees from other states as well, so the statistics likely underestimate the number of refugees living in the state and the Atlanta metro area.

Official statistics indicate that more than forty-nine thousand refugees arrived in the state between 1981 and 2002. Half came from Asia, nearly all of them fleeing the aftermath of the Vietnam War. Vietnam itself produced almost 40 percent of Georgia's refugees, with smaller numbers coming from Cambodia and Laos. European countries supplied one-quarter of Georgia's refugees, more than half of them from Bosnia (part of the former Yugoslavia). Most of the rest came from the republics that emerged after the collapse of the former USSR.

One out of six refugees resettled in Georgia came from Africa. More than half of them came from Somalia after its civil war broke out in 1991. Ethiopia supplied half as many as Somalia with the rest coming in smaller numbers from Sudan and many other African countries. Although the Middle East produced many refugees, the region sent less than 5 percent of those coming to Georgia, mainly from Iraq and Iran. Cubans and other refugees from the Americas accounted for only 1 percent of the refugees accepted into Georgia.

The forty-nine thousand refugees represented 11.7 percent of the international immigrants in Georgia. A comparison of the origins of international immigrants with those of refugees in Georgia reveals that entire blocks of international immigrants were refugees. These included the immigrants from Vietnam, Bosnia and Herzegovina, Russia, Ethiopia, and Sierra Leone. Another large block of refugees from Somalia did not appear in some counts because the census did not differentiate the national origins of all African refugees.

THE VISIBILITY OF REFUGEES

Sheer numbers alone do not determine public awareness of international immigrants. Visibility also depends on the way immigrants

Table 4.4   Refugees Immigrating to Georgia by Origin, 1981 to 2002 (Listed in Order of Declining Frequency)

	Years Recorded*	Number Arriving	Percentage of State Total
Vietnamese War Related Vietnamese, Cambodians, Laotians, and from Thailand Camps**	1981–2002	23,781	48.2%
Vietnamese by Themselves	1981–2002	19,181	38.9%
Bosnians	1993–2002	6,769	13.7%
Former USSR***	1988–2002	4,241	8.6%
Somalia	1991–2002	4,010	8.1%
Ethiopia****	1983–2002	2,003	4.1%
Asian Countries	1981–2002	24,911	50.5%
European Countries	1983–2002	12,229	24.8%
African Countries	1983–2002	7,650	15.5%
Middle Eastern Countries	1983–2002	2,066	4.2%
American Countries	1994–2002	706	1.4%
Georgia Total*****	1981–2002	49,295	100%

Notes: *Refugee statistics in Georgia start with 1981 when the state established the Office of State Refugee Coordinator and other administrative units. Refugees may have arrived in the state earlier but were not recorded as such. **Refugees noted as coming from Thailand were Southeast Asian children who were born in Thai refugee camps. ***Refugees coming from the former Union of Soviet Socialist Republics were identified (beginning in 2001) as coming from Russia and the Ukraine. The 2002 data added entries for Moldova and Uzebekistan. There are some inconsistencies in the 1981–2002 summary data for this category. ****The 1990 refugee data contained an undifferentiated "African" category, which was counted here as Ethiopian. *****The Georgia total includes 1,733 refugees (3.5% of the total) whose countries of origins were not differentiated.
Source: Georgia Office of Refugee Health

arrive and settle, their motivation to assimilate, and the integration efforts of established residents.

Since the 1800s, international immigrants arriving in Atlanta have generally blended into metropolitan society with little public notice. For decades, they arrived individually or in small groups, and with little public fanfare. Newcomers who appeared to be either black or white spoke English, dressed like Georgians, ate the same foods, and followed many of the same public customs in an effort to assimilate. Residents generally made an effort to accept the newcomers without segregating them socially.

The arrival of refugees in recent decades, however, marked the end of this relative anonymity. Although refugees represent only a fraction of international immigrants, they gained visibility beyond their numbers. An inordinate amount of media attention clearly played a role.

Refugees presented the human face of global conflicts for the local media. Half the refugees in Georgia came because of the Vietnam War. These Vietnamese, Cambodian, and Laotian refugees represented painful reminders of a war that bitterly divided the country and ended in a U.S. defeat. The refugees also stirred guilt and anguish over the desertion of local allies by U.S. forces when they left Vietnam in 1975.

When refugees from Bosnia and Herzegovina began arriving in 1993, they represented victims of a European war that Americans had witnessed on the evening news. The refugees from Kosovo, reminders of another televised international failure in Europe, arrived in 1999. Graphic photos of death and destruction preceded these refugees. The U.S. government's decision to accept specific cohorts of refugees for resettlement was publicized as proof of U.S. humanitarian intentions. When a conflict flared overseas, the local media focused on how the refugees in Atlanta were responding to renewed strife in their homelands. This continually reestablished the visibility of their international presence.

Arriving refugees often received more attention because they came in groups met by host agencies and volunteers. The arrival and reception of refugees generally attracts newspaper and television coverage.[13] Refugee arrivals, managed by the U.S. government, are also publicized by host service agencies to increase public support for the refugees and boost fund-raising. Refugee resettlement in the metropolitan area has not been dispersed, remaining concentrated around a few visible enclaves. The establishment of refugee enclaves was not a deliberate strategy, but rather an unintended consequence of restricted mass transit and housing decisions made by resettlement agencies.

As in the Minnesota case study explored in another chapter, physical and cultural differences have also been striking. Many European immigrants had physically blended into the white population, just as many African refugees could blend into the black population.[14] The Vietnamese, Cambodian, and Laotian refugees and the Korean and Chinese immigrants, however, were physically distinct and displayed cultures and languages that did not easily blend into southern black-and-white society. One clear cultural example has been the proliferation of Asian restaurants, specialty shops, shopping centers, and multilingual advertising signs.

For the Muslim and Arab refugees from Somalia, Bosnia, Iraq, and Iran, the emphasis on national security since September 2001 resulted in heightened public attention and vulnerability. Even when the refugees were Christian and received permission to attend local churches, they often preferred separate services for linguistic and cultural reasons. These separate services were publicized prominently outside the host churches.

Although some refugees to Atlanta were educated, English speaking, and wealthy enough to purchase cars, most arrived without private vehicles or the resources to buy them. Representatives from the resettlement agencies, stressing the importance of mass transit to refugee integration, encouraged placement of refugees in the two counties served by MARTA. Half of all refugees resettled in Georgia were resettled in DeKalb County, and three-fourths of all Georgia's refugees were resettled inside the perimeter in DeKalb and Fulton Counties.[15]

Within these two counties, refugee resettlement was further concentrated because of practical reasons stemming from housing issues. When church congregations sponsored a refugee, they could put up the newcomer family in a home owned by the church or a member of the congregation. But service agencies generally placed refugees in apartment complexes, which is easier when only a few selected buildings are involved.

UNDOCUMENTED IMMIGRANTS IN GEORGIA AND METRO ATLANTA

Georgia was one of three states that had "relatively few unauthorized residents in 1990" and then "experienced rapid growth of the unauthorized population" during the 1990s, according to the federal government.[16] In fact, Georgia was among the six states in this country with the largest numerical increases in undocumented immigrants over the decade. Whereas only thirty-four thousand undocumented immigrants lived in Georgia in 1990, accounting for 0.5 percent of the state's population, there were 228,000 undocumented residents by 2000. This meant that undocumented immigrants made up 2.8 percent of Georgia's population, almost a six fold increase in ten years.

Census figures showed that almost three-fourths of the foreign born in Georgia in 2000 lived in the AMA. Assuming the same ratio for the undocumented, approximately 171,000 undocumented immigrants were living in metro Atlanta in 2000. This would mean that 4.2 percent of metro residents were undocumented.

Despite the limitations inherent in estimates of an undocumented population, they do provide at least some basis for evaluating the origins of the foreign born in the AMA. The increase in undocumented immigrants during the 1990s made them a more significant portion of the immigrants in the metro area. Although refugees gained a higher profile because of media attention, they only accounted for 10.5 percent of the foreign born in metro Atlanta in 2000. The undocumented, on the other hand, constituted 40.4 percent, and 49.1 percent of the foreign born were legal immigrants admitted for employment or family reunification.

Spanish-speaking countries in the Americas sent almost half the international immigrants living in the AMA in 2000. Mexico produced more than half of the immigrants from the hemisphere and almost eight times as many immigrants as the next country, Jamaica. Some Central Americans were granted residence for reasons stemming from civil wars and national disasters.[17] All the Mexicans and most of the Spanish-speaking immigrants, in other words, were either undocumented or legal nonrefugee immigrants.

The category of undocumented immigrant captures a heterogeneous population, as noted above. There were students and tourists from every continent who overstayed their visas, individuals who fled persecution in their countries and might be recognized as worthy of asylum or temporary protection, and many who came looking for work. The influx of Hispanic men looking for day labor became a highly visible sign of the international presence in the metro area. The popular impression of undocumented immigrants in metro Atlanta was that they were all Mexican, spoke Spanish, had entered the country illegally, had low levels of education, and worked at day labor, unskilled, or semiskilled jobs.

There was a high demand for day laborers in construction, landscaping, and other jobs. The hiring process, which took place on the street, required that workers gather early in the morning and wait for prospective employers to offer employment. Once hired, the workers, who usually came on foot, piled into the employer's truck and rode to the day's worksite. As a consequence, the parking lots of many gas stations, convenience stores, and strip malls in the metro area became gathering places for Hispanic men seeking work. Metro residents, looking across a cultural divide, typically viewed the waiting men with suspicion and voiced concerns about crime, law and order, and public sanitation.

Chamblee, a small city in DeKalb County, responded to the challenges posed by large-scale immigration in a positive way that aided integration efforts. The city confronted a major influx of humanitarian and undocumented immigrants, endured a period of tension and hostility, and emerged as an integrated multicultural city with an "international village."

CHAMBLEE: A CASE STUDY

Before the expansion of the metropolitan area, Chamblee, located outside Atlanta, was a small town. After a black neighborhood was relocated to another area in the 1940s, the population of Chamblee remained primarily white until the late 1970s when Atlanta churches began resettling refugees from the Vietnam War in the area. The availability of cheap apartments and good public transportation made it an appealing resettlement site.[18]

Many Cambodian, Vietnamese, and Laotian refugees arrived in the late 1970s and early 1980s, and their presence was so widely noted that Chamblee acquired the nickname "Chambodia." The arriving refugees were culturally and linguistically different from the local residents, but the refugees tended to keep a low profile and stay together in closed groups.

Tensions escalated with the arrival of Mexicans and other Hispanics in the 1980s and early 1990s. Attracted by a construction boom in metro Atlanta, Hispanics settled in Chamblee for the same reasons that churches had chosen the city as a resettlement site: cheap housing and job opportunities. By 1990, nearly a quarter of the city's population was Hispanic and 12 percent was Asian. Residents reported that the early years of the Hispanic influx were difficult. They referred to the arrival of "busloads of Mexicans" who crammed too many people into overcrowded apartments and brought trouble to the streets. Amid rising crime, prostitution, and drug problems, some residents felt threatened and trapped inside their homes.

In a widely publicized case in 1992, a city council meeting generated the idea of using bear traps to keep day laborers waiting for work off of private property.[19] Residents complained that Hispanic men frequently were rowdy, drank, and used drugs while waiting for work near a convenience store. An elderly white woman who lived behind the store complained the men used her yard as a bathroom. The idea raised at a city council meeting was that bear traps would discourage the men from trespassing, and anyone caught in a trap could be deported to Mexico.

The incident brought out the negative perceptions of the Hispanic newcomers and the concerns of established residents. But the case also triggered public and official condemnations and marked a turning point in how Chamblee dealt with immigrants. Under criticism, city officials apologized. The U.S. Department of Justice started an investigation, and subsequent elections and appointments brought many new people into office. A local task force was also created to review the changes in Chamblee and consider how the city might respond more appropriately to the newcomer population.

The Chamblee Task Force report emphasized the positive contributions of immigrants and proposed recommendations to facilitate their integration. The report proposed hiring multilingual civil servants, more minority representation on the police force, an international community center, and orientation and English classes for immigrants. The bottom line was that the "immigrants, both legal and illegal, stimulate the economy"[20] and should be encouraged to settle in Chamblee.

Inspired by the discussion of contributions by immigrants, the DeKalb County Chamber of Commerce and Chamblee began to consider them a community resource. Studies conducted by the chamber indicated that the section of Buford Highway running through Chamblee contained "the largest concentration and variety of ethnically oriented businesses in the Southeastern U.S."[21] The area, with more than one hundred immigrant-owned retail outlets including ethnic restaurants, attracted shoppers from beyond the metro area and appeared capable of attracting even tourists.

Seeing potential, the city and chamber of commerce developed and began to publicize the concept of an "International Village" district in Chamblee. Land-use plans were developed for the entire area that included improvement of pedestrian walkways, bicycle lanes, and roadways, and new public facilities. The village was projected to become "the nucleus of a growing, multicultural, international community both within the City of Chamblee and within the greater metropolitan Atlanta area . . . home, workplace, learning center, tourist center, retail center and recreation area for individuals and businesses with a variety of cultures."[22]

The original idea was to create a larger "village" area that would include both Chamblee and the adjacent small city of Doraville. The cities, linked by a stretch of ethnic businesses along the highway, were of similar size and both took in resettled Asian refugees and Hispanic immigrants. But Doraville had not received as many immigrants. Nearly 70 percent of Doraville's population was white in 1990, compared to 45.4 percent in Chamblee. Whereas Hispanics and Asians represented 35.9 percent of Chamblee's population, they were only 16.3 percent of Doraville's inhabitants. About one-fifth of the people in Chamblee (19.3 percent) and Doraville (18.6 percent) were black.

At an emotionally charged public meeting held to present the international village concept in Doraville in 1993, opponents voiced economic and cultural objections. One participant recalled that Doraville officials made physical threats and the presenters needed a police escort to leave. As an Atlanta newspaper reported, "Doraville City Council members blasted the project as a threat to jobs for longtime residents and the town's identity."[23]

The two adjacent cities were also confronting similar integration challenges with growing populations of Asians and Hispanics. As a local newspaper reported, the same "undercurrent" ran through both cities: "the continuing struggle to adapt to—and in some cases, fight against—a tide of immigrants who have transformed the two former blue-collar, predominantly white cities."[24]

Faced with the same issues, the two cities selected different solutions. Doraville officials continued to fight the influx of immigration. A Doraville official was later quoted as saying: "The International Village wanted us to go after low-rent housing to attract more immigrants. Why would we want to attract more immigrants when we got all we want? We got plenty. We got enough to go around. If you want any in your neighborhood, we'll send you some."[25]

Officials in Chamblee, by contrast, embraced the idea. The development of the international village consequently was restricted to Chamblee, where the steady growth of the international population was marked by an increase in "ethnic" businesses. The area was designated a Targeted Employment Area by the state in 1998, which offered permanent visa status in the United States to foreigners willing to invest at least $500,000 in a business that created ten jobs or more.[26]

Instead of focusing on immigrants as a problem, Chamblee officials approached integration challenges with a broader perspective. The task force charged with reviewing the city's response to the influx of newcomers had a mandate to look at problems that affected the entire community. Community development included more than mere economic development. Public order and crime were seen as key issues. A criminal subpopulation needed to be controlled and city ordinances needed to be enforced.

Low-cost housing attracted immigrants to the area, but the poor quality and lax supervision turned some multifamily apartment complexes into slums or havens for criminal activity. The city responded by inspecting all apartment complexes and requiring landlords to repair and resolve violations. Two complexes were condemned and demolished. These initiatives eliminated focal points for problems and attracted new landlords who built and maintained better housing.[27] Significantly, the improvements were made not to eliminate housing for immigrants but to improve conditions for everyone in the city.

The Chamblee police force also adapted to the newcomers, making significant changes in its operations. A new responsiveness to the immigrant community, developed through lessons learned from experience and a change in police leadership, marked a dramatic turnaround from law enforcement's initial reaction to the influx of undocumented immigrants. When Hispanic laborers first began gathering in parking lots, police responded with an "us against them" attitude.

Antagonism marked early relations between law enforcement and the newcomers as police enforced a city ordinance against soliciting or hiring day laborers off the street. Owners of gas stations and convenience stores had complained that their customers were being bothered and the businesses were suffering because of these Hispanic trespassers. When a pickup truck pulled into a gas station, laborers surrounded the driver and offered to work. Working with the Immigration and Naturalization Service (INS), the police made repeated sweeps of the places where Hispanic men gathered and began arresting those without documents.[28] Hispanic men, who came to identify the police with the INS, scattered whenever officers appeared. Eventually, the police began to reassess their tactics. One concern was that the fleeing laborers might be struck by a car as they ran across busy streets to avoid being questioned by the police.

A more widespread concern was that police had made it difficult for themselves to fight criminals who targeted Hispanics. Immigrants often did not have bank accounts and carried their money on them, making them prime targets for robberies. The drug trade had also infiltrated some of the apartment complexes where immigrants were living, introducing a criminal element that made the buildings unsafe. Because the police were perceived as being affiliated with the INS, however, victims without legal residency would not report the thefts to the police for fear of being deported.

In a strategic departure from their initial approach, the police reevaluated how to focus on their mission to protect the community. Their policies were making it impossible to effectively fight crime and maintain law and order in Chamblee. To combat the thieves and drug dealers, the police had to gain the trust of the immigrants who were being victimized and work with them against the criminals. "Us" had to incorporate the people of Chamblee who were law abiding (if you ignore immigration laws), and "them" had to represent those causing the thefts, drug traffic, and violence.

The police cut off their relationship with the INS and oriented themselves more toward the community. The new position was that illegal immigration was a problem for the federal government, but one that lay outside the jurisdiction of the Chamblee police.[29] The priority was to establish a better relationship with the international immigrants in order to maintain law and order in Chamblee. In collaboration with Bridging the Gap, a local nongovernmental organization, the police received diversity training and hired Vietnamese-speaking and Spanish-speaking staff.

By 2003, Chamblee was an integrated, multicultural, multinational city. It had its challenges like any other city, but international immigrants and multiculturalism were no longer seen as problems. The area along Buford Highway thrived with Chinese, Korean, Hispanic, and Vietnamese shops, restaurants, shopping centers, service organizations, and other businesses and professional offices.

The trying but ultimately rewarding experience of Chamblee offers a shining example to Georgia and other Southern states of how to move beyond a black and white framework to integrate newcomers of diverse ethnicities. In many ways, the legacies of discrimination affect today's immigrants, as highlighted by the development of Atlanta's public transportation system. But the healing of race relations that has occurred since the civil rights movement has also provided a roadmap of sorts for the advancement of newcomers. Perhaps most significantly, Chamblee turned the corner in its relations with immigrants by realizing that they too offered resources that could enrich the wider community.

NOTES

1. Hispanic refers to the Spanish language or affinity, whereas Latino refers to the geographic area of Central and South America and the Caribbean (Latin America). Strictly speaking, Portuguese-speaking (from Brazil) or French-speaking Latinos are not Hispanic. Atlanta residents generally refer to themselves as Latino rather than as Hispanic.

2. The acronym AMA represents the Atlanta Metropolitan Area and is used to avoid confusion when reference is made to the metropolitan area instead of to the city of Atlanta.

3. Campbell J. Gibson and Emily Lennon, "Historical Census Statistics on the Foreign-Born Population of the United States: 1850–1990," Population Division Working Paper no. 29, U.S. Bureau of the Census, February 1999, www.census .gov/population/www/documentation/twps0029/twps0029.html (accessed January 16, 2003). A metropolitan area consists of all the communities that are highly integrated economically and socially with a core area that has a large population nucleus. Metropolitan areas (MAs) in the United States are defined and designated by the federal government's Office of Management and Budget. Except in New England, where MAs are composed of cities and towns, MAs throughout the country consist of counties.

4. F. Hobbs and N. Stoops, "Demographic Trends in the 20th Century," U.S. Census Bureau, Census 2000 Special Reports, Series CENSR-4 (Washington, DC: U.S. Government Printing Office, 2002).

5. The statistics related to language were percentages of the population five years of age or older, that is, excluding children under five.

6. Alton Hornsby, *A Short History of Black Atlanta, 1847–1990* Apex Museum, 2003.

7. William B. Hartsfield, Atlanta International Airport, www.atlanta-airport .com (accessed February 20, 2003).

8. Rebecca Dameron and Arthur Murphy, "An International City Too Busy to Hate? Social and Cultural Change in Atlanta: 1970–1995," *Urban Anthropology* 26, no. 1 (1997).

9. In 1950, 88.7 percent of the city's population lived in Fulton County and 11.3 percent in DeKalb County. Between 1950 and 2002 the absolute number of people living in the city in Fulton County grew, while the absolute number in DeKalb shrank. By 2002, 92.5 percent of the city's population and 94.7 percent of the city's territory were located in Fulton County with the rest (7.5 percent of the population and 5.3 percent of the land) in DeKalb (Atlanta Regional Commission, personal communication).

10. In this chapter, "the Americas" referred to the western hemisphere, including North, Central, and South America and the Caribbean.

11. Ronald H. Bayor, *Race and the Shaping of Twentieth Century Atlanta* (Chapel Hill: University of North Carolina Press, 1996).

12. Center for Applied Research in Anthropology (CARA), "CARA Diversity Index Quantifies the People of Metro Atlanta," *Research Applications* 3, no. 2 (Fall 1994): 1, 4.

13. The U.S. news media, especially television, had increasingly turned away from serious analysis to concentrate on "action news," human-interest stories that produced graphic photos, and the photographs of refugee arrivals fit into this new concentration.

14. Skin color similarities between residents and immigrants did not mean that the immigrants shared the same identity.

15. Data showing the county where refugees were resettled were not available for the entire twenty-two-year period (1981–2002), only for thirteen years (1988–1997, 1999, 2001–2002). The first seven years of resettlement, primarily of Vietnam War–related refugees, were absent from these data. Personal statements from

representatives of refugee agencies noted that most of these refugees were resettled around the Buford Highway, Chamblee-Doraville area.

16. INS Estimates 2003, 7. The existence and integration of undocumented immigrants was difficult to study because they knew that they were vulnerable to being deported and attempted to evade attention, even though states tried to encourage everyone to participate in the 2000 census. To compensate, the INS assumed in its calculations a 10 percent undercount of the undocumented in the 2000 census.

17. Nationals of El Salvador, Guatemala, and Nicaragua have qualified for asylum and Temporary Protected Status under the Nicaraguan Adjustment and Central American Relief Act (NACARA), which was signed into law by President Bill Clinton in November 1997.

18. Information about Chamblee was supplied by city and chamber of commerce officials during interviews in 2002. Public transit improved in 1986 when MARTA opened a train station in Chamblee.

19. The incident was reported in the New York *Village Voice* as well as the local *Atlanta Journal-Constitution*.

20. "Immigrants Lift Economy, Task Force Says," *Atlanta Journal-Constitution*, January 7, 1993.

21. 1994 market feasibility study by Arthur Andersen, "A Preliminary Feasibility Study for the Development of an International Village in DeKalb County," quoted in DeKalb Chamber of Commerce's International Village Fact Sheet.

22. International Village master plan prepared for the City of Chamblee, Georgia, by Comstar Real Estate Services and HOH Associates, Inc., August 1994.

23. "Doraville Blasts 'Village' Project," *Atlanta Journal-Constitution*, July 6, 1993.

24. "Metro's Melting Pot: Struggling with Ethnic Change," *Atlanta Journal Constitution*, December 13, 1993.

25. "Metro's Melting Pot."

26. DeKalb Chamber of Commerce news bulletin, June 8, 1998.

27. Interviews during 2002 with city and chamber of commerce officials.

28. Interview in 2002 with city police official.

29. Interview in 2002 with local police official.

5

Latinos, Africans, and Asians in the North Star State: Immigrant Communities in Minnesota

Katherine Fennelly

Immigration to Minnesota has generated an enormous amount of local interest. In the span of one recent year alone the two major newspapers[1] in the Twin Cities have published almost one thousand articles on the topic and immigration has been the subject of countless hearings, debates, and discussions in the legislature; on local radio and television programs; in community forums; and in meetings of nonprofit agencies and policy groups. Topics range from the "remarkable diversity" of the state and announcements of heritage festivals to human-interest stories about health practices, lifestyles, and the need for a range of educational, health, and social services. In some instances, letters to the editor decry the rapid increase in immigrants and the perceived drain on public services.

Judging from all the attention, one might expect Minnesota to have a significant number of immigrants. Yet the size of Minnesota's foreign-born population (113,039 in 2000) pales in comparison with the numbers in the border and coastal states. Twenty other states have larger immigrant populations; California alone has almost seventy-eight times the number of foreign-born residents.

Minnesota is a cold, northern state, remote from major U.S. ports of entry, with a history of settlement by Scandinavian and German immigrants more than a century ago. Other than these European immigrants and the historical Ojibwe and Dakota Native American tribes, the state has had relatively little ethnic or racial diversity. Non-Hispanic whites constitute 85 percent of the population (figure 5.1), while 85 percent are of European ancestry (figure 5.2).

In 2000, only 5 percent of Minnesotans were foreign born—half the national average (see figure 5.3), and well below the high percentages

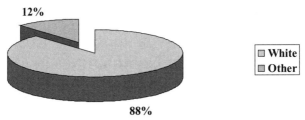

Figure 5.1   White, Non-Hispanic Population in Minnesota, 2000

Source: White, Non-Hispanic Population in Minnesota, 2000

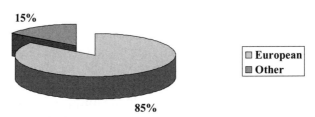

Figure 5.2   European-Ancestry Population in Minnesota, 2000

Source: U.S. Census 2000, Summary File 3
Note: Calculated by removing "American or US" from ancestries reported and dividing percent European ancestries by total percent ancestries reported.

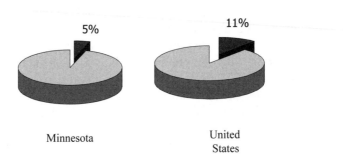

Figure 5.3   Percent of Foreign-Born Population in Minnesota and the United States, 2000

Source: U.S. Census 2000, Summary File 3

in California (26 percent), New York (20 percent), New Jersey (18 percent), and Hawaii (18 percent).[2]

What then accounts for the high degree of interest in immigration to Minnesota? The answer lies in three distinguishing demographic characteristics of the state:

1. the rapidity of the increase in foreign-born residents during the past decade,
2. the high proportion of immigrants who are refugees, and
3. the heavy concentrations of foreign-born residents in certain parts of the state.

These characteristics are described in the following pages. In the second half of the chapter, the challenges of social and economic integration of immigrants into a predominantly white, European-origin population are discussed. A case study of Faribault, Minnesota, a town of twenty thousand inhabitants sixty miles south of the Twin Cities, illustrates some of these challenges. Like many rural towns with meat-processing plants, Faribault has experienced dramatic demographic change in the past decade. Minority school enrollment increased by 273 percent between 1991 and 2002, with immigrants or their children accounting for most of the minority students.[3] In the case study, Asian, African, and Latino residents explain in their own words their motives for coming to Faribault. I also present the reactions of white community members to the presence of newcomers in the host society.

A NOTE ON DATA AND DEFINITIONS

It should be noted that Minnesota has two different immigration streams: the first is composed of individuals who come to the United States as immigrants (either directly to Minnesota or after settling in another state); the second is made up of refugees placed in the state by the U.S. resettlement program. The distinction is important because the two groups vary greatly in ethnic origin and pre- and postmigration experiences.

Many immigrants to the United States come for economic reasons. The largest numbers of economic migrants in the United States, and in Minnesota, are of Mexican origin. Canadian immigrants constitute another large, although less visible, immigrant group in Minnesota. An unknown percentage of Mexicans and Canadians (and a lesser number of other groups) also enter the United States without immigration visas or overstay visitor or work visas.

By contrast, refugees are granted entry because of a well-founded fear of persecution due to their political beliefs or group membership. Few refugees have come from the Americas in recent years, but many have been fleeing Asia, Eastern Europe, the former Soviet republics, and Africa. Minnesota is home to some of the largest groups of Hmong refugees in the United States and sizable refugee populations from Somalia, Liberia, Sierra Leone, and Tibet.

The distinction between immigrant and refugee communities, however, becomes blurred as family members of refugees enter the United States as *immigrants* under family reunification programs. Also, when refugee or immigrant adults have U.S.-born children, they become "mixed status" families. For these reasons, families commonly include a combination of refugees, immigrants, and U.S. citizens. To further complicate the issue, many programs and publications employ definitions of "immigrants" that do not correspond with the immigration status of an individual. Examples include the designation of African-born children as "African Americans" in school data, or measures of primary language spoken in the home, or counts of individuals who designate themselves "Latinos." There is a lack of data on primary versus secondary migrants, that is, individuals who come directly to Minnesota from another country versus those who settle first in other states. Even when data are available on immigrants' country of birth, they are not always accurate, as demonstrated by a recent Census Bureau follow-up survey that suggested that Minnesota has a larger margin of error in census counting than any other state.[4]

In the discussion that follows, I describe the entry patterns of immigrants and refugees separately. But I also include general discussions of the characteristics of all foreign-born residents, whether they are immigrants or refugees, and the policies that affect them. In those cases the term "immigrant" is used to cover either status.

RAPID RATE OF INCREASE IN THE
FOREIGN-BORN POPULATION

Although the absolute number of immigrants and the proportion of foreign born in Minnesota (5 percent) is quite low compared with other states, the rate of increase in the foreign-born population from 1990 to 2000 was among the highest in the country, leading one anti-immigration organization to call Minnesota a "new Ellis Island."[5] More than half of the foreign-born population entered the state in the past decade as the foreign-born population increased by 138 percent, compared with 57 percent nationwide (figure 5.4).

The rate of increase was particularly dramatic for immigrants from Africa (621 percent) and for Latinos (577 percent).[6]

Birth rates and changes in the population of English Language Learners (ELL) students in the schools have also captured the growth of the foreign-born population. In 2000, 14 percent of all births in Minnesota were to mothers born outside the United States (up from 6 percent in 1990), and in some counties the percentages were as high as 29 percent.[7] The number of school children for whom English is a second language increased 350 percent in the 1990s (figure 5.6).

STRONG ECONOMY DRAWS IMMIGRANTS TO MINNESOTA

The rapid growth in both the foreign-born and the native-born populations in Minnesota during the 1990s can be attributed to the strong economy and bounty of jobs in computers, communications, information technology, and manufacturing. In May 1999, *The Economist* published an article titled "Minnesota's Job Market: Land of 1,000

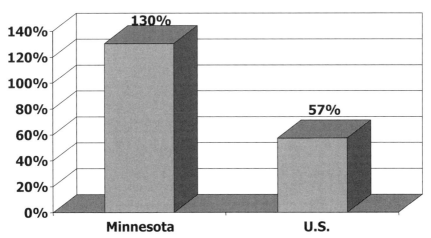

Figure 5.4   Increase in Foreign-Born Population, 1990 to 2000

Source: U.S. Census Bureau, 1990 Census of Population and 2000 Census

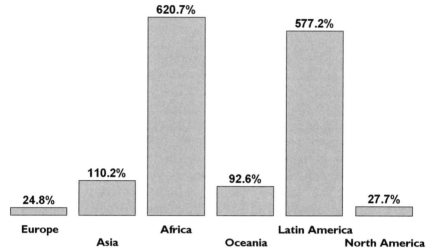

Figure 5.5   Percentage Increase in Foreign Born in Minnesota, 1990 to 2000
Source: Ronningen 2002; U.S. Census 2000

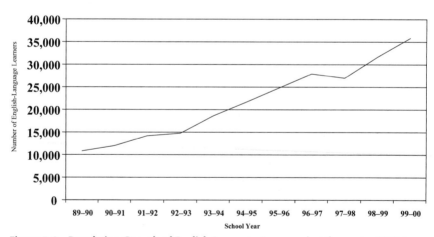

Figure 5.6   Population Growth of English-Language Learners in Minnesota, 1990 to 2000

Source: Minnesota Data Center, Department of Children, Families and Learning
Note: Figure reflects K–12 ELL students receiving services in 1999–2000.

Opportunities."[8] Prior to the current recession, the state experienced eighteen consecutive years of economic expansion amid high employment and a significant increase in the gross domestic product.[9] Seventeen companies on the Fortune 500 list are headquartered in the Twin Cities. Major employers include the Federal District banks and related financial services and insurance companies (e.g., Prudential), Northwest Airlines and its subsidiaries, grain mills (General Mills and Pillsbury), and high-technology firms (Honeywell, Ecolab, 3-M, Cray Research, and Alliant Techsystems).[10] As the booming economy and strong social services attracted new residents, Minnesota's total population increased by 12.4 percent between 1990 and 2000—the largest increase in the history of the state.[11] Eighty percent of the growth occurred in the Twin Cities metro area.

The result of the economic boom was unprecedented labor force growth for men and women of all backgrounds. Minnesota has the highest female labor force participation rate in the country (66 percent) and the fourth highest rate for men (77 percent). Rates declined by about one percentage point for men over the past decade, but the decline has been less than that for males in the United States as a whole (4 percent). Labor force participation rates among Minnesota minorities are also the highest in the nation. In 1999, 70 percent of Latinos in the state were in the labor force, compared with 61 percent nationally.[12] Immigrants were attracted to the state by a wealth of jobs in manufacturing, the hospitality industry, construction, food processing, and agriculture.

LATINOS IN MINNESOTA

The large number of jobs in food processing has been a significant attraction for Latino immigrants, particularly Mexicans, who have a long history of migration to the Midwest as seasonal agricultural workers. Most of the Mexican immigrants to Minnesota come from rural states of the Mexican Central Plateau, such as Guanajuato. With a population of about forty-two thousand in the state in 2000, Mexicans represent the largest foreign-born group in Minnesota. There were also more than 137,000 Spanish speakers. Many Latinos come to Minnesota from California, Texas, or Midwestern states in search of jobs. As farm work has given way to manufacturing and food processing jobs in Minnesota, seasonal agricultural workers have settled in small towns or moved to metropolitan areas.

Latinos are much more likely to hold low-wage jobs than other Minnesotans, and this disadvantage shows in poverty rates, homeownership rates, and other measures. As in North Carolina, the low rate of high school graduation among Latinos is particularly troubling. Just under one-third of Latino adults age twenty-five and older hold a high school diploma (29 percent), compared with 18 percent of the general adult population.[13]

Although Latinos are frequently lumped together as an undifferentiated group, they have a variety of backgrounds and legal statuses. Since the end of the wars in Guatemala and El Salvador few Latinos have entered the United States as refugees. Most enter as economic migrants, some without legal documentation. Because of the stigma and legal penalties associated with "illegal aliens," it is impossible to know what percentage of Latinos is documented. It is also difficult to distinguish documented or undocumented immigrants from Chicanos or other U.S.-born Latinos. What is clear is that Latinos of all origins are becoming more numerous in Minnesota. Only 4 percent of the total population of Minnesota is Hispanic/Latino, but their rate of growth in the state (166 percent) was the fastest in the United States between 1990 and 2000; during that same period the number of Latinos in the labor force in Minnesota almost tripled.

HIGH PROPORTION OF IMMIGRANTS
WHO ARE REFUGEES

Another distinguishing feature of immigrant populations in Minnesota is a high proportion of refugees compared with other states.[14] After World War II, Minnesota was one of the first states to respond to the federal refugee resettlement program established under the Displaced Persons Act of 1948[15] by creating the Citizen's Committee, which began a tradition of accepting refugees. Today there are seven voluntary agencies resettling refugees in the state: Lutheran Social Services, Catholic Charities, Minnesota Council of Churches, International Institute, World Relief Minnesota, Jewish Family Service, and the Jewish Family and Children's Service of Minneapolis. In the aftermath of the wars in Southeast Asia, Minnesota received large numbers of refugees from Laos and Vietnam, along with Hmong from several countries in the region. In recent years there has also been an influx of refugees from Africa and the former Soviet states.

In the 1990s the proportion of immigrants who are refugees ranged from 24 percent to 46 percent in Minnesota, compared with 6 percent to 16 percent nationwide (see figure 5.7). Once again, it is the proportion that distinguishes Minnesota rather than the absolute numbers.

Refugee resettlement in Minnesota and the rest of the country has nearly come to a halt since the September 11, 2001 terrorist attacks, but refugee arrivals have remained part of the overall increase in immigrants to Minnesota since 1999.[16] Secondary migration of refugees to the state may be a greater factor than primary resettlement. The large number of Hmong and Somali residents in Minnesota has attracted other members of these communities. Generous social benefits, training opportunities, and employment opportunities have also been strong incentives for refugees to come to the state. In 1998, the U.S. Office of Refugee Resettlement reported that Minnesota had the largest net refugee migration gain—principally from California, Virginia, and Texas. Refugees in Minnesota also had the highest utilization rates for the welfare programs Aid to Families with Dependent Children (AFDC) and Temporary Assistance to Needy Families (TANF) that year (39 percent).

Refugees come from countries where particular groups have been persecuted and the United States has political or humanitarian interests. Because of its refugees, Minnesota has a larger proportion of residents from Africa and Asia than the rest of the United States. Thirteen

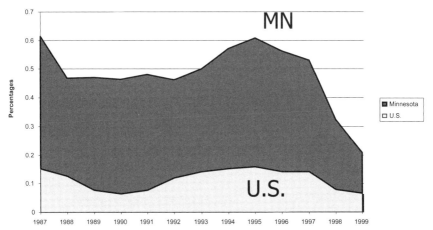

Figure 5.7 Percent of Immigrants Who Are Refugees in Minnesota and the United States

Source: INS 2002

percent of foreign-born Minnesotans are from Africa (compared with 3 percent nationwide) and 41 percent are from Asia (compared with 26 percent).[17] Large-scale immigration of non-Europeans to Minnesota began in the late 1970s. At the end of the Vietnam War, Minnesota nonprofit agencies and religious groups responded to a request by President Carter for states to accept Southeast Asian refugees.[18] In 2000, the Minnesota Department of Health estimated that 21,561 Laotian refugees (both Hmong and lowland Lao) had been resettled in the state since 1979. This figure only reflects primary refugee resettlement, but many more secondary migrants have moved to Minnesota from other parts of the United States. In the late 1990s, the state's Hmong population increased substantially with the influx of family and clan members from Fresno, California. Lee Pao Xiong, president of the Minnesota Urban Coalition, suggests that many Hmong left California to come to St. Paul because of the lower cost of living and the availability of good education and jobs.[19] The state's Hmong population grew by 255 percent in the 1990s to 42,863 residents, giving Minnesota the largest concentration of Hmong residents in the United States.

With the breakup of the Soviet Union in the late 1980s came a wave of Russian-speaking refugees—Jews, Baptists, and Pentecostal Christians fleeing religious persecution. In 1980 no Russian refugee arrivals were recorded in Minnesota, but since 1987 more than three thousand Russian-speaking Jews alone have settled in Minneapolis. Nearly half of them are older than age fifty-five and some are in their nineties.[20]

In 2000 three-quarters of the primary refugee arrivals to Minnesota were from sub-Saharan Africa. The majority came from Somalia (55 percent), but others came from Ethiopia (10 percent), Liberia (8 percent), and Sierra Leone (3 percent). Civil war and famine in the region have produced a steady stream of applications for asylum. There were an estimated 34,469 foreign-born Minnesotans from Africa in 2000, a 621 percent increase since 1990, making the state home to the largest concentration of Somalis in the United States.[21] The dress, skin color, and religion of some of the newest refugees from Africa focus attention on immigration and may create the perception that there is an even greater number of foreign-born residents in the state.

GEOGRAPHIC CONCENTRATIONS OF FOREIGN-BORN RESIDENTS

Another reason for the high degree of attention to immigration in Minnesota is that concentrations of immigrants in particular parts of the state boost their visibility. The Twin Cities metropolitan area is home to 60 percent of the total state population and 77 percent of the state's immigrants. This area has always been the site of the largest concentrations of immigrants, but the rate of increase has accelerated in recent years. Figure 5.8 shows an increase in the percentage of children speaking a foreign language at home in a one-year period (from the 1999–2000 school year). After the Twin Cities, the city of Rochester has the largest foreign-born population with settlements of immigrants and refugees from Latin America, Asia, Africa, and the former Soviet states.[22]

Several rural communities in Minnesota have also experienced dramatic increases in numbers of immigrants and nonnative English speakers (figure 5.9),[23] although this is a relatively recent phenomenon.

With the exception of Indian reservations, rural Minnesota historically has had little ethnic diversity. Recent increases in rural minority populations, however, reflect surging numbers of Asian, African, and Latino immigrants and their children in the state's rural counties between 1990 and 2000.[24] The food processing industry that has driven much of this change is described in the next section.

FOOD PROCESSING AND IMMIGRATION

The diversification of rural Midwestern communities by Latino, Asian, and African residents is due almost entirely to large food processing

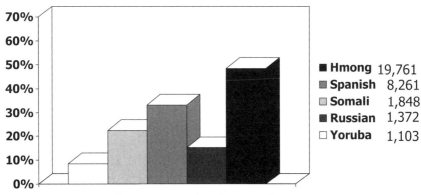

■ Hmong	19,761
▨ Spanish	8,261
☐ Somali	1,848
■ Russian	1,372
☐ Yoruba	1,103

Figure 5.8   One-Year Change Percent of Students Speaking Foreign Language at Home in the Twin Cities Metro Area, 1999 to 2000

Source: DCFL Data; Ronningen 2002

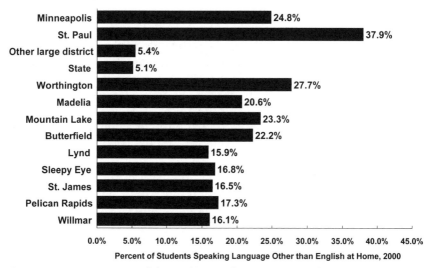

Figure 5.9   Percent Non-English-Speaking Students in Metro and Nonmetro Districts in Minnesota, 2000

Source: Reinhart and Gillaspie 2002

plants.[25] The establishment or expansion of these plants has come in the context of declining large farms, population losses, and shrinking tax bases in agricultural communities across the Midwest.[26] Fonkert calculates that between 1983 and 2000 there was a 50 percent decline in rural grocery stores, a 44 percent decline in hardware stores, and a 36 percent decline in grain elevators.[27] Also, twenty-seven hospitals in rural Minnesota closed during that period. Figure 5.10 shows Minnesota's eighty-seven counties that lost population during the 1990s. Twenty-four of these counties were in the southern and western areas of the state. At the same time, the aging of the working-age population and low unemployment rates have resulted in acute labor shortages.[28] In 2001, the state unemployment rate was 3.7 percent, compared with 4.8 percent nationwide.

Similar demographic changes across the Midwest have coincided with the food processing industry's relocation of large packing plants from urban to rural communities in search of lower transportation and labor costs. Mechanization of meat and poultry processing has also fundamentally altered those industries' social and economic structures. Greater automation and the advent of a disassembly line has reduced the need for highly skilled and well-paid butchers to prepare

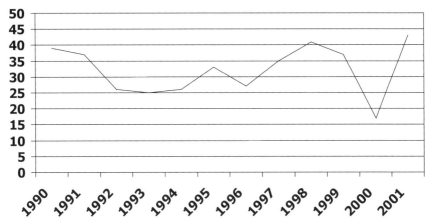

Figure 5.10   Number of Counties with Net Population Loss in Minnesota, 1990 to 2001

Source: MN Planning Indicator 49, 2002

the carcasses.[29] The decline of wages and working conditions in meat processing, coupled with population losses in rural areas, resulted in labor shortages for rural-based meat and poultry processing plants. Meat packing companies took advantage of the low-wage labor offered by newly arrived immigrants, who were also willing to tolerate poor working conditions. As a result, meat processing has become the most important manufacturing activity in rural American communities.[30] To keep labor costs low, meat processing companies have frequently closed plants and eliminated union jobs. As plants have reopened, immigrants with limited English skills have taken many of the nonunion jobs.

In Minnesota, the principal meat processing industries are pork and turkey. Although most poultry processing plants are concentrated in the southern United States, Minnesota leads the nation in turkey production. Meat and poultry processing has become a multibillion dollar business in the state, employing thousands of people in rural plants scattered across the state, with concentrations in the south-central region. In 1996 the meat processing industry in Minnesota employed 14,746 workers, representing a 32.3 percent increase in that sector. Industry employment rose only 21 percent in the United States over the same period. Figure 5.11 shows the changes in minority student enrollment in kindergarten classes in districts near food processing plants.[31] Other industries that have attracted foreign-born workers

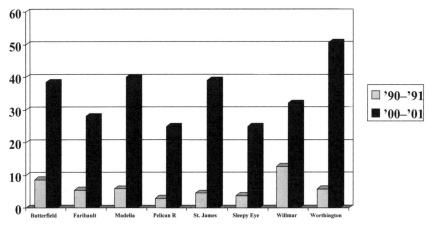

Figure 5.11   Percent Grade-K Minority Enrollment in Selected Minnesota School Districts Close to Food Processing Plants, 1991 and 2000

Source: MN DCFL 2002

include vegetable processing and ethanol plants. As Hart points out, many towns have become "small cogs in the national manufacturing system of locally produced crops and livestock."[32]

IN THEIR OWN WORDS: MOTIVES OF IMMIGRANTS FOR MOVING TO A RURAL, MIDWESTERN TOWN, AND THE REACTIONS OF NATIVE-BORN RESIDENTS

Immigrants may face the greatest challenges to social and economic integration in rural areas where there has been little ethnic or racial diversity. Acceptance of newcomers is notoriously slow to develop and even more so for immigrants and refugees. To better understand foreign-born residents' motives for moving to rural communities and the reactions of European-origin natives, Fennelly and Leitner conducted separate, bilingual focus groups with seventy-nine Cambodian, Vietnamese, Mexican, Central American, Sudanese, and Somali residents from a rural Minnesota community sixty miles south of Minneapolis.[33] This was followed by three focus groups with twenty-two white, native-born residents of the community.

Faribault, Minnesota, is a town of twenty thousand residents with a large poultry processing plant called "The Turkey Store." The plant was established in the 1940s by a co-op of local turkey growers and purchased by Jerome Foods in 1979. In 1993 the management announced plans to close the plant and asked the three hundred workers to voluntarily accept reduced wages. In December of that year, the company closed the plant, reopening it one month later as the "Turkey Store" with one hundred employees. When the union contract expired a year later, the new and remaining members of the much-reduced workforce voted to forego union representation.

In January 2001, the "Turkey Store" plant was purchased by Jennie-O, a subdivision of Hormel Foods. A second shift was added and the plant expanded to six hundred employees who process about twelve thousand tons of turkey a day. In addition to Latinos, the plant employs Cambodian, Vietnamese, Somali, and Sudanese workers. Many have settled in Faribault with their families, as demonstrated by the increase in minority student enrollments at a time when overall enrollments were declining (figure 5.12).[34]

Although foreign-born participants in the focus groups varied in English language ability, education, and length of stay in the United States, about 90 percent were employed in blue-collar jobs with salaries ranging from $5.50 to $9.30 per hour. Sixty-two percent of the women and 79 percent of the men were working and the vast majority (85 percent) of those who were employed worked at least forty hours per week. Average hourly wages for the men were $10.36 (s.d. = 2.7)

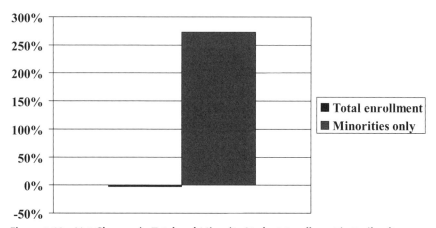

Figure 5.12   Net Changes in Total and Minority Student Enrollment in Faribault Schools, 1991 to 2000

Note: Calculations done using DCFL enrollment files

and $9.52 for the women (s.d. = 1.2). All of these disparate groups repeatedly mentioned the promise of steady employment as the prime attraction of life in Faribault, followed by the tranquility of life in a small town.

Most of the African, Asian, and Latino focus group participants were employed at the poultry plant. Company human resource records show that foreign-born workers held 96 percent of the lowest-paying disassembly line jobs and only 15 percent of the supervisory positions in the year of our study. Despite the difficult nature of their jobs at local poultry plants, canning factories, and manufacturing plants, the immigrant workers expressed a high degree of satisfaction with life in Faribault. What pleased them was the availability of steady work at hourly pay above minimum wage—a stark contrast to conditions in refugee camps, their home countries, or other parts of the United States.

> MAIA (Guatemalan): The beautiful thing here . . . is that you can start working and you see that you are earning money . . . in my country it takes me a month to earn one hundred dollars; so you tell yourself, I'm going to get ahead. If I want to buy something, I can buy it. If you want to buy a car you say, I can afford it. That's what this country gives us—the opportunity to get ahead. If you work hard, you can get what you desire.
>
> ABDULLAH (Somali): Personally I like working in Faribault for a number of reasons. I am new to the country and this job does not require English-language skills. No transportation is needed. I can walk. It's less expensive to live in small towns than bigger cities. It's safe to live here. It's easy to get a job and it's permanent, not like the short-term jobs in some bigger cities.

In contrast to the immigrants, few native-born residents in the focus groups had a positive view of work in meat processing.

> JOE: I don't know how else to put this, but this white face is probably not going to work at the turkey plant and we have people willing to come to Faribault and do the work; I'm willing to buy the turkey and eat it but I have a lot of feeling for the people willing to take these jobs.

Joe's comment reflects his perception of the difficult nature of work in meat processing plants. Unlike native-born residents, immigrant workers are unlikely to openly complain about low wages, poor working conditions, or substandard living conditions. Two African workers in the Faribault study noted this point:

JOSEPH (Sudan): Many of us have come over from Africa with lots of job experience. In our culture, it's hard to complain about not getting raises. I don't think many Sudanese complain about this. Sometimes you don't get a raise because you are discriminated against, but we don't think about it this way.

KHALID (Somalia): People complain about management and their benefits are always different than the way they were first explained. I have seen others complaining about the time sheets. They said "we work overtime and we only get paid straight time instead of overtime." Again when asked, the answer is "that's how it is."

The majority of foreign-born respondents in the Faribault study spoke little or no English and recognized that they had limited alternatives. Boupha, a Cambodian man commented: "[I don't know] where else to find a job; I am so ignorant. I don't know the language and I don't know where to go. So what else is there, but to stay there?"

In contrast to the satisfaction of foreign-born residents, some working-class residents in the community were resentful of the immigrants who came to Faribault to work in the plant.[35] As one resident, Daniel, said: "They shouldn't be treated better than we are. We're the ones that are payin' for what they're gittin. If they're gonna run around, act like they're better than we are, we ain't gonna, we ain't gonna appreciate that at all."

Other researchers describe similar white, anti-immigrant sentiment in towns with large food processing plants.[36] In Faribault there is little interaction between white residents and the African and Latino workers. The segregation is less pronounced for the Vietnamese residents who have been in the community for generations, but it is still a factor for groups of isolated, non-English-speaking Cambodians. Socioeconomic differences between low-wage workers of color in the meat plants and white, middle-class native-born residents exacerbate tensions.

SOCIAL AND ECONOMIC INTEGRATION

Bean and Bell-Rose suggest that the United States is experiencing a new and complex system of stratification in which "immigrants, because of their limited proficiency in English and other characteristics are channeled into certain sectors of employment, labor market segmentation along nativity lines, as well as along racial and ethnic lines."[37] Stratification in housing is another major barrier to social integration. As one white resident in the Faribault study stated:

> SHARON: I feel like we have maybe three communities existing right here, and you know, we overlap at the grocery store or the gas station or whatever, but basically they kind of go to their little areas, and we kinda go to our little areas, and . . .
> MODERATOR: What are the three communities?
> SHARON: Well, actually there are probably more, but I mean you know, the European—the white Europeans—the Hispanic, and I would say the African. Because, like I said, I think that the Asians have really become almost part of the European.

These divisions not only preclude close social interactions, they foster negative stereotypes that lead to fear and xenophobia:

> ANDREA: A lot of people on the streets. Lot of blacks, lot of Mexicans hanging out on the street corners in front of storefronts.
> LILLY: There's a lot of [people] that they don't even care to go downtown anymore.
> MODERATOR: How come?
> LEANNE: I think they're afraid of 'em too. You know. They don't really know them, so. . . .

Some white residents of Faribault also fear the economic impacts of an increase in foreign-born residents that would accompany plant expansion.

> DALE: One of our largest industries . . . is planning on expanding and about doubling their size and most of their employees are, uh, immigrants. And um, we see some concerns on that in the fact it's going to put pressure on the school system because they're having to teach a language and whatever. And getting worried—is it temporary?—if the plant cuts back and then you got a whole slug of 'em on unemployment, or welfare. It makes you think. It's unfortunate, but that's what happens.

The preceding quote reflects a significant barrier to the integration of immigrants into both urban and rural communities—the notion that African, Asian, and Latino immigrants are not full-fledged members of the community, but rather temporary residents who are expendable when their labor is no longer needed. This sentiment has been brought to the foreground in Minnesota with the election of fiscally and socially conservative state legislators. Cuts in benefits to poor families that began with welfare reform have had a strong negative impact on the state's documented and undocumented immigrants. A recent study found that immigrant families who are no longer eligible for public assistance have a particularly difficult time finding jobs because of language barriers and the inability of the welfare system to meet their needs. What many legislators may not realize is that the primary victims of such cuts are U.S. citizens such as children in mixed-status families. Nevertheless, at the federal level, in the Minnesota legislature, and across the United States, programs for undocumented immigrants and even legal immigrants have been first on the chopping block.

The events of September 11, 2001 and the subsequent recession have led to an anti-immigrant backlash and put proimmigrant groups on the defensive. Some virulently anti-immigrant groups have used the new political landscape to their advantage, disseminating exclusionary messages that resonate in rural communities already stressed by rapid demographic change. Several white nationalist groups have moved into the political mainstream on the crest of anti-immigrant sentiment, according to the Center for New Community in Chicago.[38] Their rhetoric is frequently found in letters to the local newspaper editors in towns with large numbers of immigrants.

One example appeared recently in Owatonna, a meatpacking town in Minnesota with a large population of Latinos and Somalis. The following letter written by the founder of an anti-immigrant group called Project USA, published in the *Owatonna People's Press and Shopper*, includes verbatim text found in letters to the editor signed by other individuals:

> With unemployment at 5 to 8 percent in America, it is stupid to bring in nearly 1 million legal immigrants per year plus two hundred thousand anchor babies, about five hundred thousand illegal aliens and fifty-five thousand refugees per year. I have researched the immigration issue for more than eight years. Whenever I give a speech, people always ask "why is our government doing this to us?"

When the Minnesota Department of Finance established a state website for public input on ways to address the state budget deficit, several postings had a similar anti-immigrant tone. Excerpts from two such letters are quoted below:[39]

> We have thousands of illegal immigrants who have children. They come and request assistance for their children and lie, stating that they do not have any income. These are the same people that are working illegally.

> We have a shortage of housing. We have an excess of people driving with-
> out drivers license and insurance each day. We have a huge demand on the
> schools because they have to provide services to undocumented children. Our
> infrastructure (police, highways, roads, sewer) is getting overwhelmed.

Even more disturbing is the implication by state and federal officials
that immigrants are a security threat. When Governor Tim Pawlenty
was inaugurated in 2003, he immediately proposed a bill to record visa
expiration dates on immigrant drivers' licenses as an "antiterrorism"
measure. In Owatonna, in response to a newspaper column advocating
tolerance toward foreign-born residents, a woman wrote: "As for education on crime she should read Michelle Malkins *Invasion*. There she
will find thousands of documented cases where illegal aliens have
harmed, and yes, killed, American citizens, plus those killed during
the September 11 attacks."

CONCLUSIONS

Two countervailing influences may reduce the trend toward increased
numbers of refugees in Minnesota. The first is the xenophobia induced
by the attacks on the World Trade Center and the Pentagon. In the
aftermath of September 11 media attention focused on Minnesota's
Somali population and the arrests of a few individuals involved in
Muslim charities and international money exchange outlets. Meanwhile, the number of refugees admitted to the country has declined
significantly. For fiscal year 2002 the administrative ceiling for refugee admissions to the United States was seventy thousand, but fewer
than half that number were admitted.[40] Minnesota has felt the impact
of this reduction in both numbers of refugees and funding for agencies
that serve refugees.

The onset of a national economic recession has also affected international immigration to the state. As noted earlier, many immigrants
and refugees came to Minnesota because of the availability of jobs and
generous social programs. Since March 2002, when economists say
Minnesota's recession began, the state has lost more than fifty-four
thousand jobs, two-thirds of them in manufacturing.[41] Besides elimi-
nating jobs, the economic troubles have also slowed rates of immigration by heightening xenophobia and feeding political efforts to reduce
benefits for documented and undocumented immigrants. It is difficult
to forecast the length or extent of this erosion of liberal social policies

or its future impact on the number of foreign-born residents coming to the state.

Despite the uncertainty, current demographic trends suggest that Latino immigration will continue to have an impact on the state. Minnesota is the fastest-growing state in the Midwest, and several key industries will only increase their dependence on foreign-born workers as the general population ages, school enrollments decline, and labor shortages persist. Many industries actively recruit Mexican and other foreign-born workers who respond with alacrity, eager to come to Minnesota to find work and forge a future. Latinos accounted for 24 percent of the growth in the labor force between 1990 and 2000.[42] While labor force participation increased by 16 percent overall in the state during that period, it increased by 335 percent for Latinos.

The increasing use of technology in agriculture has reduced the demand for seasonal and migrant workers, but this has been offset by the demand for year-round workers in growth industries such as food processing, construction, hospitality, and health care. The demand for low-wage labor in these industries is likely to be slowed, but not halted, by the current economic recession. Further dependence on immigrant labor is likely under Governor Pawlenty's proposal for tax-free "enterprise zones," designed to encourage businesses to relocate to Minnesota by offering tax exemptions in ten rural zones.[43] These zones create further incentives for new manufacturing and food processing businesses to take advantage of low-wage, immigrant workers.

Latinos are the largest foreign-born population in Minnesota and their numbers are projected to increase significantly in the next ten years. Minnesota Department of Planning projections for 2000 to 2010 show an increase of 67 percent in the Hispanic population, compared with 3 percent among non-Hispanic whites.[44] The integration of this important and rapidly growing segment of Minnesota society requires opportunities for upward mobility. In his research on Latino migrant workers, Chavez identifies several essential "links of incorporation" including opportunities for secure employment, family formation, the establishment of credit, competency in English, legal status, and capital accumulation. These links are unlikely to come about as the result of largesse on the part of the host community unless immigrants themselves organize and demand fair treatment. *Centro Campesino* in southern Minnesota, acting in response to employer discrimination and some public opposition to benefits for immigrants, sponsored an innovative program based upon this principle. The program advises Latino agricultural workers of their legal rights so they can advocate for better working conditions, immigration reform, workplace safety, affordable housing, and childcare.

As suggested by other case studies in this book, another essential precursor to successful integration is programs that help white, native-born residents accept immigrants as legitimate members of society and acknowledge their economic and social contributions. Though rarely documented, these contributions are dramatic. Foreign workers pay income, property, and sales taxes; they open new businesses and send their children to local schools, revitalizing shrinking communities. The director of the Center for Rural Policy at Minnesota State University has noted that while south-central Minnesota grew by seven thousand people during the 1990s, only 470 of these new residents were non-Hispanic whites.[45] Minority children account for all of the growth (or reversal of declines) in the region's school enrollments. Still, discussions of the challenges of immigrant integration are rarely balanced with discussions of positive impacts.

At the national level, the federal treasury reaps financial benefits from immigrant labor that are not shared with the states and local communities that bear the costs. In their careful analysis of the fiscal impact of immigration in the United States, a National Research Council panel concluded that many of the fiscal advantages of immigrant labor accrue at the federal level through income taxes, while costs are greatest in local areas. In the report summary, Smith and Edmonston note that

> under most scenarios the long-run fiscal impact is strongly positive at the federal level, but substantially negative at the state and local levels. The federal impact is shared evenly across the nation, but the negative state and local impacts are concentrated in the few states and localities that receive most of the new immigrants. Consequently, native residents of some states, such as California, may incur net fiscal burdens from immigrants, while residents of most states reap fiscal benefits.[46]

Smith and Edmonston also point out that most fiscal analyses tend to overstate costs because they include U.S.-born children of immigrants while they are in school, but do not estimate their future positive contributions to the economy.

The future health of Minnesota depends on acknowledgment of the economic contributions of foreign-born residents and the establishment of equitable policies that promote their full economic and social potential. Achievement of this vision requires major shifts in public opinion. It will also require recognition by policymakers that the full integration of immigrants in general, and Latinos in particular, is essential for the future of the state as a whole. Barriers to this integration will impose limitations on the economic and social success of a rapidly growing portion of the Minnesota population and a majority of the state's future labor force.

NOTES

1. *Minneapolis Star Tribune* and *St. Paul Pioneer Press.*
2. Elizabeth Grieco, "Characteristics of the Foreign Born in the United States: Results from Census 2000," Migration Policy Institute, December 1, 2002.
3. Minnesota Data Center, PowerPoint slides on School Enrollments in Minnesota, 2002.
4. Associated Press, "Census Overcount in Minnesota Could Be Overstated," *Minneapolis Star Tribune*, April 16, 2003.
5. Steven A. Camarota and John Keeley, "The New Ellis Islands Examining Non-Traditional Areas of Immigrant Settlement in the 1990s," Center for Immigration Studies, September 2001.
6. Barbara J. Ronningen, "Immigration Trends in Minnesota," State Demographic Center, Minnesota State Planning Agency, 2002.
7. Barbara J. Ronningen, PowerPoint presentation on immigration trends in Minnesota, St. Paul, MN, 2002.
8. Anonymous, "Minnesota's Job Market: Land of 1,000 Opportunities," *The Economist*, May 29, 1999.
9. Dave Senf, "Minnesota's Recipe for an Expanding Economic Pie: Four Parts More Labor and Three Parts Higher Productivity," *Minnesota Economic Trends* (December 2001–January 2002), www.mnwfc.org (accessed March 29, 2003).
10. BestJobsUSA, "Minneapolis/St. Paul Minnesota: Major Employers 2003," BestJobsUSA.com (accessed March 24, 2003).
11. James Hibbs, "Unprecedented Population Growth Revealed by Census," *Population Notes*, Minnesota Planning Agency, December 2001.
12. Martha McMurray, "Minnesota Labor Force Trends 1990–2000," Minnesota Planning Agency, December 2002.
13. Chicano Latino Affairs Council and Urban Coalition, "The Chicano Latino Community in Minnesota: Recent Trends," St. Paul, MN, 2000.
14. Immigration and Naturalization Service, www.immigration.gov (accessed March 2003).
15. Immigration History Research Center, "Citizens Committee on Displaced Persons Records, 1946–1953," www1.umn.edu/ihrc/inventories/ihrc60.htm (accessed April 26, 2003).
16. Ronningen, PowerPoint presentation on Immigration Trends in Minnesota.
17. Grieco, "Characteristics of the Foreign Born."
18. David Griffith, "Impacts of Immigrants on Rural Communities: A Compar-

ative Discussion of Marshalltown, North Carolina, and Hardee County, Florida," Greenville, NC, East Carolina University, 2002.

19. Lee Pao Xiong, "Goodbye Fresno: More Hmong Americans Make St. Paul Home than Any Other U.S. City," *Asian Week Archives*, August 17–23, 2001.

20. Barbara Ronningen, "Immigrants in Minnesota: An Increasingly Diverse Population," Minnesota Planning Agency, December 2000 http://server.admin.state.mn.us (accessed March 2001).

21. Grieco, "Characteristics of the Foreign Born."

22. Martha McMurry, "2000 Census Shows a More Racially and Ethnically Diverse Minnesota," *Population Notes*, Minnesota Planning Agency, May 2001.

23. Hazel Reinhart and Tom Gillaspie, PowerPoint presentation on Minnesota Population Trends, St. Paul, MN, 2002.

24. Martha McMurray, "Migration a Major Factor in Minnesota's Population Growth," *Population Notes*, Minnesota Planning Agency, July 2002.

25. Katherine Fennelly and Helga Leitner, "How the Food Processing Industry Is Diversifying Rural Minnesota," *JSRI Working Paper #59*, The Julian Samora Research Institute, Michigan State University, 2003.

26. Fred Gale, "Small and Large Farms Both Growing in Number," *Rural Conditions and Trends* 10, no. 2 (2000): 33–37.

27. Jay Fonkert, "Patterns of Rural Livelihood," Paper read at presentation at Minnesota State Planning, St. Paul, Minnesota 2001.

28. "Minnesota Labor Shortages Are Likely to Continue," Minnesota Planning Agency, May 1999.

29. Katherine Fennelly and Kimberly Ford, "Poultry Processing in a Rural, Midwestern Community: Perspectives of Immigrant Workers," Hubert H. Humphrey Institute of Public Affairs, University of Minnesota, 2003.

30. Alan Barkema, Mark Drabenstott, and Nancy Novack, "The New U.S. Meat Market," Federal Reserve Bank of Kansas City, Economic Review Second Quarter, 2001.

31. "School Enrollment Data 2003," Minnesota Department of Children, Families and Learning, www.educ.state.mn.us/ (accessed 2003).

32. "Refugee and Immigrant Communities" (part of a Resource Kit for Preventing Sexual Violence), Minnesota Department of Health, www.health.state.mn.us/svp/commrefugee.html (accessed June 1, 2000).

33. Katherine Fennelly and Helga Leitner, Research Report to the Russell Sage Foundation, University of Minnesota, 2002.

34. The numbers of minority children increased every year from 1991–1992 through 2001–2002. In 2002–2003, the number of minority students did not increase, but the number of non-Hispanic white students declined.

35. Helga Leitner and Katherine Fennelly, "Narratives of the Immigrant Other in Small Town America: Racialization and the Defense of Identities, Privilege, and Place," paper read at Association of American Geographers, Los Angeles, 2002.

36. Frank D. Bean, Mark A. Fossett, and Kyung Tae Park, "Immigration and Race: New Challenges for American Democracy Labor Market Dynamics and the Effects of Immigration on African Americans," in *Immigration and Race: New Challenges for American Democracy*, ed. G. D. Jaynes (New Haven, CT: Yale University Press, 2000).

37. Frank D. Bean and Stephanie Bell-Rose, *Immigration and Opportunity: Race, Ethnicity and Employment in the United States* (New York: Russell Sage Foundation, 1999).

38. Center for New Community, http://www.newcomm.org (accessed 2003).

39. Website for public comment on budget cuts 2002, Minnesota Department of Finance www.finance.state.mn.us (accessed December 9, 2002).

40. Chris Smith, Statement on Congressional Refugee Caucus, www.refugeesusa.org/who/govt/statement_smith.pdf, 2003.

41. Bill Catlin, "Manufacturing Downturn Hits Entire State," Minnesota Public Radio, December 2, 2002.

42. McMurray, "Minnesota Labor Force Trends 1990–2000."

43. Bob von Sternberg, "Tax-Free Zones: No Panacea," *Star Tribune* (Minneapolis-St. Paul, MN), January 18, 2003.

44. Tom Gillaspie, Presentation at CHARIS Center, Minnesota State Planning Agency, St. Paul 2001.

45. Jack Geller (director of the Rural Policy Center), personal communication with the author, 2002.

46. James P. Smith and Barry Edmonston, *The New Americans: Economic, Demographic and Fiscal Effects of Immigration. National Research Council* (Washington, DC: National Academy Press, 1997).

6

From Temporary Picking to Permanent Plucking: Hispanic Newcomers, Integration, and Change in the Shenandoah Valley

Micah N. Bump

"The reality is we don't care what nationality they are. . . . If they were Martians and they could do the job, we would be happy."

—Virginia business owner commenting on Hispanic[1] participation in the Virginia workforce

"I believe that everyone should pay their taxes. I do not like people who do not pay their taxes but use our services."

—Virginia chief of police commenting on the newcomer community

"We meet monthly and work to develop coordinated efforts to provide culturally and linguistically appropriate services and inclusion in the decision-making process for the Spanish-speaking members of our community."

—Virginia Hispanic advocacy group

North American settlement patterns were originally established by waves of European immigrants that came from the colonial period through the first two decades of the twentieth century. Threads of continuity and discontinuity relate today's immigration to that last great wave. Then as now, a few nationalities dominate, but today the leading immigrant groups are Latinos and Asians instead of Southern and Eastern Europeans.

New regional patterns of settlement, employment and integration challenges were well known by the 1980s.[2] Theorists expected that immigrants would continue to concentrate in a few metropolitan areas, and the central cities of today's seven major immigration states: Arizona, California, Florida, Illinois, New Jersey, New York, and Texas. After all, immigrants' location choices are predicated not only on wages but also the advantageous concentration of prior immigrant support networks.[3] Research supports the notion that wages are even less important to location choices than the presence of prior immigrant communities.[4]

In the late 1980s, however, researchers noticed a growing number of immigrants were moving to states and small communities that had very small foreign-born populations. These geographic pioneers tend to be Latino and to a lesser extent Asian. The former have made their mark in both metropolitan and rural regions in southern, middle, and Rocky Mountain states, while Asians have gravitated to suburban metropolitan areas in new destination states. In the 1980s some industries relocated themselves from the north-central states to the southern and south-central states to be closer to the feedlots and nonunion, low-wage labor.[5] Located in small, rural communities with little local labor, food processing companies have recruited immigrant workers from California and Texas, as well as directly from Mexico and Central America. Such communities as Winchester, Virginia; Rogers, Arkansas; and Georgetown, Delaware now have sizable immigrant populations.

Another common industry in new settlement areas is agriculture, particularly labor-intensive crops. The multiple forces driving this process have included a broader net cast by growers to find workers and a heretofore unprecedented "settling out" of new immigrants in diverse places. The Latinization of agriculture has occurred in the apple groves of Washington State, the mushroom sheds of New England, the grape and row crops of Southern California and the orange groves of southern Florida.[6] Amnesty in 1986 for nearly three million formerly unauthorized workers revealed several settlement zones with distinct demographic and employment patterns.[7]

This resettlement has occurred over a relatively short period, bringing significant numbers of the foreign born into communities that were often unprepared for them.[8] The pressures on small towns in Southern and Middle America, like the distress of immigrants, can be significant. Institutions in long-homogenous communities have not been prepared to cope with sudden changes in their populations and new demands placed on schools, housing, law enforcement, and social services. Local governments have not had any significant experience with newcomers and nongovernmental organizations have been overburdened or simply nonexistent.

In the northern Shenandoah Valley, Winchester, Virginia, is no exception. A tragic incident there in May 2002 illustrates the difficulties that newcomers and established residents face in new settlement communities. A woman in labor arrived at the emergency room at the local hospital with hopes of giving birth to a healthy child, but complications during delivery claimed the lives of both mother and child. Life had been lost for the third time in a year in the Winchester emergency room as a result of complications during the birth process. The three separate instances shared common characteristics: the women involved were immigrants, they had no medical insurance, and they had little or no access to prenatal care.

Most residents of the city and the surrounding county never learned of these tragedies because the local media did not cover them. But concerned citizens were well aware of the problem. The successful efforts of a local advocacy group to address the lack of prenatal care for uninsured immigrant women demonstrate that the sociodemographic transformation of the Shenandoah Valley and the challenges inherent in this process have not gone completely unnoticed in Winchester and the surrounding areas.

SETTING THE STAGE: A THEORETICAL FRAMEWORK FOR ANALYZING NEWCOMERS AND ESTABLISHED RESIDENTS IN WINCHESTER, VIRGINIA

Winchester, an independent city in Frederick County, has long been exposed to immigrant populations through contact with seasonal agricultural labor migrants working in the local fruit industry. Frederick County is Virginia's largest producer of apples, and Winchester has been home to the principal migrant labor camp in the region since 1946 when a former prisoner-of-war camp was converted to a housing facility for migrant workers. Given the transient existence of the seasonal migrants, the community was able to ignore the impact of migrants on the host society and regarded the challenges faced by migrants as intrinsic to the fruit industry, dealing with them in an ad hoc manner. Winchester, like many other towns in the South, focused its community efforts instead on the relationships between African Americans and Caucasians.

In the South today, however, community relations involve far more than Caucasian/African American dynamics. The change in the socio-demographic composition of the South as well as other parts of the country has been well documented.[9] One of the most salient character-istics of the country's changing landscape is a shift from longstanding ethnically homogenous or biracial communities to multiracial commu-nities. Like many other areas, Winchester has had to grapple with soci-etal tensions accompanying the settlement of newcomers. By the mid-1990s, several Hispanic newcomers began settling in the area perma-nently, many of them former seasonal agricultural workers seeking more stable jobs in the burgeoning local food (poultry and fruit) proc-essing, manufacturing, construction, and service industries. By the beginning of the new millennium, the demographics of Winchester had changed dramatically. It had the highest proportionate growth in Hispanic population in the greater Washington, D.C., metropolitan area.

MEDIATING INSTITUTIONS

This study analyzes the response of the city of Winchester and Freder-ick County to the community relationship and integration challenges resulting from the influx of newcomers in the 1990s. The focal point of this analysis is the Latino Connection, a local advocacy group embodying an important community response to newcomer settle-ment. The examination of the organizational history and undertakings of the Latino Connection draws upon the concept of "mediating insti-tutions" set forth by Peter L. Berger and Richard John Neuhaus and more recently adapted to newcomer-established resident relations by Louise Lamphere. Berger and Neuhaus use the term "mediating struc-tures"[10] to refer to "those institutions, [good or bad], that stand between the private world of individuals and the large impersonal structures of modern society."[11] These institutions operate as a two-way street in the sense that they protect the individual from the "alien-ations and anomie of modern life" while simultaneously exposing the large societal institutions, the state included, to the values of ordinary people.

   Lamphere adapts the concept of "mediating structures" to new-comer-established resident relations by focusing on formal institutions and organizations within communities that are hierarchal in nature and extend beyond the lives of the individuals involved with them at any particular point in time.[12] These institutions, such as the corporate workplace, local school systems, health care infrastructure, and local governments, have a mediating function with regard to newcomers and established residents for two reasons. First, they "channel" macro-level economic and political forces into their daily environments, impacting their lives as individuals. Second, they shape the interactions between newcomers and established residents because they comprise the societal space in which "people from diverse backgrounds are thrown together to live, work, learn, and participate in local government or community activities."[13]

This case study of Winchester, Virginia, demonstrates that the newcomer voice is often overlooked or misunderstood within the context of mediating institutions such as schools, hospitals, the corporate workplace, and local government. Institutional shortcomings may be attributed in part to negative attitudes toward newcomers that may pervade particular mediating institutions. More commonly, however, a mediating institution may desire to serve newcomers better but lack the information and resources necessary to effectively meet the needs of a new population group. Just as mediating institutions are often unprepared to serve newcomers, immigrants and refugees who come from places with vastly different religious and cultural norms may also be ill prepared for their new lives in unfamiliar communities.

Taking this predicament as a point of departure, this study seeks to explore solutions to the service gap caused by a lack of understanding between community mediating institutions and newcomer populations. The recent deaths of the immigrant mother and three newcomer children at the Winchester Medical Center demonstrate the consequences of an unaddressed service gap. An effective community response to such situations is crucial to avoid escalating tensions between newcomers and established residents and to facilitate newcomer integration into community life.

The analysis of Winchester emphasizes the role of the Latino Connection to illustrate the value of a local advocacy group comprised of individuals who are familiar with the needs of the newcomer population (with some being newcomers themselves). The group became a mediating institution in its own right by intervening in larger community institutions to improve relations between newcomers and established residents and facilitate newcomer integration into community structures. In contrast, when the Latino Connection has been uninvolved, newcomers' needs have often not been properly met. The evidence suggests that successful integration of newcomers into community mediating institutions is greatly facilitated when a separate mediating entity with knowledge of the new population groups takes an active role in newcomer advocacy.

This study has focused on Winchester and surrounding areas to provide insights into the community response to the immigrant-related changes affecting rural America and Virginia's Shenandoah Valley in particular. This chapter includes three sections. The first section provides an overview of the demographic changes in Virginia over the last decade, both at the state and local level in the Shenandoah Valley. The second part includes an analysis of the regional economy and its dependence on immigrant labor, which demonstrates how the Latino Connection was born out of the interrelationship between local fruit and poultry industries and their reliance of immigrant workers. The final segment centers on the impact of the newcomer population on local mediating institutions. It pays particular attention to the Latino Connection's role as a mediator between the newcomer Hispanic population and other community mediating institutions such as the public school and health care systems, and law enforcement. It concludes with an analysis of the limits of the Latino Connection's role as mediating institution and thoughts on the future prospects of the newcomer advocacy group.

VIRGINIA'S POPULATION, 1990 TO 2000: GREATER NUMBERS, GREATER DIVERSITY

"Old timers like to say Northern Virginia isn't Virginia—it's a different state. And the latest census figures show they're not terribly wrong—by the numbers, at least."[14]

—*Washington Times*, August 15, 2001

From 1990 to 2000 the Commonwealth of Virginia's population grew from 6,187,358 to 7,078,515, an increase of 14.4 percent.[15] As table 6.1 shows, the foreign-born population in Virginia fueled 30 percent of this surge by growing 82.9 percent over the decade. Over the last three decades, the foreign-born population in Virginia has changed significantly. In 1970, more than half of Virginia's foreign-born residents were European and less than 20 percent were Asian. North and Central Americans comprised 15 percent of the foreign born, and the other 14 percent came from South America, the former Soviet Union, and Africa.[16]

Figure 6.1 shows that by 1990, the European and Asian concentra-

Table 6.1   Virginia Total and Foreign-Born Population, 1990 to 2000

	1990		2000		1990 vs. 2000	
Subject	Number	Percent	Number	Percent	Numeric Difference	Percent Change
Total population of Virginia	6,187,358	100.0	7,078,515	100.0	891,157	14.4
Native[1]	5,875,549	95.0	6,508,236	91.9	632,687	10.8
Foreign Born[2]	311,809	5.0	570,279	8.1	258,470	82.9
Region of Birth of the Foreign Born in Virginia						
Total Foreign Born[3]	299,626	100.0	570,271	100.0		
Europe	64,759	21.6	86,612	15.2	21,853	33.7
Asia	134,526	44.9	235,374	41.3	100,848	75.0
Africa	13,220	4.4	42,509	7.5	29,289	221.6
Oceania	2,047	0.7	2,807	0.5	760	37.1
Latin America	75,309	25.1	189,809	33.3	114,500	152.0
North America[4]	9,765	3.3	13,160	2.3	3,395	34.8

Sources: U.S. Census Bureau, 1990 Census of Population and Housing and Census 2000; Migration Policy Institute, "Fact Sheet on the Foreign Born: Virginia," www.migrationinformation.org/USfocus/statemap.cfm.
Notes: 1. The term "native" refers to people residing in the United States who were U.S. citizens in one of three categories: (a) people born in one of the fifty states and the District of Columbia; (b) people born in the U.S. Insular Areas, such as Puerto Rico or Guam; or (c) people who were born abroad to at least one parent who was a U.S. citizen.
   2. The term "foreign born" refers to people residing in the United States on census day who were not U.S. citizens at birth. The foreign-born population includes immigrants, legal nonimmigrants (e.g., refugees and persons on student or work visas), and persons illegally residing in the United States.
   3. For both 1990 and 2000, the total for the region of birth of the foreign born is different from the total foreign born. This is because the 1990 total excludes those who did not report a country of birth and those born at sea, while the 2000 total excludes those born at sea. In 2000, in contrast to 1990, individuals who did not report a country of birth were allocated (or assigned) a country (and thus a region) based on various characteristics. Because of allocation in 2000, but not in 1990, the increase for a specific region is overstated by a small (but unknown) amount.
   4. North America includes Canada, Bermuda, Greenland, St. Pierre, and Miquelon.

tions had reversed: 44 percent of Virginia's foreign born were Asian and only 21 percent were European. The number of immigrants from Latin America had also risen significantly, comprising 25 percent of the foreign born. The 2000 Census showed that those demographic trends only intensified during the 1990s. Immigrants from Latin America had the largest absolute growth with an increase of 114,500 people between 1990 and 2000. Asians saw a similar increase, totaling just fewer than 101,000. Africans comprised the fastest-growing immigrant group with a 221.6 percent increase. The vast demographic transformation of the Commonwealth is largely a reflection of the changes that have swept Northern Virginia.

   Slightly more than one-quarter of Virginia's seven million residents live in the nine northern counties and independent cities adjacent to

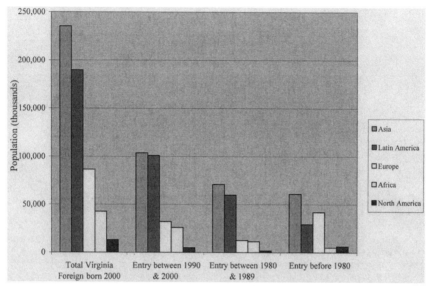

Figure 6.1   Virginia Foreign-Born Population by Region of Birth and Entry Year

Note: Total 2000 foreign-born population in Virginia: 570,279.

the District of Columbia. These counties contain an infinitely more diverse population than the rest of the predominantly Caucasian state. While the foreign born comprise 8.1 percent of the total Virginia population, they now account for over 18 percent of the total population of Northern Virginia. Fairfax County's foreign-born population surpasses 237,000. In areas such as Bailey's Crossroads and Seven Corners, the immigrant population outnumbers the native population. In Fairfax County, Arlington, Alexandria, and Fairfax City, 20 percent of the total population was born outside the United States. In Prince William, Loudoun, Falls Church, Manassas, and Manassas City, 10 percent of the residents are foreign born.[17]

Although other regions of the state have far fewer foreign-born residents, many have experienced large proportionate growth in their foreign-born populations. Areas such as Norfolk, Virginia Beach, Henrico, and Chesterfield counties each have more than ten thousand foreign-born residents. The University of Virginia's graduate school caused the foreign-born population to double in Albemarle County and Charlottesville, Virginia. Rural areas of the state also experienced significant growth. Many towns in the Shenandoah Valley, such as

Harrisonburg, Galax, and Winchester, saw large increases in their Hispanic populations. Harrisonburg's foreign-born population jumped approximately three thousand in the 1990s; Galax's foreign-born residents surged from 46 to about 600; and Winchester's foreign-born population almost tripled.

WINCHESTER AND FREDERICK COUNTY, VIRGINIA: A NEW DESTINATION FOR HISPANICS

Winchester, on the western edge of the Washington, D.C., metropolitan statistical area, comprises part of the northwest corner of the Shenandoah Valley along with Frederick, Clarke, Shenandoah, and Warren counties. Between 1990 and 2000 Winchester experienced the highest proportionate growth in Hispanic population in the greater Washington, D.C., region. According to the 2000 Census, Winchester's Hispanic population grew by nearly 600 percent between 1990 and 2000.[18]

In Winchester, the increase from 219 people in 1990 to 1,527 in 2000 indicates that Hispanics now represent approximately 6.5 percent of the city's population.[19] As shown in table 6.2, 58.4 percent of the Hispanic newcomers are of Mexican origin. El Salvadorans comprise the second most populous Hispanic group with 217 residents or 14.2 percent of the population.

Table 6.2   2000 Hispanic or Latino by Type: Winchester, Virginia

Population by Type	Total	Percent of Total
Total population	23,585	100.0
Hispanic or Latino (of any race)	1,527	6.5
Not Hispanic or Latino	22,058	93.5
Hispanic or Latino by Type		
Hispanic or Latino (of any race)	1,527	100.0
Mexican	892	58.4
Puerto Rican	97	6.4
Cuban	18	1.2
Salvadoran	217	14.2
Other Hispanic or Latino	303	19.8

Source: U.S. Census Bureau, Census 2000 Summary File 1, Matrix PCT11

Frederick County's Hispanic population also grew significantly with a 245 percent surge during the 1990s. The 2000 Census indicates that the combined population growth in the area was approximately 24,200 people.[20] Frederick County displays the greatest absolute growth in the region with an increase of 13,486 residents, from 45,723 recorded in the 1990 Census to 59,023 in the 2000 version.[21] This represents a 29.5 percent surge over the decade.

Winchester saw its overall population increase by 7.46 percent. The 2000 Census put the total number of residents at 23,585, a jump of 1,638 residents from 1990.[22] This increase reflects the steady but moderate growth that Winchester has experienced over the last twenty years. Between 1980 and 1990 the population increased 9.2 percent to 21,947 residents.[23] But in contrast to earlier population growth, which was due largely to increases in Caucasian and African-American residents, Hispanic newcomers constituted 80 percent of the overall population growth in the 1990s.

MIGRATION FROM THE ORCHARD TO THE POULTRY PLANTS: HISPANIC PARTICIPATION IN THE SHENANDOAH VALLEY LABOR FORCE

"Potential workers can find jobs almost anywhere they choose."[24]

—John Marker, president of the Frederick County
Fruit Growers Association, August 2002

"They [Hispanics] start off as migrants and decide they don't want to move around."

—Angela Tejeda Rose, daughter of a migrant worker, who in
1992 became the first Hispanic graduate of a rural Virginian
high school. She now teaches French and civics there.

Over the last five years, the historical trend of using seasonal farm workers from Florida and Texas for agricultural work in the Shenandoah Valley has been considerably altered. The economic boom of the 1990s yielded increased industrialization, rock-bottom unemployment rates, and encroaching development. These factors have driven fruit growers in the Shenandoah Valley to shift their employment base from migrant farm workers and locally based seasonal workers to H-2A guestworkers (see figure 6.2 for definitions).[25] This shift is an indication of the permanent settlement pattern that has emerged as former

Migrant farm workers are U.S. residents who travel from their permanent residence to their place of work and are unable to return home the same day. Commonly, migrant farmworkers are residents of Florida or Texas who travel to Virginia for summer employment. National origin and primary language of the farmworkers do not classify them as immigrants.

Seasonal farm workers are nonmigrant workers: They return to their permanent place of residence the same day. They earn the majority of their annual income from farmwork, and work at least twenty-five days per year, but not year-round, for the same employer. Many seasonal workers are former migrant farmworkers who have settled in the community and continue to perform farmwork.

H-2A guest workers are not U.S. residents and can only be employed when a shortage of labor exists in a particular region. They are prohibited by law from taking other employment within the United States upon completion of their contract. Employers must pay for H-2A workers' transportation to and from their country of origin, must provide them with housing, and must pay them a guaranteed wage.

Figure 6.2   U.S. Department of Labor Definitions of Migrant, Seasonal, and H-2A Farmworkers
Source: Department of Labor, www.dol.gov/dol/allcfr/ETA/Title_20/Part_633/20CFR633.104.htm

seasonal migrant farm workers have found year-round employment opportunities in the area.

The process follows a well-established pattern. At the end of every August, approximately one thousand fruit pickers arrive in the Winchester region. They revive the dormant migrant labor camps dotting the region, the largest of which is located within the city limits and is operated by the Frederick County Fruit Grower's Association. From the camps they proceed to the orchards, where they toil for about two months until the trees are picked clean.

The migrant workers were initially an all-Caucasian labor force from Florida, but have evolved to include Haitian, Jamaican, and Hispanic workers. In some instances, migrant laborers have been augmented by seasonal farmworkers drawn from a local labor force of poorly educated African Americans or Caucasians from the Appalachians. During the last two years, the predominant practice of using migrant workers ended and increased employment of H-2A workers from Mexico and Jamaica began.[26]

The experience of a local fruit grower illustrates the trend toward guest workers. In 1996, Kent Barley Inc., a Frederick County orchard, relied entirely on migrant workers from Florida and Texas to fill its seventy-five picking slots. By 2002, all the pickers came from the H-

2A program. Although the H-2A program has been in existence since 1986, local orchard owners have begun to depend on it only in recent years amid the tight labor market.

The annual influx of farm workers is vital to the region's economy. Growers in the Shenandoah Valley, who produce approximately three-fourths of the state's apple crop, depend on the workers' labor for the yearly apple harvest. In the fall of 2001, growers in the Shenandoah Valley produced 227,854 pounds of apples generating cash receipts of approximately $34 million.[27] Frederick County alone accounted for more than half of the harvest, with a harvest of 127,727 pounds of apples.

Despite this production, the strong economy did not shield fruit growers from mounting difficulties. Low prices, increased global competition, rising production costs, and encroaching development have steadily lowered the number of acres used for farming over the past twenty years, both nationally and locally. Labor shortages have been a particular problem. Between 1992 and 2000 Winchester and Frederick County saw an overall job increase of 31.6 percent, outpacing Virginia as a whole, which grew only 22.8 percent during the same period. The growth in Winchester and Frederick County has been concentrated in the manufacturing, services, construction, trade-wholesale, and trade-retail sectors. Figure 6.3 portrays the growth in these sectors in terms of employment; the statistics demonstrate that the Winchester-Frederick County increase (25.7 percent) in manufacturing employment greatly surpassed the negative 4.6 percent posting of the entire state. The boom in construction, manufacturing, and services contributed to the labor shortage of the fruit industry.

The surging economy created jobs in the service industries and residential construction, two sectors that draw on the same labor pool as the fruit industry. Unemployment statistics from 1992 to 2000 illustrate that labor shortages led the construction, manufacturing, and service industries to tap the labor force historically employed by agriculture. Table 6.3 shows the dramatic drop in unemployment that the region has experienced since 1992. Unemployment in Winchester dropped from 9.9 percent in 1992 to 1.8 percent in 2000. Joblessness fell at a similar clip in Frederick County, from 7.7 percent in 1992 to 1.6 percent in 2000. With tight labor markets and better job possibilities available in other sectors, many individuals who would otherwise work in seasonal agriculture took year-round positions. Data from the field research show that the poultry processing plants that dot the Shenandoah Valley have been the primary source of permanent

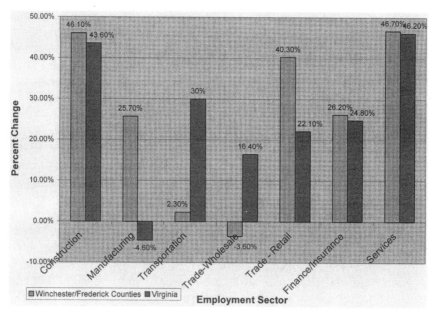

Figure 6.3   Change in Average Employment, 1992 to 2000

Table 6.3   Winchester and Frederick, Virginia, Unemployment Statistics, 1992 to 2001

Year	Civilian Labor Force	Employment	Unemployment	Unemployment Rate (%)
2001	48,280	46,978	1,302	2.70
2000	46,875	46,082	793	1.69
1999	45,464	44,456	1,008	2.22
1998	46,215	44,979	1,236	2.67
1997	43,984	42,251	1,733	3.94
1996	43,590	41,742	1,848	4.24
1995	43,700	41,720	1,980	4.53
1994	42,251	40,260	1,991	4.71
1993	41,022	38,820	2,202	5.37
1992	41,641	38,160	3,481	8.36

Source: Winchester-Frederick County Economic Development Commission Annual Report 2002, Virginia Employment Commission

employment, while construction, landscaping, plastics manufacturing, and nonpoultry food processing constitute the secondary employment niche for the Hispanic newcomer population.

Five major poultry processing companies have had a presence in the region since two corporate mergers in 2001. The industry leader in the United States, Tyson Foods, operates a processing plant in Harrisonburg, Rockingham County, about sixty miles south of Winchester. Pilgrim's Pride Corporation, the third-largest poultry operation in the United States, owns two plants: a turkey processing facility in Hinton and a chicken facility in Broadway, both in Rockingham County. Carghill Turkey Products and Perdue Farms have processing facilities in Harrisonburg and Bridgewater, respectively. George's Chicken, operates a chicken processing plant in Edinburg, a township equidistant between Winchester and Harrisonburg. Its proximity to Winchester has made it an ideal place of employment for that city's growing Hispanic population. A human resource representative from George's Chicken said that Hispanics comprise approximately 70 to 80 percent of the one thousand workers employed by the Edinburg plant.[28] According to the Virginia Poultry Federation, the eight poultry processing facilities owned and operated by these firms employ approximately 8,200 people. Each individual plant processes between 600,000 and 1.2 million chickens per week.[29]

VIRGINIA'S HISTORY WITH MIGRANT WORKERS: A MIXED BLESSING FOR NEWCOMERS

The Shenandoah Valley's long history with migrant workers has been a mixed blessing for the many Hispanics settled permanently in the region. On one hand, a comprehensive support services network for migrant farm workers has developed over the last twenty years. The network and its directors have provided the base for the Latino Connection, the most significant community response to Hispanic permanent settlement in the region. On the other hand, it has conditioned local business leaders and the community at large to view Hispanic employees as temporary residents. Conceptualization of the newcomers as short-term residents and not permanent settlers has adverse implications for integration.

With decades of experience with Hispanic migrant workers, established residents in the Shenandoah Valley have come to view the newcomers as temporary. This perception has been reinforced by the demands of corporate profitability.[30] Burawoy argues that business leaders tend to view Hispanics as transient because low-wage labor best enhances corporate profitability when other sojourners can readily replace existing workers.[31] Access to a large pool of low-skill newcomer labor in job sectors such as poultry is beneficial to businesses and host communities because it shifts the costs of labor force development from the host community to the workers' communities of origin. In a business with slim profit margins, it also provides management with a pretext for externalizing indirect labor costs such as housing, health care, language instruction, skills training, and other human services.[32] Griffith shows that corporate profitability benefits from such a practice.[33]

Even though Hispanics in Winchester and Frederick County have obtained permanent employment in sectors including plastics manufacturing, retail, construction, landscaping, health care, social services, and local government, the perception that Hispanics comprise a transient workforce still prevails among business leaders and the community at large. This slanted assessment has, in some cases, been transformed into a "denial of responsibility" for Hispanic health care, education, security, job continuity, English-language instruction, housing, and retirement needs.[34]

Inadequate housing, health care, education, and security for seasonal migrant farmworkers are problems endemic to the national agricultural industry. Even after Cesar Chavez and Edward R. Murrow's documentary "Harvest of Shame," the plight of seasonal migrant workers continues. Suárez-Orozco frames the struggle for farmworker dignity as a tension between two meaning systems: one that constructs the workers and their families as invisible, and another that insists on their humanity.[35] In Winchester and Frederick County, an infrastructure consisting of a local division of the Migrant Education Program, a Migrant Medical Clinic, the Migrant Head Start Program, and housing, youth, and employment services offered through the Telamon Corporation have provided migrant workers and their families with services to meet basic human needs. That many of the newcomer residents in Winchester are former seasonal migrant workers and, thus, trapped in the "invisibility versus humanity" construct, naturally positioned the service providers to also help meet the needs of permanently settled newcomers. In a sign of this evolution, a group of migrant service providers founded and are now a sustaining force of the Latino Connection.

THE ORIGIN, ORGANIZATION, AND OPERATION
OF THE LATINO CONNECTION

In 1998, Valley Health System, a nonprofit organization of health care providers serving residents of the northern Shenandoah Valley in Virginia, West Virginia, and western Maryland, organized a coalition of outreach workers familiar with the Hispanic community to help the recently settled Hispanic population. It quickly became apparent that information about the health needs of the Hispanic community was scarce, and Valley Health System decided that more data were needed before they could seek funding.

The coalition of outreach workers initially assembled by the Valley Health System served as the foundation for the Latino Connection, created in 1999. The Latino Connection has evolved into a networking and advocacy group that works on quality-of-life issues affecting the Hispanic community in Winchester and Frederick County. The mission of the Latino Connection is twofold: (1) to strengthen the community by coordinating efforts to provide culturally and linguistically appropriate services to Hispanic newcomers in Winchester and Frederick County and (2) to uphold the power of diversity in decision making by providing a forum that disseminates accurate and meaningful information among the newcomers, established residents, and community mediating institutions.

The Latino Connection is comprised of about thirty-five representatives from various community organizations, mostly from the fields of education and health care. Its members, approximately 50 percent Hispanic and 50 percent Caucasian, have permission from their employers to meet during normal working hours on a monthly basis and for special events such as community information fairs targeting the Latino population. Valley Health System allows the group to use its facilities to hold meetings free of charge. The members of the Latino Connection are all employed independently of the advocacy group, which allows it to remain informal and do without paid staff or incorporation as a nonprofit entity. This allows the group to concentrate all its energy at monthly meetings and community events on issues facing the newcomer Hispanic population without being distracted by its own economic preservation.

The group has made a conscious effort to remain an informal coalition because its members feel that is the best way to ensure that the nonhierarchical structure of community representatives remains intact. By not actively seeking funds to support its work, the Latino Connection also avoids what Berger and Neuhaus call "the fatal embrace of regulation" experienced by many mediating institutions.[36] Steering clear of stipulations imposed by government regulations and private philanthropists means the group does not have to reconfigure its organization to meet the agenda of anyone else. According to its members, this framework also gives the Latino Connection greater legitimacy in the eyes of its members and the community it represents.

Although informal in its own right, the Latino Connection is one of three community groups that have formed the nonprofit Regional Intercultural Alliance. This alliance, comprised of the Latin American Community Outreach Service of Shenandoah County, the Harrisonburg Area Hispanic Services Council, and the Latino Connection, was formed to gain greater access to funding opportunities not for their own use, but for specific initiatives. Members of each of the three participatory groups form the board of the Regional Intercultural Alliance with members participating on a rotating basis.

The Latino Connection's outreach initiatives focus on closing the gap between mediating institutions ill prepared for serving newcomers and immigrants ill prepared for life in their new communities. In this sense their work is both "bottom up" and "top down" because it targets both community institutions and the individual newcomers. Most of the group's members are employed by traditional mediating institutions such as schools, hospitals, and different sectors of local government, which allows them to deal directly with newcomers and newcomer issues as part of their regular employment. This places members of the Latino Connection in strategic positions to help newcomers directly while simultaneously educating their colleagues on integration issues. Such education has the potential to activate the institutional change needed to address the challenges posed by a newcomer population.

The Latino Connection sought members who had previous experience with the migrant agricultural worker community to form a working group that was familiar with the day-to-day needs of the Hispanic community. As a result, issues could be raised in a setting conducive to constructive dialogue and mutual assistance in problem solving. Since the conception of the Latino Connection, its modus operandi has been to draw upon the knowledge of its member network to find solutions to problems raised by the same members and, in turn, provide information that administrators and public officials need to carry out necessary changes. Much of the Latino Connection's work has

focused on problems stemming from the established community's perception that the Hispanic newcomers are a transient group.

IMPACT AND (NON)RESPONSE: INTEGRATION AND CHANGE AMONG NEWCOMERS, ESTABLISHED RESIDENTS, AND MEDIATING INSTITUTIONS

"Students' Changing Needs Challenge Winchester Schools"

—*Winchester Star*, October 31, 2001

"Promotoras de Salud lay health promoters . . . bridge gap to save lives . . . [of] immigrants in the Winchester area."

—*Winchester Star*, November 25, 2002

"[The Winchester chief of police] has been worried about the influx of illegal immigrants since 1997."

—*Winchester Star*, January 5, 2002

"Employment Opportunities Here Attract Illegal Aliens"

—*Winchester Star*, January 5, 2002

The local newspaper quotes listed above point to several different social arenas where newcomers interact with established residents: schools, the workplace, law enforcement, and health care. As areas of interface they create community boundaries between the different groups and form the social space in which assimilation and change, on one hand, or isolation, containment, and conflict, on the other, take place. For this reason, Lamphere conceptualizes these social spaces as mediating institutions. By analyzing the interaction between newcomers and established residents within this framework it becomes clear that integration and change "do not . . . take place in some abstract way, through unspecified exposure to or contact with American culture and society."[37] Rather, they occur in defined areas of social exchange. Because interaction between the two groups is inherently a two-way street, the scope of analysis includes the possibility for transformation of established residents within mediating institutions. Once transformed, individuals within mediating institutions play an essential role in transforming the institution as a whole to better meet the needs of newcomers. This is the type of activity that Berger and Neuhaus describe when they argue that mediating institutions constitute "a vehicle by which personal beliefs and values [can] be transmitted into . . . institutions."[38]

In Winchester, the Latino Connection has played a vital role as a mediating institution between the newcomer Hispanic community and traditional institutions such as the public school and health care systems, law enforcement, and the corporate workplace. The latter four are examples of institutions that (1) funnel macro-level political and economic forces into micro-level settings where they may impact the relations between newcomers and established residents and (2) mediate the interaction between newcomers and established residents.[39] The Latino Connection has had different levels of success in helping community institutions respond more effectively to the needs of newcomers, depending on the extent to which group members have engaged them. Some institutions, particularly local law enforcement, have been more difficult to influence.

AN EAR TO THE GROUND:
A PROJECT IN ACTIVE LISTENING

"One way to achieve peace is to separate the act from the person."

—Geoff Huggins, Winchester resident

The first action taken by the Latino Connection was to conduct a needs assessment of both the Latino population and the greater community of Winchester. The goal was threefold: (1) to increase the understanding and communication among individuals, groups, and organizations concerned with newcomers; (2) to facilitate a constructive dialogue among newcomers and established residents; and (3) to help members of the Hispanic community organize to improve their neighborhood. The method for conducting the needs assessment was based on a version of the Quaker Model of Compassionate Listening developed by Herb Walters, a Quaker peace activist at the Rural Southern Voice for Peace, in North Carolina. Numerous communities have used the Quaker "Listening Project" model successfully as a conflict resolution and community organization tool.[40] It attempts to engage participants in processes that allow them to see the humanity of the other, even when they disagree. This requires questions that are nonadversarial and listening that is nonjudgmental. With this model, the Latino Connection stressed the need for the community to listen to the voices of the diverse ethnic groups of Winchester. The "Listening Project" conducted by the Latino Connection used in-depth interviews to ask questions regarding housing conditions, education, public safety, resident–police relations, and general quality-of-life issues.

The Active Listening Project produced two immediate results. The first was a "Welcome to Winchester" resource guide for newly arrived Hispanics. Written in both English and Spanish, the guide has undergone annual updates since 1999 and is distributed at agencies serving Hispanic clients. The second immediate product of the project was a bilingual guide to renter rights that the Latino Connection researched and developed in collaboration with another advocacy group from Harrisonburg.

NEWCOMER ADULT EDUCATION

"The [adult] ESL classes are important not only for the students, but for the entire community."

—Director of Northern Shenandoah Valley Adult Education

The information obtained from the Active Listening Project indicated that Adult English as a Second Language (ESL) infrastructure was highly improvised and in need of improvement. At the time of needs assessment adult ESL classes were held at a variety of locations, including church basements, school cafeterias, and different workplaces, with no continuity from week to week. No mechanism was in place to group ESL students according to their ability levels and class inscription was completely open. Beginner students shared classroom time with advanced students and class sizes varied considerably, holding back the progress of Adult ESL students at all levels.

The needs assessment called for implementation of an ability-based curriculum with pre- and postassessment testing that would allow students with different language skills to progress at their pace. Other needs identified in the course of the survey included: permanent locations for ESL classes, block enrollment,[41] affordable rates, and free childcare during classes. In accordance with its mission to serve as a conduit of information, members of the Latino Connection presented the results of their survey to the Winchester City Schools, Frederick County Schools, Literacy Volunteers, and Shenandoah Valley Adult Education administrators. The Teachers of English to Speakers of

Other Languages (TESOL) director from the local Shenandoah University acted as a facilitator of this information exchange. The process described above demonstrates the mediating role of the Latino Connection between the newcomer Hispanic community and other traditional mediating institutions. Before the establishment of Latino Connection, the educational needs of adult newcomers were not being met by the organizations that had the institutional capacity to address them. The involvement of the Latino Connection in the adult education infrastructure catalyzed the different mediating institutions and amplified the newcomers' voices. The process has yielded impressive results.

Acting on information provided by Latino Connection, ESL administrators made changes that have substantially affected the enrollment and academic progress of adult ESL students. Since July 2001 Winchester Public Schools (WPS), Frederick County Public Schools, and the Northern Shenandoah Valley Adult Education (NSVAE) have cosponsored classes held at a central location, in a formal school setting. This was made possible by the collaborative efforts of the Latino Connection and the WPS with regard to the 21st Century Grant, a three-year federal grant from the U.S. Department of Education that provides academic enrichment and youth development to at-risk students. This funding enabled WPS and NSVAE to offer evening ESL classes at a local middle school. The classes are consistently held in the same classroom and educational childcare services are provided for students with families. There are four levels of ESL instruction: new beginner, high beginner, intermediate, and advanced. The ESL program and students' progress are subject to periodic assessment. Block enrollment was implemented in 2002 to allow for improved progress.

Beyond textbook English, the classes focus on pertinent living skills. Susan Martin demonstrates that programs emphasizing literacy, English-language acquisition, and basic skills increase the potential of unskilled immigrants to advance in the U.S. economy.[42] For this reason the classes focus on "very practical learning" and teach students how to use local banking services, handle parent–teacher conferences, write a note excusing a child's absence at school, prepare a résumé, and deal with tax issues.[43] A section of the curriculum also focuses on techniques for improving child literacy at home, a process that helps adults practice their own literacy skills while helping their children. Adult ESL program directors emphasize that newcomers who learn the

English language, life skills, and local culture are more likely to contribute to the advancement of the local workforce and community.

In March 2002, Latino Connection organized an information fair to publicize the Adult ESL Program and promote other services available in the area. Written flyers, pamphlets and oral presentations promoted topics including nutrition, school enrollment, health care, transportation, migrant education services, Hispanic support services, and adult ESL classes. The information fair coincided with the opening of the Multicultural Resource Center, which is also supported by the 21st Century Grant and serves as a clearinghouse of information to help integrate newcomers to the area. To renew interest in fall classes, a Spanish-language announcement about the availability of ESL classes was published in the local newspaper. As a result, student enrollment in the Adult ESL classes has increased significantly, from 228 students in January 2001 to 314 students one year later, an increase of 72.6 percent. Furthermore, the ability-based curriculum and block enrollment has helped lower student dropout rates. Current efforts are focusing on organizing a daytime adult ESL class that follows the same program as the evening classes already in place.

NEWCOMER EDUCATION IN
WINCHESTER PUBLIC SCHOOLS

"We need to deal with these [ESL] kids; we owe them an excellent education."

—ESL coordinator for Winchester Public Schools

Members of the Latino Connection indicated that although Adult ESL instruction was in dire need of improvement, the school-age ESL program of the WPS has adapted very well to the challenges posed by the demographic changes. The Latino Connections deserves some of the credit for educating school-age ESL students in Winchester through the individual work of its members and active collaboration with the WPS as evidenced by the 21st Century Grant. The positive response of the school system, however, should in no way discount the tremendous challenge the increased number of immigrant children has placed on the school district.

Overall enrollment in the WPS grew from 3,338 in 1996 to 3,542 in 2003, a small increase compared with public schools in larger cities but one that pushed the school system to classroom capacity. At the beginning of the 2002–2003 school year, the kindergarten to fifth-grade enrollment reached maximum capacity. The middle school (sixth to eighth grade) exceeded its maximum enrollment by 250 students and the local high school was approximately three years from reaching it capacity.[44] The School Board's Building and Grounds Committee began to discuss options to alleviate these problems. The short-term suggestion was to increase class size and freeze new programs, and focus on building new schools and renovating others.

A soaring number of ESL students has paralleled the overall enrollment increase. The Winchester Public Schools' K–12 ESL student population has grown approximately 500 percent over the past five years. At the beginning of the 2002–2003 school year, the WPS had 338 ESL students, representing approximately 10 percent of the total student population. Projections for the 2003–2004 school year estimated the ESL population at 460 students. As indicated in table 6.4, the majority of ESL students are elementary school pupils. At the beginning of the 2002–2003 school year, 222 students were enrolled in the elementary school.

Until the 2001–2002 school year, each designated site of ESL instruction in Winchester schools ran its own program autonomously. Particular emphasis was placed on oral proficiency, with less structured instruction in reading and writing. A revamped curriculum has changed WPS ESL instruction to embrace an integrated, competency-based literacy model that focuses on building fluency, comprehension, writing, and vocabulary knowledge of a second-language learner from the very beginning. According to the WPS ESL director, the goal of implementing a competency-based ESL program was to break the

Table 6.4   Winchester Public Schools ESL Enrollment by Grade Level, 1996 to 2003

Year	Grade K–5	Grade 6–8	Grade 9–12	Total	% Increase per Year	% Increase Cumlative	ESL % of Total Enrollment
2002–2003	222	64	52	338	41	493	9.54
2001–2002	160	42	37	239	54	319	6.75
2000–2001	107	29	19	155	38	172	4.56
1999–2000	80	18	14	112	49	96	3.31
1998–1999	52	11	12	75	6	32	2.25
1997–1998	49	9	13	71	25	—	2.13
1996–1997	34	10	13	57	—	—	1.71

Source: Winchester Public Schools

cycle of students spending the entire day, with the exception of art and physical education, in ESL classes. The content-based program, in this sense, will facilitate the transition from ESL to mainstream classes for nonnative English speakers.

ESL students enrolled in the Winchester school system expressed desire to move into a mainstream course of study. A fifteen-year-old student interviewed in June 2002 enthusiastically displayed works of art that he completed while attending local public schools. Despite obvious talent and a demonstrated passion for art, the student spoke of his real desire to take the same academic classes as the mainstream, nonimmigrant students. He longed to sit in an integrated classroom where he could practice his English with native speakers and make friends with American students. His younger sister, who displayed fair command of the English language, complained of boredom in her ESL class. She too wanted to learn in the company of American students. Asked about her friends, she indicated that all of the kids she played with during recess and talked to at school were Mexican. Although the interaction between nonnative and native students depends on individual personalities as well as language skills, the mainstreaming objectives of the WPS are an important step to facilitate meaningful interactions between newcomer and established resident students.

The increasing enrollment of ESL students has forced the WPS to expand its ESL program. The high concentration of newcomers in the Bellview-Montague neighborhood led to an uneven distribution of ESL students among the four local elementary schools. This resulted in overwhelming enrollment at the Frederick Douglass and John Kerr Elementary Schools. Altered attendance zones partially resolved this issue in the 2002–2003 school year by ensuring approximately the same number of ESL students in each elementary school.

Two of the four elementary schools had no prior experience with ESL students, requiring a proactive approach to staff development and new hiring. At the end of the 2001–2002 school year, the WPS had two full-time ESL teachers at the elementary level. Three new ESL teachers and one ESL aide were hired for the 2002–2003 school year bringing the total to five ESL teachers and three native Spanish-speaking aides. To address staff inexperience, a comprehensive development plan was put into place in 2002–2003 to ensure systematic and effective instruction of the ESL student body. ESL administrators also made site visits to Fairfax County and Arlington public schools, two Northern Virginia school districts with a record for model ESL programs, to study grading strategies for ESL students and different approaches to retention issues. The Winchester school board's willingness to redistrict the ESL student population and provide funds to hire additional ESL teachers, a commendable approach to staff development, bodes well for the accommodation of the newcomer population's educational needs.

NEWCOMERS AND HEALTH CARE

"The Latino Connection developed out of this need for agencies to do something because we were all being hit hard—the social services, the hospital, the health department, and the school system—because nobody had prepared themselves for the seasonal migrants to stay here."

—Bilingual nurse from the Winchester Health Department

The observations of the bilingual nurse underscore that as more newcomers have settled permanently in the area, the health care system has come under increasing pressure to provide health services to the Latino community. As indicated above, Valley Health System and the Winchester Health Department are the principal mediating institutions in the local health care system. Valley Health operates Winchester Medical Center, a 405-bed regional referral hospital in the city of Winchester; the Surgi-Center of Winchester, an ambulatory surgery facility located on the Winchester Medical Center campus; and the Winchester Rehabilitation Center, a thirty-bed comprehensive medical rehabilitation facility. The Winchester Health Department, a branch of the state health department, also provides numerous health services including free blood pressure checks, adult and childhood immunizations, HIV testing, pregnancy tests, and tuberculosis risk assessments. The major difference between Valley Health System and the Health Department is that the former does not offer walk-in nonemergency care, whereas the latter provides many services on a walk-in basis. According to a health care employee, this distinction has made the Health Department "the first stop for facilitating any kind of service" to newcomer residents, which is consistent with other research.

Three health care personnel interviewed for this project indicated that the newcomers in Winchester are by and large a healthy population. But they stressed that to maintain their good health, the population required health education, especially on preventative care. A nurse practitioner with over ten years of experience working with seasonal agricultural migrants noted that former seasonal agricultural migrant workers suffer from work-related illnesses as well as hypertension, respiratory diseases, heart diseases, muscular and skeletal problems, certain cancers associated with chemicals used in fertilizers and excessive sun exposure, and tuberculosis. For poultry workers, the hurried pace of the disassembly lines at processing plants, as well as the repetitive nature of the work, can cause muscular and skeletal problems.

A 2001 survey of Hispanic health and quality of life in the region conducted by the Health Community Council in Central Shenandoah Valley indicated that high blood pressure, back problems, asthma, arthritis, and alcoholism were the top-five medical problems faced by the Hispanic community in the area.[45] The survey points out that these problems are exacerbated by the fact that 44 percent of the respondents had not had a general checkup in two years. As an illustration of why the newcomer community suffered from these problems, a Salvadoran member of the Latino Connection stated that many people from her culture did not know about diabetes, infection, nutrition, and preventative medicine. Asked why they were not getting general checkups, 31 percent of the respondents declared that they did not seek health care services because they felt that providers did not speak their language.

The survey results show that more than 60 percent of the Latinos interviewed were married and under thirty-five years of age. Given the demographics of the newcomer population in Winchester, including a high percentage of women of childbearing age, prenatal care was determined to be the number one health care need among the local Latino population. Before November 2002, all expectant women in Winchester were eligible for one visit to the obstetrician at the Health Department. Under state guidelines, the Health Department was obligated to refer them to a private OB-GYN provider. While there are three different obstetricians in Winchester, they all require approximately $500 as a deposit from anyone lacking private health insurance and Medicaid eligibility. A follow-up visit also costs about $500 and every subsequent visit comes with a price tag around $180. It costs approximately $2,700 to $3,000 to have a baby in Winchester.

Many of the expectant Hispanic mothers, who are often young and not employed, do not have the money to pay for prenatal care.[46] Those who work, usually in a low-wage, entry-level position, or are supported by their husbands, boyfriends, or other family members, do not have enough income to cover a $3,000 birth expense. As a result, pregnant women were arriving at the emergency room in labor with no prenatal care, or at most, the single visit to the Health Department. This has had drastic consequences. As described above, three infants and one mother from the Hispanic immigrant community lost their lives during childbirth in 2001 and 2002.

The deaths revealed the weakness of the existing system and prompted concerned members of the Latino Connection to ask Valley Health System for a prenatal care program that would ensure access to health care and improve the health of immigrant mothers and infants in the Winchester/Frederick County area. The program targets pregnant immigrant women who are uninsured, ineligible for Medicaid, and unable to pay for proper care out of pocket. Through a community-based effort initiated by a bilingual nurse from the Winchester Health Department, Valley Health System obtained a $570,860 grant from the Department of Health Resources and Services Administration. The grant funds the Partners in Prenatal Care Program (PIPC), a consortium of local medical providers that was implemented in November 2002. The program, which hired a full-time bilingual nurse, a part-time administrator, and three interpreters, provides transportation to the health care facilities and interpretation during prenatal visits, delivery, and postpartum and newborn care. It also provides assistance with Medicaid and birth certificate applications. The goal is to provide a continuum of quality prenatal care and an opportunity for information sharing among health care providers, community advocates, and client groups.

Lack of access to quality prenatal care, of course, is not exclusive to the newcomer population. Responding to the state's high infant mortality rates, the Virginia General Assembly formed a taskforce in the early 1990s that found that many pregnant women in poverty-stricken areas were unable to afford prenatal care. The group found that mortality rates declined with the availability of midwifery services, a low-cost option for those without access to care provided by OB-GYN doctors. Midwifery also represents a culturally appropriate, holistic approach to prenatal care. Despite the presence of a renowned midwifery program at the Shenandoah University in Winchester, the Latino Connection is still urging the local health care mediating institutions to accept midwifery as a cost-effective and culturally sound approach to obstetric care. According to one nurse involved with the PIPC program, a midwifery birthing center in Winchester "would be something wonderful that would probably solve a lot of our providing problems."[47]

Even in cases where financial costs were not an issue, language barriers have obstructed access to adequate health care. Traditionally, the

Valley Health System facilities relied on a limited number of bilingual personnel, family members, or a list of paid but untrained and untested interpreters to assist their non-English speaking patients. But amid the recent influx of newcomers, it became apparent that the lack of uniformity and professionalism among the various interpreters was leaving patients and providers confused and frustrated.

In 2001, Valley Health System began seeking solutions to its interpretation needs. With help from the Blue Ridge Health Education Center in Harrisonburg they began to use the "Bridging the Gap" medical interpreter training program that originated in Seattle, Washington. The forty-hour course covers a wide spectrum of issues including communications styles, medical terminology, professionalism, ethics, confidentiality, health care insurance, and the importance of listening. To enter the course, bilingual speakers must pass tests in both oral and written comprehension of the two languages and demonstrate basic knowledge of medical terms and familiarity with common childhood and adult diseases. As of January 2003, Valley Health System required its interpreters to have passed the "Bridging the Gap" training course. The Latino Connection developed a companion training piece, "Effective Use of Interpreters," which addresses the need for English-only speakers to understand how to use interpreters and to judge the quality of interpreted communication. The training, which led to more direct contacts between Latinos and established residents, has been provided to all local schools and several hospital departments and is scheduled for social services and other community agencies.

The 2001 survey and other local data confirm that, as in other areas of newcomer settlement, the impersonal, institutional system of delivering health care so common in the United States does not always work with immigrants.[48] The primary health care system in the United States assumes a level of trust in hospitals, clinics, and doctors and is particularly intimidating for immigrants who have rarely experienced institutional health care. As a community, Winchester has been challenged to dispel fears and foster immigrant trust in the American health care system.

A program directed by a Salvadoran member of the Latino Connection has begun to address this issue. Through a federal grant and a four-way partnership between Valley Health System, James Madison University, Shenandoah University, and the Lord Fairfax Health District,[49] members of the local Winchester/Frederick County Hispanic community have been trained as *promotoras de salud* (or health educators). The community views the program, which began in 1999 in

Harrisonburg, as a positive step in educating the newcomer community on health-related issues and making the sometimes daunting local health care system more accessible. The director said the nine most recent graduates of the program have already made contact with four hundred members of the Latino community in an effort to improve "access to health care and health education for all Hispanics in [their] locality."[50]

AN ILLEGAL FIXATION:
NEWCOMERS AND LAW ENFORCEMENT

The police chief in Winchester, Virginia, went through a self-proclaimed culture shock when he came to Winchester from Lynchburg, Virginia. According to the chief, Lynchburg was a "true black and white community," with a demographic breakdown of 33 percent black and "the rest white."[51] When he was appointed chief of police in Winchester in 1997 he was "shocked" to discover that he had to deal with Salvadoran, Honduran, and Mexican populations. Having no prior experience serving newcomer communities, the chief and the police force under his command have faced constant challenges to effectively carry out their mission of community policing.

As the chief quickly realized, he was not the only Northern Shenandoah resident treading unfamiliar water. Other established residents were also alarmed by the influx of newcomers whose actions sometimes transgressed the deep-seated sense of acceptable behavior in Winchester. This problem has been exacerbated because recently arrived Latino newcomers often carry entrenched fears of law enforcement stemming from abuse and corruption in their countries of origin. In the Northern Shenandoah Valley, the history of INS raids exacerbates the high level of mutual suspicion between newcomers and law enforcement.

This mutual mistrust has deepened misunderstandings. An anecdote related by a member of Latino Connection underscores the sensitivity of the issue. Several years ago, an advocacy group called Para el Bien de la Comunidad (For the Good of the Community), a precursor to the Latino Connection, held a community forum for newcomers to interact with local government officials, including police officers. When asked about their understanding of U.S. law, one Latino man stated through an interpreter that, given the difficulty of obtaining a driver's license, the only law members of his community routinely broke was driving without a license. The next day the police department set up a road block outside an apartment complex that housed a large number of Latino newcomers and checked licenses and car registrations, which resulted in numerous citations and arrests.

Law enforcement efforts to improve communication with the Hispanic population have not had as much success as the initiatives seen in North Carolina's Triad area, which are discussed in another chapter. For instance, upon taking office in 1997, the police chief wanted a better understanding of the newcomer community in Winchester. He directed police officers to conduct a series of satisfaction and community protection surveys, which largely missed the Hispanic community because they were handed out by uniformed officers and were not printed in Spanish. The language barrier has proved to be a major and constant challenge. According to the police department's website, the Winchester police force was comprised of seventy-one full-time officers and ten reserve officers yet as of March 2002, Winchester had no Spanish-speaking officers. Officers do carry a small booklet titled *Emergency Translation Guides for Law Enforcement* that includes translations of the most common warnings, questions, and orders issued by the police. Although helpful on occasion, the utility of basic phrase guides is extremely limited in emergency situations.

In another example of a missed opportunity, the police department produced a short video in 2001 with the help of Spanish-speaking local residents to familiarize Winchester's Hispanic population with some of the available services. The Spanish-language video, paid for with surplus funds from a $423,000 state grant to weed out crime and seed community development, features step-by-step information on calling 911 and dealing with medical and fire emergencies, assorted crimes, and traffic stops. The video also provides helpful information about services provided by the Winchester Commonwealth's Attorney's Office, the Virginia Employment Commission, Winchester Public Schools, and Winchester Medical Center. The police department, however, failed to distribute the video effectively. Asked about the percentage of the Hispanic population that had actually seen the video, the chief did not have concrete information but said that he "would like to think 50 percent."[52] As of January 2003, the Latino Connection, the only ethnic community-based organization in town, had not received a copy of the video.

Making matters worse, a series of high-profile crimes involving undocumented migrants in the Winchester area heightened a sense of insecurity among the local police department and established residents. In October 1999, an undocumented migrant from Jamaica with a long-standing criminal record murdered a highly decorated police sergeant. The event received national media coverage and prompted the INS to station an agent in Winchester. In January 2002, an undocumented man from Honduras living in Winchester was arrested on two counts of statutory rape of a twelve-year-old Caucasian girl.[53]

Good intentions for effective community policing have clashed with concern over the "illegal" status of many newcomer residents. The exact number of undocumented residents in the area is impossible to know, but the police chief's estimates have ranged from "hundreds" in March 2002 to a "thousand" in June 2002.[54] Several times, representatives of the police department have publicly stated that the presence of "illegal" immigrants in Winchester was a problem and the chief has allegedly been "begging" for help from the INS since 1998.[55] In an official meeting with the Winchester Community Safety Network Committee in September 2002, a supervisory special agent for the INS informed the community that arresting every "illegal alien" they encounter is not a priority for the INS. According to the press coverage of the meeting, the Winchester police chief was "bothered" by this prioritization and the fact that local law enforcement did not have the authority to enforce federal regulations.[56]

Law enforcement agencies in many newcomer settlement areas have looked to the INS to solve their problems with immigrant communities. But real advances in community law enforcement are not made until local law enforcement accepts that the INS is incapable of rounding up and deporting all those without proper documentation. However, concern raised about proper documentation for residents in the Winchester area has not fallen on deaf ears. The INS apparently planned to establish a regional office in Harrisonburg. It was unclear, however, how the reorganization of the INS under the new Department of Homeland Security would affect these plans.

INTEGRATION AND CHANGE IN WINCHESTER, VIRGINIA: THE FUTURE OF THE LATINO CONNECTION AND THE PROSPECTS FOR NEWCOMER ACTIVISM

Hackenburg points out that newcomer growth can become either a community burden or a coveted political resource capable of providing its own representation.[57] In Winchester, the police chief has expressed frustration about his department being the only local service entity on call twenty-four hours a day. He has said the obligation to be first responders to any newcomer-related issue, from a broken-down car to domestic violence, was stretching his resources tremendously. In essence, the chief was calling the newcomer population a burden. School and health care representatives have echoed his sentiment, noting the economic challenge of serving newcomers. While there is no overt hostility toward the newcomers in Winchester, there is a general consensus that they have strained the service community's resources. Notably absent from this picture is the business community, which benefits directly from the presence of newcomers. The remaining challenge for Winchester, and other rural newcomer communities in similar situations, is to make the transition between burden and valuable resource a reality.

An effective community approach to achieving this transition should consider the following questions: What makes a newcomer community a valuable political and economic resource? What role do newcomers play in ensuring that they are not a community burden? What role do established residents play in facilitating the newcomer transition to a political and economic resource? What action can be taken on the local, national, and international governmental levels to ensure newcomers become this resource?

A newcomer community becomes a valuable resource as it mobilizes the collective resources of its members to become a political and economic force capable of representing itself and asserting its rights. Sullivan argues that activism emerging within the newcomer community is essential to this transition.[58] In part, activism is contingent on the presence of a critical mass of newcomers proportionate to the total population. However, activism is not only a function of population size and density; it also correlates with immigration status and length of residence. In communities like Winchester where former migrant workers employed in low-wage food-processing jobs comprise the bulk of the newcomer population, the "length of time in residence" variable directly relates to the high incidence of undocumented residents.

As the newcomer population establishes itself more permanently, normalizing the immigration status of individuals within the group becomes a priority. In the past, pressure for legalizing undocumented immigrants resulted in the 1986 Immigration Reform and Control Act (IRCA) amnesty that allowed 2.7 million people to regularize their immigration status under the Legally Authorized Workers and Special

Agricultural Workers Programs. The resolution of undocumented immigration with amnesty supports the notion that over time, instances of lack of documentation tend to drop. The increased access to legal channels of civic and social participation that accompany the transition from lack of documentation to legal immigration status encourages greater newcomer activism. In this sense, it is the proportion of Latinos in the community as well as their legal status that create opportunity for activism. The failure of the 1986 amnesty to stem undocumented migration has intensified the contentious nature of the immigration amnesty debate and, in turn, contributed to a political reluctance to address the issue. This trend has become even more pronounced in the post–September 11 environment.

Despite this reluctance, advocacy groups such as the Latino Connection support amnesty measures because they feel newcomers will become better integrated, in both a civic and an economic sense, if they are unafraid to openly engage community institutions. Yet even when newcomers have proper documentation, learning the norms of community life takes time, effort, and significant will on behalf of the newcomers.[59] Thus, the sooner newcomers are accepted and able to participate the better.

In light of these conditions, the mutually reinforcing relationship between newcomer activism and length of residence becomes even more apparent. This poses two important interrelated questions about newcomer activism and representation: (1) Given the lag between newcomer arrival and newcomer participation, what entity mediates between the newcomers and society at large in the meantime? and (2) Once newcomers are able to represent themselves, what is the nature of the transition in representation that occurs between the mediator and the newcomers? These processes most likely play out differently depending on the characteristics of the newcomer population and its particular settlement community.

In Winchester, the Latino Connection serves as the mediating institution representing the newcomer population vis-à-vis the greater community. Although the membership is in large part Latino, few represent the latest newcomers to arrive. The Latinos working in the advocacy group represent instead a category of Latinos that Sullivan calls "activists."[60] These are long-term residents invested in the United States through home ownership, ties to banking institutions, children in local school systems, and other measures. They speak English fluently and by most measures are active in the political and social affairs of the wider community. They form an important bridge between newcomers and the established community because of their familiarity with newcomer culture, their bilingualism, and their knowledge of the larger host society. In urban areas they provide the financial and political foundation of what Portes and Stepick call ethnic enclaves, communities where ethnic businesses and residences are geographically concentrated.[61] The intraethnic contact permitted by geographical proximity allows members even to keep a significant number of their monetary transactions within their own community. The accumulation of purchasing power fosters Hispanic business ownership, which, in turn, promotes increased profits, savings, and further investment within the community. This financial concentration allows members of the community to grow to a point where they can organize themselves to pursue a common political and economic plan.

To date, no ethnic enclave exists in Winchester. Although Latino newcomers form the majority in several apartment complexes, they are tenants and not landlords. Although a handful of Latino-owned businesses have sprouted, their concentration is not great enough to keep economic activity predominantly within the Latino community. For purposes of newcomer integration, the organizational approach taken by the Latino Connection bypasses the system of self-sustenance promoted by ethnic enclaves. The advocacy group's alternative approach of uniting newcomers and established residents in the decision-making processes early in the integration process has benefits for both newcomers and established residents. On one hand, it allows established residents in the position to provide newcomer services to channel pertinent information to the newcomer community. The newcomers benefit through improved access to health care, education, financial services, and public safety. Established residents working in the mediating institutions where newcomers and the established residents interact are transformed to meet the needs of a more diverse society. Both groups aid in the newcomer transition from burden to valuable political resource.

The Latino Connection's modus operandi is to address issues relating to the well-being of the newcomer community one at a time until resolved. Effectively addressing issues related to newcomer empowerment facilitates integration and imparts the means for newcomers to provide their own representation. In this sense, the group's approach has the potential to create a system where integration issues could be addressed by newcomers themselves. The organization of the Latino Connection as a noninstitutional, nonhierarchical, and nonexclusive entity could facilitate the newcomer transition to self-representation.

On one hand, newcomers interested in participating in the existing representative mechanism can be easily incorporated. On the other, if the newcomers choose to form their own representative entity, it would underscore the Latino Connection's success in providing the means for the newcomer population to participate in community affairs, which, according to Hackenburg, would make them an important political resource.[62] Further analysis of Winchester over the next decade would provide the necessary data for measuring long-term newcomer integration.

Still, it is important to note that in a post–September 11 world, newcomer-related issues are increasingly complex. Forces at play go beyond the power of a single community-based advocacy group. In Winchester and the greater Shenandoah Valley, newcomers have settled permanently for jobs in corporate food processing, an industry marked by extremely fierce competition and increasing corporate consolidation. If a major change occurs in the region's poultry industry, the newcomer presence may vanish just as quickly as it appeared. This precarious economic situation exists against a social backdrop of heightened alarm and suspicion of foreign-born newcomers among established residents and law enforcement. Mitigating these tensions is the Latino Connection. If in ten years the children of newcomers are in the position to provide services to the newest of newcomers, it will be a testament to the effectiveness of the group's work.

NOTES

1. In this chapter the terms "Hispanic" and "Latino" will be used interchangeably when referring to Virginia residents whose native language is Spanish. This reflects local practice in Winchester and the Shenandoah Valley.

2. B. Lindsay Lowell. "Regional and Local Effects of Immigration," in *The President's Comprehensive Triennial Report on Immigration* (Washington, DC: U.S. Government Printing Office, 1989).

3. Alejandro Portes and Ruben Rumbaut, *Immigrant America: A Portrait* (Los Angeles: University of California Press, 1990), 28–56.

4. Ann P. Bartel, "Where Do the New U.S. Immigrants Live?" *Journal of Labor Economics* 7, no. 4 (October 1989): 371–91.

5. Michael J. Broadway, "From City to Countryside: Recent Changes in the Structure and Location of the Meat- and Fish-Processing Industries," in *Any Way You Cut It: Meat Processing and Small-Town America*, ed. Donald D. Stull, Michael J. Broadway, and David Griffith (Lawrence: University Press of Kansas, 1995), 17–40.

6. David Griffith, "Hay Trabajo: Poultry Processing, Rural Industrialization,

and the Latinization of Low-Wage Labor," in *Any Way You Cut It: Meat Process-ing and Small-Town America*, ed. Donald D. Stull, Michael J. Broadway, and David Griffith (Lawrence: University Press of Kansas, 1995), 129–51.

7. B. Lindsay Lowell, "Circular Mobility, Migrant Communities, and Policy Restrictions: Unauthorized Flows from Mexico," in *Migration, Population Struc-ture, and Redistribution Policies*, ed. C. Goldsheider (Boulder, CO: Westview Press, 1992), 137–58.

8. James. H. Johnson, Karen D. Johnson-Webb, and Walter C. Farrell Jr., "Newly Emerging Hispanic Communities in the United States: A Spatial Analysis of Settlement Patterns, In-Migration Fields, and Social Receptivity," in *Immigra-tion and Opportunity: Race, Ethnicity, and Employment in the United States*, ed. Frank D. Bean and Stephanie Bell-Rose (New York: Russell Sage Foundation, 1999), 261–62.

9. Betsy Guzman, "Census 2000 Brief: The Hispanic Population," in *U.S. Census Bureau* 2001, www.census.gov/prod/2001pubs/c2kbr01-3.pdf (accessed November 29, 2002).

10. Berger and Neuhaus use the term "mediating structure," while Lamphere uses "mediating institution." In this chapter the latter will be used.

11. Peter L. Berger and Richard John Neuhaus, "Peter Berger and Richard John Neuhaus Respond," in *To Empower People: From State to Civil Society*, ed. Michael Novak (Washington, DC: AEI Press, 1996), 148.

12. Louise Lamphere, "Introduction," in *Structuring Diversity: Ethnographic Perspectives on the New Immigration*, ed. Louise Lamphere (Chicago: University of Chicago Press, 1992), 1–34.

13. Lamphere, introduction, 4.

14. Stephen Dinan and August Gribbin, "Virginia Diversity Clustered in North: Job Opportunities Draw Immigrants." *Washington Times*, August 15, 2001.

15. U.S. Census Bureau, "U.S. Census 2000 Summary File 1 (SF 1) 100-Per-cent Data P1. TOTAL POPULATION [1]—Universe: Total population," factfind-er.census.gov/servlet/DTTable?_ts = 62526482024 (accessed August 4, 2002); and U.S. Census Bureau, "U.S. Census 1990 Summary Tape File 1 (STF 1)—100-Per-cent data P001. PERSONS—Universe: Persons," factfinder.census.gov/servlet/ DTTable?_ts = 62526633642 (accessed June 4, 2002).

16. Donna Tolson, "Increased Immigration: An Asset for Virginia." *The Vir-ginia News Letter* 73, no. 3 (April 1997): 1–8. Available at www.ccps.virginia.edu/ publications/NLtrs/Mar97NL.pdf (accessed September 4, 2002).

17. Group Demographics and Workforce Section, "Foreign-Born Growth in Northern Virginia Helps Drive State's Population Increase; Latin Americans the Fastest Growing." *Weldon Cooper Center for Public Service, University of Virginia*, www.ccps.virginia.edu:16080/demographics/analysis/DemoProfiles/ Foreign/Foreign.html (accessed September 4, 2002).

18. U.S. Census Bureau, "Virginia Population of Counties by Decennial Census: 1900 to 1990," www.census.gov/population/cencounts/va190090.txt (accessed June 7, 2002); and U.S. Census Bureau, "American Fact Finder, GCT-PL. Race and Hispanic or Latino: 2000, Data Set: Census 2000 Redistricting Data (Public Law 94–171)."

19. U.S. Census Bureau, "Virginia Population of Counties by Decennial Census: 1900 to 1990," www.census.gov/population/cencounts/va190090.txt (accessed June 7, 2002); and U.S. Census Bureau, "American Fact Finder, GCT-PL. Race and Hispanic or Latino: 2000, Data Set: Census 2000 Redistricting Data (Public Law 94–171)."

20. U.S. Census Bureau, "Virginia Population of Counties by Decennial Census: 1900 to 1990," www.census.gov/population/cencounts/va190090.txt (accessed June 7, 2002); and U.S. Census Bureau, "American Fact Finder, GCT-PL. Race and Hispanic or Latino: 2000, Data Set: Census 2000 Redistricting Data (Public Law 94–171)."

21. U.S. Census Bureau, "American Fact Finder, GCT-PL. Race and Hispanic or Latino: 2000, Data Set: Census 2000 Redistricting Data (Public Law 94-171)."

22. U.S. Census Bureau, "American Fact Finder, GCT-PL. Race and Hispanic or Latino: 2000, Data Set: Census 2000 Redistricting Data (Public Law 94-171)."

23. U.S. Census Bureau, Virginia Population of Counties by Decennial Census: 1900 to 1990, www.census.gov/population/cencounts/va190090.txt (accessed June 7, 2002).

24. Ann Schimke, "Orchardists Picking New Way to Hire Labor." *Winchester Star*, August 9, 2002.

25. Griffith, "Hay Trabajo," 129–51.

26. For further discussion on the H-2 Visa, see Philip Martin, "Guest Worker Programs for the 21st Century," *Center for Immigration Studies* (Washington, DC), April 2000; and Philip Martin, "U.S. Guest Workers: Experience and Issues," *University of California, Davis* 1995, www2.smu.edu/tower/P_Martin.html (accessed December 8, 2002).

27. Virginia Agricultural Statistics Service, "Commercial Apple Production by Counties, 2000–2001," www.nass.usda.gov/va/pg5202.pdf (November 29, 2002).

28. Micah Bump, phone interview notes with George's representative, January 29, 2003.

29. Malcom Gay, "Poultry $24 Billion Industry." *Richmond Times-Dispatch*, September 15, 2002, p. A-8.

30. Robert A. Hackenburg. "Joe Hill Died for Your Sins," in *Any Way You Cut It: Meat-Processing and Small-Town America*, ed. Donald D. Stull, Michael J. Broadway, and David Griffith (Lawrence: University of Kansas Press, 1995), 246–49.

31. Michael Burawoy, "The Functions and Reproduction of Migrant Labor: Comparative Material from South Africa and the United States." *American Journal of Sociology* 81, no. 5 (1976): 1050–87.

32. Hackenburg, "Joe Hill Died for Your Sins," 238.

33. Griffith, "Hay Trabajo," 145–49.

34. Hackenburg, "Joe Hill Died for Your Sins," 238.

35. M. M. Suárez-Orozco, "State Terrors: Immigrants and Refugees in the Postnational Space," in *Ethnic Identity and Power: Cultural Contexts of Political Action in School and Society*, ed. Y. Zou and H. T. Trueba (New York: State University of New York Press, 1998), 302.

36. Berger and Neuhaus, "Peter Berger and Richard John Neuhaus Respond," 150.

37. Lamphere, introduction, 17.

38. Berger and Neuhaus, "Peter Berger and Richard John Neuhaus Respond," 148.

39. Lamphere, introduction, 4–6.

40. Gene Knudsen Hoffman. "Essays and Articles on Compassionate Listening and Reconciliation," www.coopcomm.org/listening.htm (accessed November 4, 2002).

41. Block enrollment refers to the organization of the different levels of adult ESL classes in three twelve-week time blocks with class enrollment closed after each section is filled. This promotes continuity in instruction and class size because students at different levels of ESL are placed accordingly and students are not permitted to drop into any class at any time.

42. Susan Martin, "Immigrant Integration: Options for Rural Communities." Paper presented at the Immigration and the Changing Face of Rural California Conference, University of California, Davis, September 2–4, 1999.

43. Kelly Cupp, "New Adult ESL to Focus on Life Skills." *Winchester Star*, August 17, 2002, www.winchesterstar.com/thewinchesterstar/020817/area_adult.asp (accessed September 6, 2002).

44. Jodi L. Sokolowski, "New Building Recommended for DMMS." *Winchester Star*, August 21, 2002, www.winchesterstar.com/thewinchesterstar/020821/area_dmms.asp (accessed September 6, 2002).

45. Healthy Community Council. *The State of the Community: Harrisonburg and Rockingham County, Virginia: Hispanic Survey Data, December* (Harrisonburg, VA: Rockingham Memorial Hospital Planning and Community Health, 2001).

46. Of the sixty-plus female clients of the Partners in Perinatal Care program only two were unmarried and not in partnership with the baby's father. However, many of the couples are not officially married. The ideal matrimonial process within the newcomer Latino population requires a return to the country of origin and a large family/community celebration. Actual circumstances have created a situation in which the couple is viewed as married in the eyes of the community and even the church, unofficially, with a long-term plan for a big wedding when the money is saved and the time is right. Often, children and the day-to-day pressures take over and the big wedding in the source country never occurs. In this case, many couples resort to a civil ceremony.

47. Micah Bump, Elżbieta Goździak, and Miguel Guzman, fieldnotes, June 6, 2002.

48. Dan Telvock, "Graduates Bridge Gap to Save Lives." *Winchester Star*. November 25, 2002, www.winchesterstar.com/thewinchesterstar/021125/area_gap.asp (accessed January 3, 2003). For information on the health care impact of newcomers in other areas, see Mark A. Grey, "Pork, Poultry, and Newcomers," in *Any Way You Cut It: Meat Processing in Small-Town America*, ed. Donald D. Stull, Michael J. Broadway, and David Griffith (Lawrence: University Press of Kansas, 1995), 109–27.

49. Lord Fairfax Health District is one of thirty-five health districts in the state of Virginia. For more information, see www.vdh.state.va.us/lhd/02.htm.

50. Telvock, "Graduates Bridge Gap to Save Lives," 2002.

51. Micah Bump and Miguel Guzman, fieldnotes, June 6, 2002.

52. Micah Bump and Miguel Guzman, fieldnotes, June 6, 2002.

53. "Honduran Charged in Rape of Child." *Winchester Star*, January 25, 2002, www.winchesterstar.com/thewinchesterstar/020125/area_charged.asp (accessed November 9, 2002).

54. Daniel M. Telvock, "City Police Get New Communication Tool." *Winchester Star*, March 7, 2002, www.winchesterstar.com/thewinchesterstar/020307/front_communication.asp (September 4, 2002); and Micah Bump and Miguel Guzman, field notes, June 6, 2002.

55. Daniel M. Telvock, "Suspects Identified in Dunlap Driveby." *Winchester Star*, July 16, 2002, www.winchesterstar.com/thewinchesterstar/020716/area_driveby.asp (accessed September 8, 2002).

56. Daniel M. Telvock, "INS Prioritizing Terrorists, Lets Lesser Cases Go." *Winchester Star*, September 27, 2002, www.winchesterstar.com/thewinchesterstar/020927/area_ins.asp (accessed October 10, 2002).

57. Hackenburg, "Joe Hill Died for Your Sins," 249.

58. Teresa Sullivan, "Stratification of the Chicano Labor Market under Conditions of Continuing Mexican Immigration," in *Mexican Immigrants and Mexican Americans*, ed. H. Browning and R. de la Garza (Austin: University of Texas Press, 1986), 55–73.

59. Alejandro Portes and Rubén Rumbaut, *Immigrant America: A Portrait,* Second Edition (Los Angeles: University of California Press, 1996), 193.

60. Sullivan, "Stratification of the Chicano Labor Market under Conditions of Continuing Mexican Immigration," 55–73.

61. Alejandro Portes and Alex Stepick, "Unwelcome Immigrants: The Labor Market Experiences of 1980 (Mariel) Cuban and Haitian Refugees in South Florida." *American Sociological Review* 50, no. 4. (August 1985): 498–501.

62. Hackenburg, "Joe Hill Died for Your Sins," 246–50.

7

At the Gates of the Kingdom: Latino Immigrants in Utah, 1900 to 2003

Armando Solórzano

Immigrants have always posed a challenge to the state of Utah, where a religious heritage shared by 71 percent of the population drives the allocation of political and economic resources. Analyzing the integration of recent Latino newcomers in Utah, I use the conceptual framework of Leonard Arrington, who argued persuasively that Utah's Mormon economy "represents one of the few regional economies in modern history founded for a religious purpose, dominated by religious sentiments, and managed by religious leaders."[1] In his conceptualization, religion plays a fundamental role in understanding the economic development of a state.

The symbiotic relationship between economics and religion sets the experience of Latino immigrants in Utah apart from that of Latinos elsewhere in the Southwest. While Latino immigration to the region is commonly understood in political, racial, and economic terms, in Utah these issues are obscured by religious abstractions. Upon their initial arrival to Mexico's far-northern frontier, Mormons perceived the territory of Utah as their gathering place, the "New Zion" where "God's selected people" should build the Kingdom. More significantly, the Mormons perceived themselves as heirs to the land. All others were "immigrants" who might contribute to the creation of the Kingdom after they accepted the principles of the "renewal of the land" and the regulation of property by the Mormon Church. This theology, however, was challenged and transformed by the incorporation of Utah into U.S. capitalism and by the influx of immigrants looking for a place to work and freely practice their beliefs. My analysis locates immigration in Utah within the context of religious forces to examine the extent to which religion has been a magnet for immigrants and influenced their integration. I focus on the development of Latino immigration patterns in Utah and the role the Latter-Day Saints (LDS) Church has played in facilitating or impeding immigrants' integration.

Originally, Latino immigrants were excluded from the creation of the Mormon Kingdom because it was reserved exclusively for Anglo-Europeans. This image of the Kingdom was eventually transformed by capitalist enterprises that took advantage of nonreligious immigration to guarantee higher rates of capital accumulation. Though Latino immigrants were excluded from the creation of the religious Kingdom, their labor was indispensable to the establishment of the economic empire in Utah. To compete with out-of-state capitalists, Mormon industries turned to the cheap labor provided by Hispanics and Latinos.[2] From 1910 to 1940, non-Mormon capitalists, primarily railroad and mining companies, brought thousands of Latinos to Utah. These companies were more tolerant of religious representation and facilitated the creation of Latino social and cultural institutions. During World War II, religious boundaries were relaxed in Utah and Latinos were incorporated into the communities as long as they continued to work and support the U.S. war effort.

Latino immigration to Utah rose dramatically in the 1980s and 1990s as a consequence of violent conflicts in Central American and the collapse of the Mexican economy. Utah's Hispanic population grew from 60,302 in 1980 to 84,597 in 1990, an increase of 40.3 percent. The growth was even more rapid during the 1990s when Utah's Hispanic population more than doubled, from 84,597 in 1990 to 201,559 in 2000. Overall, Utah's Hispanic population grew 234.2 percent between 1980 and 2000 and Hispanics now constitute 9 percent of the state's population.[3] Many of the Latino immigrants were attracted to Utah because of its economic growth and the rise in service industries.

The integration of Latino immigrants during the 1990s has had mixed results, probably because the majority of Latino immigrants are Catholics, but also because the LDS Church is not as enthusiastic to accommodate its Latino followers as it was in the 1970s. The aftermath of September 11 has also impacted immigrant integration in Utah. The host community has adopted contradictory approaches toward newcomers and the state has sponsored inconsistent immigrant policies. Other factors that have affected immigrant integration include efforts by the Latino community to develop a more humanitarian approach toward Mexican undocumented workers, the position of the Catholic and LDS Churches, and changes in the political climate of the state.

THE MORMON EXODUS AND THE BUILDING OF THE KINGDOM

When the first Mormons arrived in 1847, Utah was a Mexican territory. In September 1847, a band of 1,681 Mormons fleeing religious persecution in Illinois and Iowa entered Mexico and settled in the Great Basin area.[4] After five months of Mormon occupation of northern Mexico, the U.S. and Mexican governments signed the Treaty of Guadalupe Hidalgo, which annexed half of the Mexican territory to the United States, including modern-day California, New Mexico, Arizona, Texas, Nevada, and Utah.

Expanding the population was one of the Mormons' first tasks in Utah. The Mormon Church created the Perpetual Emigrant Fund, which became the most important vehicle for "recruiting and supplying the laborers needed in building the Kingdom."[5] Church authorities orchestrated the immigration of 30,000 converts from England, while at the same time encouraging European Mormon capitalists to start an exodus to the United States. By 1870 the number of European immigrants in Utah had almost doubled, creating an immigrant community that fully identified with the Mormon economic plans. Looking at the organizational skills applied to bringing immigrants to Utah, Katherine Coman declared that Mormons' migratory practices were "the most successful example of regulated immigration in United States history."[6] Thus, the expansion of the Kingdom through European immigrants also became a successful way of building an economic empire. After several years, however, Mormons restricted immigration from Europe because of high fertility rates and scarce resources in the valley.[7]

Despite the early attempts to stimulate population growth through immigration, Mexicans and other immigrants from Central or South America were not invited to participate in the creation of the Kingdom. They had to wait to be invited. Utah's state constitution granted legitimacy only to "white male citizens of the United States," and

Mexican civil authorities were depicted as weak, imbecilic, anarchical, and unworthy.[8] These characterizations made Mexicans unsuitable for the Kingdom. More importantly, Mexicans lacked the capital, tools, and resources that Mormons from Europe offered, and they were Catholic with no interest in converting to a new religion. Thus, Utah-Zion was primarily a theocratic Anglo-European project that excluded Native Americans, Mexicans, and other Latinos.

AMERICAN CAPITALISM IN UTAH:
A DIFFERENT KIND OF KINGDOM

During the 1870s and 1880s, the theocratic Mormon commonwealth was seriously challenged by the introduction of the Pacific Railroad and the developing mining industry. By 1872, almost all the minerals deposited in the Great Basin were owned by non-Mormon capitalists. The large-scale exploitation of mines produced an important population shift. While 79 percent of the state population was Mormon in 1880, Mormons represented fewer than half of Utah's residents by 1920.[9] To maintain population equilibrium, the Mormon Church continued recruiting converts from Europe. In 1880, large numbers of immigrants came from England, Scandinavia, Switzerland, Germany, Holland, Ireland, and France. With their eyes toward Europe, the LDS Church authorities did not contemplate the immigration of Mexicans to Utah. Mexicans were a low priority since they were not European, and their culture was immersed in the "Indian culture," which was only "minimally culturally compatible" with the Mormons' belief system.[10]

In 1894 the Mormon Commonwealth joined the Union as the State of Utah. Political and economic control of the state by Mormons had come to an end, at least theoretically. What emerged was a political entity where ecclesiastical and political affairs were allegedly separated. According to Arrington, these transitions greatly impacted immigration patterns, and resulted in the promotion of new economic development to compensate for the end of the Mormon frontier.[11]

The Perpetual Emigrating Fund, the most important Mormon immigration organization, was dismantled in 1887. The State Bureau of Immigration was created in its place in 1911. One of the goals of the bureau was to control the flow of Mormon immigration from abroad. Thus, Mormon immigration was transformed into a secular enterprise and Utah was promoted as "a splendid state for the best classes of immigrants."[12]

WORKING FOR THE KINGDOM: THE FIRST HISPANIC IMMIGRANTS IN UTAH

To accommodate U.S. industrial development at the beginning of the twentieth century, the Mormon Church reinvigorated its entrepreneurial character by creating new industries, including salt mining, sugar production, farming, and expanding livestock production. Livestock production was concentrated in southwestern Utah, especially in San Juan County. The county's population skyrocketed as a result of both the increased entrepreneurial activities and the Mexican Revolution beginning in 1910. In contrast to the rest of the Southwest, the Mexican Revolution did not result in the immigration of Mexicans to Utah. Rather, it drove the Mormons living in Mexico to return home.[13] Along with this group of Mormons, a large cohort of Hispanic families skilled in sheep raising arrived in San Juan County. Families with surnames like Gonzales, Gallegos, Manzanares, Vigil, Jaramillo, and Garcia arrived from New Mexico and Colorado. These "Hispanic immigrants" to Utah increased the San Juan County population by 120 percent between 1910 and 1914.[14] Loyal to their cultural traditions, the Hispanic immigrants started changing the social and religious landscape of the county. The settlement of Monticello became the Hispanic cultural and religious center and a gateway for Hispanic migration to the rest of the state.[15]

Amid the influx of Hispanic sheepherders in Utah, the Mormon Church made significant adjustments to deal with a diversified labor force, changing the image of the Mormon Kingdom. According to the original design, only Anglo-European Mormons were to build the Kingdom. However, now Catholics and Hispanic laborers were also included. These changes were theologically unsound, but socially and economically necessary.[16] Researchers have reached different conclusions regarding the integration of these early Hispanic immigrants in Utah. According to McPherson, the growing religious and cultural diversity did not result in conflict and Hispanics "were generally accepted by local residents."[17] Other studies, however, indicate a great deal of discrimination against Hispanics in areas heavily populated by Mormons. As the burial patterns in the Monticello cemetery indicate,

Hispanics "were separated from the Anglo community in death as they often were in life."[18]

FROM REVOLUTION TO DEPRESSION: MEXICAN IMMIGRANTS, 1910S TO 1930S

With the outbreak of World War I, the demand for copper increased exorbitantly. Utah copper mines in Bingham Canyon responded by transforming their local mining enterprises into international corporate operations.[19] Until 1910, the mining labor force included Japanese, Croatian, Serbian, Greek, and Italian immigrants. Poor working conditions and low wages forced the European-origin workers to call a general strike in September 1912. The Utah Copper Corporation reacted by bringing 4,000 Mexican strikebreakers to the Canyon.[20] Mexicans were assigned the lowest-paying jobs. Records of the Kennecott Copper Corporation show that 80 percent of the Mexicans were assigned to laying tracks, blasting rocks, and drilling. Employers justified this practice by alleging that the Mexicans "didn't have the education to work in other jobs."[21] Incidentally, employers assessed the Mexicans' level of education based on their ability to speak English, not the formal education they received in Mexico.

All evidence shows that the first generation of Mexican *mineros* struggled to gain the acceptance of the mining community. Mexicans lived in the poorest camps of Bingham and in boarding houses, experiencing the same segregation and exclusion that Hispanics from Monticello endured at the beginning of the twentieth century. While the Hispanics in Monticello were discriminated against on the basis of their religion, the Mexican miners were marginalized because of their darker complexion and low economic status. The Hispanics of San Juan County and the Mexicans from Bingham Canyon found many of the same integration and community development challenges. Hispanic sheepherders and Mexican miners arrived in a land void of Catholic heritage and the host community consistently questioned the immigrants' religion. As Hunter and Ferguson said, the "Spaniards" and their religion were "an example of the wrong manner of carrying forward the work of the Lord."[22] Latinos in Utah quickly realized that Mormonism, the religion of the state's settlers, was considered inherently superior to Catholicism.

Between 1915 and 1930 the Latino immigrant experience in Utah roughly paralleled that of Mexican immigrants elsewhere in the Southwest. Mexicans started working in the traditional industries, including agriculture, railroads, and mining.[23] In 1918, sixty Mexican families were brought to Box Elder County in northern Utah to work in the Utah-Idaho Sugar Company, recruited by Mexicans and Mexican Americans who had arrived as *mineros* but ventured into other economic activities. One such recruiter, Alfred Córdova, an LDS convert from New Mexico, created his own employment agency under the auspices of the Utah-Idaho Sugar Company. The company paid the rent for his employment agency and he soon hired other labor recruiters. These *enganchistas* drafted families from Mexicali, Juarez, and Chihuahua, charging the immigrants a commission of $2 per person and 10 percent of the value of the railroad or bus ticket.[24] Entire Mexican families worked in the sugar beet industry. At the end of the season, Mexican families remained in Garland, thirty miles from Ogden, and were able to survive because Mexican women worked in domestic jobs.[25]

Appalled by the Mexican workers' squalid living conditions, the U.S. Labor Department in 1920 prohibited the recruitment of Mexicans "for the exclusive purpose of cultivating and harvesting sugar beet crops in Colorado, Wyoming, Utah, Iowa, and Nebraska."[26] But the children born to Mexican immigrants already living in Utah transformed the demographic composition of the state; by 1930, Latinos had become the state's largest ethnic minority.[27] Still other Mexicans came to work on the construction of Utah's railroads. As early as 1923, the Union Pacific payrolls showed that at least 40 percent of the workers laying railroad tracks in Utah were Latinos. By the end of the decade, the percentage of Latinos working for the Union Pacific increased to 50 percent.[28]

After forty years in Utah, Latinos were successfully creating social and political organizations in industries controlled by non-Mormon capital, including mining and railroads. However, they were less successful in establishing organizations in enterprises supported by Mormon capital such as sheepherding, agriculture, and the sugar industry. One explanation is that the non-Mormon capital opened opportunities for people of different backgrounds. Mormon enterprises, on the other hand, attracted other Mormons, making it difficult to create organizations serving people of a different faith. But whether they worked in Mormon-controlled enterprises or not, Latinos in Utah were not fully integrated into the social, political, economic, and religious institutions of the state. Latinos were invisible; they lived in the shadows of a state that did not even acknowledge their presence. This condition was challenged by the new wave of Latino immigrants who started arriving in Utah at the onset of World War II.

ALMOST IN THE KINGDOM: WORLD WAR II AND BEYOND

In Utah as the rest of the nation, the Great Depression ended with the U.S. involvement in World War II. The federal government spent more than a billion dollars in Utah on projects including construction of federal facilities, promotion of the mining industry, and improvements in transportation. This economic infusion led to increased employment rates and 103 percent growth of per capita income.[29] The enrollment of Utah males in the military and the high demand for labor also opened new doors for Latino immigrants who began arriving in greater numbers. This time, however, it was a "domestic migration" to Utah since the majority of Hispanic newcomers came from rural areas of the adjacent states of New Mexico and Colorado. Many Mexican immigrants were also expected to come to Utah under the U.S.-Mexico Bracero Program of 1942, but in the end only seven hundred Mexicans arrived under this agreement.

All the efforts to attract Latinos to Utah were not enough to meet the existing labor shortages, particularly after Utah railroad companies and mines denied jobs to Japanese Americans. In 1943, Bingham mining companies launched another effort to recruit Latino workers, dispatching recruiters this time to Puerto Rico and New York City. William Blair estimated that during World War II, Latinos in Bingham Canyon represented at least 65 percent of the Canyon's population.[30]

Latinos who arrived in Utah in the 1940s found themselves in better positions than those who migrated at the beginning of the nineteenth century. This new generation of Latino immigrants traveled with their families and sought permanent settlement in the state. In 1944, with the assistance of Father James E. Collins, the new arrivals transformed Our Lady of Guadalupe Mission into Our Lady of Guadalupe Parish, which became the cornerstone of the Latino Catholic community in Utah. At least 1,800 Latinos lived within the parish boundaries in 1944. As in the past, the majority of Latinos in Utah were Catholic. A study conducted in 1947 by Joseph E. Allen, a sociologist at the University of Utah, found that at least 84 percent of the Latinos who participated in the study identified themselves as Catholics.[31] For the first time, the hierarchy of the Catholic Diocese in Utah, dominated by Irish priests, took an interest in the Latino population.

The Mormon Latino congregation in Utah also grew considerably. Most of the efforts to convert Latinos came from the office of the First LDS Presidency, which was interested in preaching the Mormon gospel to the Mexicans.[32] The Mormons also adopted new proselytizing strategies, looking for Latino converts among the miners and railroad workers. As a result of World War II, their proselytizing efforts focused less on foreign countries and more on missionary work in Utah and other parts of the United States.[33]

The Latino immigrants of the 1940s created *barrios* on the west side of Salt Lake City, in Provo, and in Ogden. But Latinos were still invisible to other Utahans. Discriminatory practices and Latino stereotypes were mitigated, to an extent, by the tendency to view Mexico and Mexican immigrants as allies in the war against fascism and other anti-democratic evils.[34] In other words, Latinos were tolerated as long as they "worked" and supported the nation during the war. But to reclaim their rights, "Utah's New Americans" had to wait until the late 1960s when they organized themselves and articulated their concerns in the language of civil rights.

RECLAIMING THE KINGDOM: LATINO IMMIGRATION IN UTAH, 1960S TO 1980S

Five million Mexican farm workers entered the United States under the Bracero Program between 1942 and 1964. At the end of the program, however, officials from both countries were unwilling to negotiate new immigration agreements. This produced an influx of illegal migrants that challenged U.S. immigration policies but provided an important profit-making mechanism for agricultural corporations in the Southwest.[35] Although statistics are scarce, it is safe to assume that Utah followed the same migration patterns as the rest of the Southwest, where undocumented migrants outnumbered documented migrants by a ratio of four to one.[36] A large number of immigrants from Uruguay, Peru, Chile, and Argentina started arriving in Utah as a consequence of political turmoil in those countries. With the political refugees arrived also a good number of undocumented workers, many affiliated with the LDS Church.[37]

Intrigued by the increasing number of Latin American LDS members in Utah, John D. Glassett, a graduate student at the University of

Utah, attempted to ascertain what attracted South Americans to Utah. In 1970, he interviewed 272 of the 1,417 South American immigrants registered in Utah. Of the study participants, 41 percent came to Utah looking for job opportunities, and the same percentage immigrated because of the influence of the Mormon Church. When asked about their religion, 85 percent of the South Americans indicated that they were Mormons and only 12 percent identified themselves as Roman Catholics. Glassett also found that 45 percent of the South American immigrants were professionals, technicians, or clerical workers; only one survey participant said he was a farm laborer in his home country.[38]

Glassett's findings underscore the importance of the Mormon religion and its role as a magnet for Latino immigrants to Utah. His data also suggest that Latino Mormon immigrants have different socioeconomic backgrounds from the predominantly Catholic Mexicans and Hispanics who settled in Utah at the beginning of the twentieth century. Incidentally, not all Mexicans are Catholics and not all South Americans are Mormons. Both groups have different economic and religious backgrounds and, consequently, find different opportunities for integration.

While Latino Mormons find the support of a Mormon infrastructure already in place, the Latino Catholics are on their own to find the support they need to adapt socially and economically. Latino Mormons can aspire to positions of leadership because Mormons constitute the majority of Utah's politicians and civil servants. Since the creation of the Governor's Hispanic Advisory Council in 1973, at least 50 percent of its members also have been members of the LDS Church. One of the most prominent leaders of the Civil Rights Movement in Utah during the 1970s and 1980s, Dr. Orlando Rivera, is a member of the Church, as is the educational equity coordinator with the State Office of Education, Richard Gomez. Local newspapers and Latino activists estimate that most of the three thousand members of the Hispanic American Chamber of Commerce are also affiliated with the LDS Church. This is not to assert that LDS Latinos monopolize the political representation of Latinos in the state, but to corroborate that LDS Latinos are in those positions because of the support they receive from the LDS Church or appointments by state politicians who share the same religion.

Catholics and other non-LDS Latinos, who were disenfranchised for decades, tend to look to grassroots community-based organizations and ethnic leaders for support. Others ally themselves with LDS politicians in Washington such as Senator Orrin Hatch. John Florez, for example, became a member of the Presidential Commission on Hispanic Education during the administration of George H. W. Bush. As a consequence, Catholics and other non-LDS Latinos tend to create or enroll in political organizations, while Latino Mormons gravitate toward existing religious associations that might garner them a political appointment.

During the 1960s and 1970s immigrants from South America outnumbered those from Mexico. In 1970 only 18 percent of Latinos in Utah identified themselves as Mexicans. But the Latino population increased 80 percent over the next decade due to the unprecedented increase in the Mexican population, which grew 367 percent. Two main factors account for the exodus of Mexicans to the United States: the collapse of oil prices that exacerbated Mexico's foreign debt and the 15 percent drop in per capita income, which pushed unemployment and poverty to new levels. The economic crisis south of the border coincided with the boom in Utah's economy, which has been transformed from "government jobs and goods producing industries [to] private employment and service producing industries" starting in 1985.[39]

CHALLENGING THE KINGDOM: LATINO IMMIGRATION SINCE 1990

From 1990 to 2000, the Latino population in Utah increased 140 percent, due in part to the large influx of Latino immigrants. The 2000 Census reported that at least 55 percent of the foreign-born population in Utah was from Mexico and Latin America, and Latino immigrants made Spanish the second most spoken language in the state.[40] The growth of the Latino population was fueled by the arrival of asylum seekers and undocumented migrants from El Salvador, Guatemala, Nicaragua, and Panama fleeing the consequences of U.S. military involvement in Central America. The Governor's Office of Hispanic Affairs claimed that, in addition to economic and religious reasons, the rapid growth of the Latino population was due to "the abundance of higher education opportunities offered throughout the state; the economic recession California experienced in the late 1980s and early 1990s; and a high birth rate among Utah's Hispanic community."[41] Other explanations included the economic boom bolstered by the construction industry, the proliferation of hotels and restaurants, and the revitalization of the agricultural sector. This economic expansion was sustained by the 2002 Winter Olympic Games, the reconstruction of interstate I-80, and the promotion of Utah as a tourist destination. This bonanza increased the demand for labor and as always, the Latino immigrants responded without trepidation. Figure 7.1 depicts Latino immigration to Utah since 1970.

Among Latinos, those of Mexican origin represent 68 percent of the total population, followed by South Americans and Central Americans. Table 7.1 represents the different nationalities of Latinos in Utah in the year 2000.

The majority of Latino immigrants worked in entry-level jobs with low salaries. In 1990, the average weekly wage for Caucasians was $500, while Latinos earned only $325 per week. The overrepresentation of Latinos in low-paying jobs was also reflected by the 15 percent of Latinos who lived below federal poverty levels. Only 2.6 percent of Latinos in Utah occupied executive, administrative, or managerial positions.[42] Interestingly, Hispanic women reported higher weekly salaries than Hispanic men, who earned the lowest weekly wages in Utah. Figure 7.2 shows the average weekly wages for different race and gender groups in 1991.

Working in low-wage, entry-level jobs, Latino immigrants found no

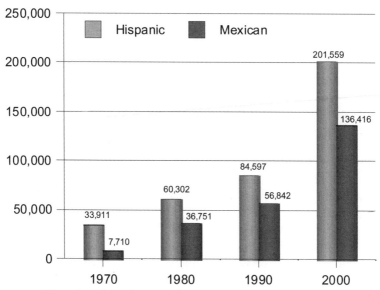

Figure 7.1   **Hispanic and Mexican Population in Utah, 1970 to 2000**

Table 7.1   Latino Population in Utah, 2000

Origin	Number	Percentage
Mexican	136,416	67.7
Puerto Rican	3,977	2.0
Cuban	940	0.5
Dominican Republic	352	0.2
CENTRAL AMERICAN:		
Costa Rican 406		
Guatemalan 2,137		
Honduran 613	6,645	3.3
Nicaraguan 330		
Panamanian 232		
Salvadoran 2,670		
SOUTH AMERICAN:		
Argentinean 1,626		
Bolivian 385		
Chilean 1,504		
Colombian 1,304		
Ecuadorian 637	9,620	4.8
Peruvian 2,276		
Uruguayan 261		
Venezuelan 1,224		
Other S. Americans 403		
SPANIARDS	859	0.4
HISPANICS OR LATINOS	42,750	21.2
TOTAL	**201,599**	**100.0**

possibility of economic or social improvement. Of all the migrants who found jobs through the Department of Employment Services, 70 percent were placed in jobs paying fifty cents above minimum wage. Latinos were hired for jobs in food processing, meatpacking, livestock, and crop production. The underrepresentation of Latinos in professional, technical, and managerial jobs was commensurate with income levels. On average, Latino families made 78 cents to every dollar earned by a Caucasian worker; the median annual income for a Caucasian household in Utah was $41,100, while the median income for Latino families was $31,500.[43]

Utah's educational system was unprepared for the challenges posed by the massive immigration of Mexicans, and Central and South

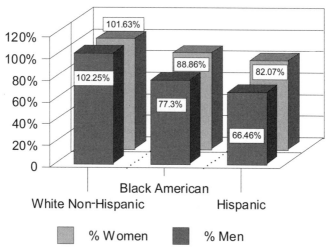

Figure 7.2   Average Utah Weekly Wages, 1991

Sources: Utah Governor's Hispanic Advisory Council, 1991
Notes: Hispanics in Utah. Utah Governor's Hispanic Advisory Council. Board Training and Applied Strategic Planning Program. Escalante Management Associates, Bonneville Research, 1991, 8.

Americans. As in other new settlement states, integration struggles were reflected in poor school retention rates. In public schools, the dropout rate for Latinos was 4.1 percent, compared to the statewide dropout rate of 1.6 percent. The situation was most alarming in high schools, where 40 percent of Latinos were leaving school before they finished their sophomore year. Utah did not have the infrastructure in place to facilitate the educational success of Latino children.

The deficiencies of Utah's educational system vis-à-vis the needs of immigrant students became most acute in the mid-1990s, when almost twelve thousand Spanish-speaking students were enrolled in Limited English Proficiency (LEP) classes. The U.S. Department of Education, through the Office of Civil Rights, reviewed seven Utah school districts and found that none complied with federal requirements to assess the needs of students whose primary language was not English. The Utah State Legislature responded by directing $1.6 million to bilingual education throughout the state.[44] These funds were insufficient, especially in the Salt Lake City School District where at least 44 percent of the students in 2000 were children of Latino immigrants and other minorities. In January 2002, President Bush signed the No Child Left Behind Act, which allows students at schools that failed state standards to be transferred to other schools in the district, with transportation paid for by federal funds. In Utah, twenty-two schools with a high concentration of immigrant children failed to pass the test and the students were transferred to schools with qualified teachers.[45]

One of the biggest concerns in the community remained the high percentage of high school dropouts. In 1990, 60 percent of Latinos earned a high school diploma, but by 2000 the number had dropped to 56.5 percent. School administrators concluded that the new immigrants "were driving the numbers down."[46] However, evidence indicates the dropout rates were directly related to the socioeconomic conditions of Latinos in the state, the underfunded educational system in Utah, and the lack of a high school curriculum that addresses the cultural and intellectual proclivity of Latino high school students.[47]

Integration problems also emerged in the health care system. As in the case study of Winchester, Virginia, the shortage of prenatal and infant care has posed a particular challenge. In Utah, 30 percent of Latinas who delivered babies between 1989 and 1991 did not receive prenatal care and Latino infant mortality rates reached 8.5 percent. By 1990 the percentage of Latinos who died of pulmonary diseases, birth defects, prenatal conditions, cirrhosis, diabetes, pneumonia, and accidents was greater than that of any other racial or ethnic group.[48]

Most Latino immigrants settled in the Salt Lake City area, where they first established a visible presence in the northwestern neighborhood of Rose Park. The foreign-born population swelled from 310 in 1990 to 3,162 in 2000, and the Latino population of Rose Park tripled. A gentrification process emerged slowly. Some Anglo-Americans moved out, citing a lack of security in the neighborhood, the deterioration of property values, and the influx of multifamily groups. Figure 7.3 denotes the racial and ethnic transformation of Rose Park from 1990 to 2002.

As in the rest of the state, the majority of immigrants in Rose Park were employed in entry-level jobs. The median household income for the neighborhood increased only 5 percent in ten years, from $33,600 in 1990 to $35,500 in 2000. This small increase contrasted with the statewide median income per household increase of 34 percent. Longtime residents in the neighborhood, like Lee Martinez, a former director of the state Office of Hispanic Affairs and Salt Lake City Council member, became fervent defenders of the neighborhood, especially against allegations that Rose Park was a cradle for Latino gang activity. The efforts of Latino activists were endorsed by long-established organizations like Centro Civico Mexicano that organized soccer leagues for Latino immigrants. Tournaments have included more than

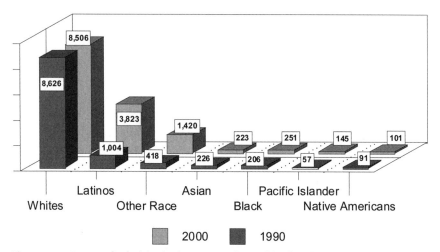

Figure 7.3   Race and Ethnicity in the Rose Park Neighborhood

three hundred Latino soccer teams. For the players, success was not just about winning tournaments, but also recovering the identity of Rose Park and promoting the reputation of Salt Lake City.[49] Maria Garcia, director of the Neighborhood Housing Services, revitalized the neighborhood by mobilizing volunteers and taking advantage of federally funded construction programs. Her ambition was to prepare the immigrants for self-sufficiency and independence from governmental support.

As the number of Latino immigrants in Utah increased, questions about racial profiling and abuse by law enforcement and the legal system became more prominent. In 1995, when Latinos made up 6.3 percent of the state population, almost 18 percent of all Latinos were incarcerated. Community leaders voiced concerns about miscommunication between the new Latino immigrants and law enforcement officers. The Utah legal system did not have enough bilingual officers. Court interpreters, clerks, and attorneys were seen by the Latino community as insensitive and unwilling to retool their skills to serve the immigrant population. Pressure from the Latino community compelled the Utah Task Force on Racial and Ethnic Fairness to organize twenty-eight forums throughout the state to make police officers more sensitive to the Latino culture and community.[50] The Office of Ethnic Affairs (OEA) also recommended recruiting ethnic youth from high schools and referring them to universities that offered criminal justice training. Additionally, the OEA petitioned to create community-based crime prevention programs and hire more ethnic employees with bicultural and bilingual skills.

As state officials slowly responded to the presence of new immigrants, Latino politicians and grassroots leaders challenged the 2000 Census data, arguing its population was miscounted. Neil Ashdown, director of the Governor's Office of Planning and Budget, acknowledged that "We definitely missed a large number of immigrants, and a large number of them were probably Latinos."[51] The count becomes even less accurate when undocumented workers are considered. In Utah's hotel industry alone, an estimated 70 percent of the service workers are undocumented.[52] In some counties, such as San Juan, 80 percent of the migrants are believed not to have appropriate immigration documents. In 1991, the Office of Hispanic Affairs (OHA) calculated that at least 40 percent of Latinos were not included in the 1990 Census because they were either undocumented or seasonal agricultural workers.[53]

Since 1990, undocumented Latinos have moved closer to the center of political attention in Utah. The Office of Hispanic Affairs, under the leadership of Leticia Medina, has become the strongest advocate for the Latino immigrant community. The office facilitated passage of a law that allows Latinos who do not qualify for a social security number to receive a Temporary Identification Number (ITIN), which allows them to obtain an Identification Card and a driver's license. This measure united different constituencies in defense of immigrant rights. The Consuls from Mexico and Guatemala supported the process. As a result of the new law, eighty thousand new applications were submitted to the Driver License Division of the Department of Motor Vehicles, and the number of uninsured drivers in Utah dropped by 32 percent.[54] An unexpected consequence of the ITIN cards was that financial institutions such as banks and credit unions started accepting them to open accounts and transfer money overseas. According to Banco de Mexico, Mexican immigrants sent home $10 billion in 2002 alone.

The ITIN measure also helped immigrants overcome driving-related obstacles familiar to many other new settlement states. Previously, many Latino immigrants were stopped while driving without documents and reported to the Immigration and Naturalization Service (INS). Documented Latino immigrants were also affected by police profiling and claimed that the cumbersome application process made it difficult to obtain a license. In Park City, a small town thirty minutes from Salt Lake City, it was difficult for immigrants to get a driver's license because the officers did not speak Spanish and the exams were conducted in English.[55] The ITIN opened the doors for immigrants to be recognized as members of the community, and in case of traffic violations, they were treated according to the nature of the violation and not their immigration status.

One of the most significant accomplishments of the Office of Hispanic Affairs (OHA) was the defeat of the "Memorandum of Understanding," which would have allowed local law enforcement to carry out functions reserved for INS agents. In 1998, Utah was selected to run a pilot project in which city officers routinely enforced immigration laws. Officials from the Salt Lake City police, the county sheriff, and the INS were called on to identify illegal immigrants arrested for committing a crime, or to transport undocumented workers to INS detention centers in Las Vegas and Denver.

Latino activists and the OHA opposed this project, arguing that the cross-deputation activities would lead to racism and increased police harassment of Latinos. John Medina, the chair of the Utah Coalition of la Raza, argued that the cross-deputizing project would only exacerbate the fragile relationship between Latinos and the police. To widen the gap between these groups was "too high a price to pay for, at best, a questionable improvement in immigration law enforcement."[56] Under persistent pressure from the Latino community, members of the Salt Lake City Council met on July 13, 1998 and voted against cross-deputizing the police. City council members were concerned with the validity of the statistics and the definition of "criminals" submitted by the Salt Lake County Commissioner. Nonetheless, in some parts of Utah, including Washington County, sheriffs implemented the cross-deputation mandate by using the 2001 decision of the 10th U.S. Circuit Court of Appeals, which granted state and local agencies the right to intervene in processes that enforced the federal immigration laws. Latino activists and grassroots organizations multiplied their advocacy efforts to protect Latino immigrants.

While activists successfully advanced programs and services for Latino immigrants, they were unable to defeat an English-only bill. Utah politicians, troubled by the notion that the unprecedented increase in immigrants would transform the state's cultural and linguistic foundations, promoted the declaration of English as the official language of the state. One of the bill's principal advocates was Representative Tammy Rowan, who received a $280,000 contribution in 2000 from U.S. English, a Washington-based organization chaired by

Mauro Mujica. Three attempts to pass the bill that would "prohibit state agencies from conducting government business and printing information in any other language but English" were defeated.[57] But on November 7, 2000, English became the official language of Utah: "English is declared to be the official language of Utah [and] as the official language of the State, the English language is the sole language of the government."[58] The law also mandates that the State Board of Education and the State Board of Regents promote policies ensuring that "non-English speaking children and adults read, write, and understand English as quickly as possible."[59] Given the number of exceptions in the English-only initiative, its implementation became largely symbolic, reflecting a considerable level of political paranoia among government officials. Judge Nehring, the third district judge, declared that English as the Official Language "is largely symbolic because it was descriptive rather than proscriptive, prohibitive of nothing."[60]

Not all the political actions responding to immigrant growth have been negative. The presence of Latino immigrants in Utah inspired a law that allows undocumented immigrant students to attend universities and colleges and pay in-state tuition, which benefits the whole state population. The bill was approved by the Utah State Legislature under the provision that undocumented students must be enrolled in a public high school for at least three years. Support for the measure rallied behind the figure of Silvia Salguero, an undocumented high school student in Park City who dropped out of the University of Utah to work as a housekeeper. She was in no position to pay $8,800 in tuition, more than three times the resident rate of $2,900. Working with teachers, legislators, members of Congress, and presidents of Utah's universities, Salguero and other immigrant students established a precedent in the nation. Utah Senator Orrin Hatch brought the bill to the U.S. Senate and stated that the undocumented status of the children is "no act of their own." To close his presentation to the Senate he added: "Many [undocumented children] have been in the United States for many years, if not the majority of their lives. By and large, these children are assimilated into American culture."[61]

As politicians and social service agencies were trying to catch up with the needs of the new immigrants, Latino businesses proliferated throughout the state. The last decade witnessed a twofold increase in the numbers of Latino restaurants, markets, tortilla factories, newspapers, and radio and TV stations. At the same time, Latinos diversified the religious composition of Utah. Immigrants from Central and Latin

America brought an impressive number of churches based on Pentecostal traditions, including *Iglesia Bautista El Sembrador, Iglesia Cristiana Pentecostal, Iglesia de Dios Rios de Agua Viva, Iglesia del Dios Vivo,* and *Primera Iglesia Apostólica.* This transformation of Utah's religious landscape confirms the studies of anthropologist David C. Knowlton, who claims that Latin America, through its immigrants, became an exporter of religious beliefs and movements. Latin American immigrants "carry with them the religious culture and institutions of their homeland."[62]

There is a strong correlation between religion and nationality among Latino immigrants. Sixty percent of Latinos in Utah are Catholic and Mexican; 30 percent are LDS converts, mainly from South America; and the remaining 10 percent are Pentecostals, mostly from Central America. The 1991 economic profiles of LDS Latinos seem to corroborate the economic and social differences between LDS and non-LDS Latinos of the 1970s. That is, LDS Latinos report more years of formal education, better paying jobs, better accommodation, and more people in professional occupations.[63] In sociological terms, these indicators measure levels of adaptation and integration into the host society, which leads to the conclusion that LDS Latinos integrate faster and more successfully in Utah. Jessie L. Embry, an LDS historian and researcher at Brigham Young University, put it in the following terms:

Mormons have . . . usually supported assimilation. Nineteenth-century Swedish immigrants were told to leave behind their culture and "adopt the manners and customs of the American people, fit themselves to become good and loyal citizens of this country, and by their good works show that they were true and faithful Latter-Day Saints."[64]

Fuller integration of LDS Latino immigrants in Utah is also explained by the fact that Latino Mormons do not perceive themselves as "outsiders" since they share mainstream religious beliefs and some components of the Mormon culture. Having achieved a higher socioeconomic position, they tend not to interact as much with Mexicans because "to be a Mexican" implies illiteracy, underdevelopment, and lower status. Mike Martinez, a Latino lawyer and activist, considers that "Mexicans in Utah are sort of the outcast . . . South Americans who are Mormons get advantages and people take them under their wings." As an example he cites the support given by Utah's Chamber of Commerce to the publication of LDS Latino newspapers and the creation of the Hispanic Chamber of Commerce.[65] Recently released information corroborates that the LDS Church is the largest employer in the state, which has implications for employment opportunities for Latino immigrants at LDS corporations. As we already know, the overwhelming majority of the employees is required to be church members in good standing and must have the predisposition and "desire to help build the Lord's Kingdom."[66]

THE IMPACT OF SEPTEMBER 11, 2001, ON UTAH'S INTEGRATION PRACTICES

The events of September 11, 2001, sparked several transformations for Latino immigrants in the state and revealed contradictions in immigration and integration policies. The preoccupation with national security prompted several raids, which confirmed the high rates of undocumented immigrants in Utah working even in "high security" positions at the Salt Lake International Airport. To protect the rights of undocumented workers, the Mexican Consulate and long-established organizations such as Centro Civico Mexicano emerged as key actors in the negotiation of immigrant rights. With the high visibility of the Mexican Consulate came also the reevaluation of the role that Latino political organizations created during the 1970s should play in Utah's political arena.

Three months after the attacks on New York and the Pentagon, Utah's Office of Homeland Security in collaboration with federal agencies launched "Operation Safe Travel." The goal was to improve airline passenger safety and identify potential terrorists. In one sweep, 208 workers lost their jobs due to their undocumented status and sixty-nine others were charged with falsifying employment records. Robert Flowers, the coordinator of the raid, alluded to the possibility that undocumented individuals working in secure areas of the airport were vulnerable to extortion by international terrorists. Nonetheless, the use of force in the raid raised the indignation of the Latino population who went to the State Capitol to protest the "window-dressing" tactics used to address the problem of undocumented workers. Latino politicians reminded Utahans that the U.S. Constitution and the Bill of Rights are applicable to "All people living in the U.S." James Yapias, chairman of the Governor's Hispanic Advisory Council, called for a one-day statewide work stoppage during the 2002 Winter Olympics. Such an action would have paralyzed the hotels, restaurants, and the transportation services of the state, demonstrating the central role that documented and undocumented Latino immigrants play in Utah's economy.

An evaluation of "Operation Safe Travel" by April 2002 reported mixed results. Most of the charges against immigrants swept up in the raid were dropped, some cases were dismissed and others were left unresolved, with the undocumented workers still facing the possibility of deportation. Moreover, the security level at the airport did not satisfy federal officials. All parties involved in the raid concluded that it only showed the "humanitarian concerns" of involved agencies. U.S. Attorney Paul Warner confirmed that prosecutors dismissed charges against families who suffered hardships resulting from the raid. Salt Lake City Mayor Rocky Anderson inaugurated a program entitled "Family to Family" for undocumented workers affected by the "unfair and inhumane" persecutions. Representatives Chris Cannon and Jim Matheson attempted to put a "human face" to the raid, calling for a balance among sensible immigration, security, and the law.

No matter how the raid was interpreted, the fact is that undocumented workers showed their deepest sorrow for the U.S. citizens who died in the September 11 attack. According to the *Salt Lake Tribune*, the "illegal" workers attended memorial services in honor of the victims, sent $50 to the Red Cross, and donated blood for the attack victims.[67]

Looking at the raid from a religious perspective, Rev. Robert Bussen, a pastor of St. Mary's Catholic Church in Park City, remarked that it brought to the surface how much the economy of Utah relies on undocumented immigrants. "They are here illegally because we want them here, we need them here. . . . We want them here illegally because Americans want to live on the cheap."[68] Another priest at the same church voiced strikingly compassionate support for the undocumented workers on October 17, 2002. Fr. Jim Flynn, proclaiming love for one's neighbor as one of the greatest commandments, asked the congregation, "Who's my neighbor?" Fr. Flynn recalled a time when the Israelites became foreigners and he quoted one of the laws that Moses gave them: "You shall not molest or oppress an alien, for you were once aliens in Egypt." Again, rhetorically, Fr. Flynn asked, In 2002, who is my neighbor? He volunteered the answer.

> You and I do show extraordinary love for undocumented Mexicans or other Latinos and Latinas. After all, you've welcomed so many Latinos here. This Church is filled each Sunday night at the 7 o'clock Spanish Mass mostly with Mexicans. Some of us hire the Latinos. We've put up a huge image of Our

Lady of Guadalupe there in back of the church. Some of us are even learning Spanish. . . . But there's another level of love for the foreigner, the Mexicans around us. We've allowed a whole economic and political system to oppress illegal and undocumented people. Many of us had ancestors who were undocumented. Many of our ancestors were oppressed and molested by an unjust economic and political system . . . It behooves us . . . to show extraordinary love, compassion and kindness to the undocumented people around us.[69]

While some sectors of the Catholic Church demonstrated commitment to the cause of the undocumented workers, the LDS Church remained silent on the issue. For Michael Clara, director of the League of United Latin American Citizens in Utah, the LDS residents of the state were confused by the legal complexities and economic implications of the issue. "Mormons are big on upholding the law, so it gets blurred on what we are supposed to do here. Everyone wants to stick to the law, but everyone knows the economic reality."[70]

At least six other massive campaigns to deport undocumented workers followed the 2001 raid. In the most publicized campaign, INS agents entered the Champion Safe Company in February 2002 and arrested 75 percent of its work force. After the raid the company hired Anglo workers who were not able to "sustain the work" and quit. To avoid bankruptcy and keep Champion competitive in the labor market, its owner, Ray Crosby, considered "following its deported workers and moving to Mexico."[71]

The controversial implementation of programs such as "Operation Safe Travel," led the federal government to create a national program to verify social security numbers in 2002. At the end of the year, the Social Security Administration sent 750,000 letters across the nation advising employers that the social security number of their workers did not match federal records. Officials stressed that the program was not aimed at undocumented workers; its goal was merely to verify the authenticity of social security cards. But Angela Kelly, deputy director of the National Immigration Forum in Utah, interpreted these measures as "silent raids." Within three months, between five hundred and seven hundred Mexican nationals who were notified that their social security numbers were invalid contacted the Mexican Consulate in Salt Lake City. Martin Torres, the Mexican Consul, observed: "Unfortunately, we must tell people that if their documentation is improper, there is nothing we can do except make sure that employers do not take advantage of the situation, that they pay whatever wages are owed."[72]

During those three months, the consul also confirmed that at least one hundred companies approached him for information on how to legalize workers, or how to read the intentions of the U.S. government. Some firms, such as Merit Medical System, trained teams of supervisors on how to talk to their employees about the issue in the most appropriate way. Privately, the company told employees about their invalid numbers, said they did not have to leave the company immediately and promised to help resolve their status. Meanwhile, employers argued the federal government should check the documents of immigrants coming across the border more aggressively, shifting the burden of responsibility away from them.[73]

Since becoming involved with the legal issues surrounding the raid, the Mexican Consul has taken a larger role in Latino community affairs, organizing cultural activities and holiday celebrations in downtown Salt Lake City. On the night of September 15, 2002, Martin Torres made public his intention to bring Anglo-Americans to share the heritage and traditions of Mexicans and make Salt Lake City a more inclusive place. His engagement was also noticeable in rural areas, where the Mexican Consulate registered all Mexicans for the sake of protection and precise records. These activities were extended to Wyoming and Idaho, two states within the jurisdiction of the consulate. The consulate also became active in the implementation of the Double Citizenship Program, which allows Mexican and Mexican-Americans to have dual nationality but citizenship in one country. Torres also played an instrumental role in planning the visit of Utah's governor to Mexico to foster business, educational, and cultural collaborations.

Some Latino activists have accused the consulate of overstepping its boundaries, fearing that its involvement could impede the integration of Mexicans into Utah's mainstream institutions. While activists like Mike Martinez do not doubt the consul is genuinely concerned about the immigrants' security, they feel he indirectly encourages immigrants to continue sending money to Mexico. It is a well-known fact that remittances are the second largest source of revenue for the Mexican government. Martinez argues that the money and resources should be spent locally instead: "Get acclimated. Get your kid educated. Keep your money here. That is what you need to do if you are ever going to be assimilated."[74] Investing in their new community is essential for the first generation of immigrants who need to establish strong foundations for their families. Rather than sending money to Mexico, according to Martinez, the Latino politicians should seek expanded benefits for immigrants. Only by gaining entitlements will immigrants come to feel welcome in Utah.

The increasing visibility of the Mexican Consul in Utah's political arena questions the role of Latino organizations created in the early 1970s, especially the Governor's Council of Hispanic Affairs and the Office of Hispanic Affairs. The dramatic change that Mexicans brought to the state has reduced the influence of these organizations with Utah bureaucrats. In the 1970s, Mexicans constituted only 24 percent of the total Latino population, but in 2002 Mexicans reached 59 percent. The community leadership represented all of the Latino population in the 1970s, but the growth of the Mexican population was not represented until the Mexican Consul took a larger role. During civil rights movement, the state's political climate was progressive and Governors Cal Rampton and Scott Matheson worked with Latinos to transform Latino communities. Now, Latino leaders, such as James Yapias, believe that "the governor and other state officials still resist the influence of the Latino community."[75] Utah's government still provides the same funds to Latinos as it does other minority groups, without considering the demographic composition of the groups. The 2002 Census clearly shows that in Utah, the Latino population is five times greater than the Asian-American community, ten times greater than the black population, and fifteen times greater than the Pacific Islanders cohort.

To facilitate inclusion of Latino immigrants into the larger society, Latino activists have relied on the tactics of protest and negotiation.[76] Confrontational tactics are generally not part of the equation in a state whose political culture is based on religious patronage and top-down nominations. Utah bureaucrats are suspicious even of the Office of Hispanics Affairs. In the words of Ruben Jimenez, one of the founders of the Chicano Civil Rights Movement: "If the office gets too active in the community, it tends to irritate government officials."[77] Catholic immigrants have similar suspicions about the religious affiliations of Utah's Latino leaders. Latino Catholics distrust the Latino LDS leadership since the Church's members constitute only 30 percent of the predominantly Catholic Latino population in Utah. Beyond religion, this distrust is related also to the differences in socioeconomic backgrounds, nationality, political alliances, levels of education, and the perception that LDS Latinos have more support integrating in mainstream Utah.

The future of Latino political institutions in Utah depends on the integration of different types of leadership. Different strains of Latino leadership currently operate independently and without coordination or a sense of mutual support. A decentralized form of leadership that has emerged to navigate the political storms of the state coexists with the leadership of the Mexican Consul, who attempts to protect the rights of documented and undocumented Mexican workers. Strong leadership has also been demonstrated by individuals of different religious denominations who need to learn the dialogue of tolerance and inclusion. These well-established forms of leadership should work together to create the political space for the new immigrants whose children represent the future of Utah's communities.

CONCLUSION

Studying the history of the United States, Oscar Handlin wrote, "Once I thought to write a history of the immigrants in America. Then I discovered that the immigrants were American History."[78] The same can be said about Utah. Ethnocentric statements too often credit the Church of the Latter-Day Saints and its members as the only heirs to the land. The state's historical annals occasionally forget that Mormons were also immigrants seeking refuge from religious persecution. Since the Mormons created a religious kingdom and an economic empire, migration has been understood as a virtuous act full of religious and economic connotations. But when the "Other" sees Utah as a land of opportunity, migration becomes a threat.

At the time the state was settled, 90 percent of the immigration was Anglo-European and Mormon, but in 2000 immigration was 90 percent Latino and Catholic. This discontinuity has made integration almost unattainable for some new immigrants. The Catholic Latinos do not mix with mainstream society in churches or in the workplace; even their children attend segregated schools. Mike Martinez sees complete disenfranchisement between Mormons and Catholics: "they don't see each other at church, they don't see each other in the workplace, and they don't see each other at the education level." For Martinez, the root of the problem is not the LDS religion per se. The region's culture, he argues, becomes "a way of life, and we are not part of that way of life."

Some LDS cultural activities, such as preparing male youths for missions, promote an appreciation of different cultures that does not extend to foreigners living in Utah. Martinez observes, "We have the largest international institute of foreign languages," but when the missionaries return to Utah they are not willing to talk or work with the immigrant population of the countries they visited. Martinez adds: "They want to eat their [immigrants'] food but they don't want to socialize with them." There is no sense of acceptance. In his final analysis, Martinez understands that immigrant integration in Utah is a formidable task because identity in the state is centered by the Mormon religion. "If you are a Mormon, you are not a worker, you are not a Hispanic, you are not a Mexican, you are not Irish; you are a Mormon first and foremost."[79]

With the LDS religion come other traditions that have delayed the incorporation of immigrants into the mainstream society. These traditions, elevated by Mormon values, include conservatism, Republican Party affiliation, middle-class status, and geographical and intellectual isolation. Ethnocentrism in Utah becomes Mormocentrism, which entails the judgment of other people according to the expectations of the LDS Church. The cool response to the Latino immigrants underscores how strongly LDS members try to preserve those traditions. Dale F. Pearson, in his study of gangs in Utah, found that when Utah bureaucrats attempt to understand the relationship between Hispanic immigration and gangs, they create negative images to discredit the Hispanic immigrants. This mischaracterization of immigrants becomes the official response to the structural changes in Utah's communities. In his conclusion Pearson wrote:

> I find the signs of a society struggling to maintain its traditional identity: Utah ranks first among U.S. states in measures that tap general levels of conservatism; Mormonism—in practice, a related phenomenon, being the predominant religion, ranks first in measures gauging religious, and therefore political dominance; a stable economy provides a base for comfortable middle-class values; and the overwhelming Anglo population lives protected from the outside world with the help of the geophysical barriers of the Wasatch Front and miles of desert to the West.[80]

But the question remains: Who is going to facilitate the full integration of the new Latino immigrants in Utah? The state government considers only the immediate needs of immigrants, providing low-paying jobs, low-quality housing, and in sporadic occasions, food and clothing. The state lacks a comprehensive strategy to fully incorporate immigrants into the state's mainstream institutions. Some analysts agree that government officials are doing everything in their power to advance the well-being of Latino immigrants, but they face opposition from constituencies that are unwilling to support the economic cost of such efforts. If the state government and the host society fall short, what remains is the power of grassroots Latino organizations to advocate for the betterment of the new Latino arrivals.

With the motto "Invest in your future, not your past," Latino leaders are attempting to promote long-term goals for the immigrants to feel more accepted and secure in an environment where their families will not be raided and their children will be educated. As Martinez said: "Ultimately what we are talking about is not me and you; it is our children."[81] The challenge, however, lies in the tactics employed by Latinos who are attempting to bring about social change. Any assessment that suggests Utah has fallen short in immigrant integration is going to be perceived as an accusation against the local culture and religion. To accept the marginalization of immigrants in Utah is to admit that the LDS religion has failed. Martinez puts it eloquently:

> You can't attack the culture, or the infrastructure, or the strata without attacking the religion that is behind it because everyone that runs the system is a member of that religion. You become a troublemaker by saying the schools system is failing. You become a troublemaker because you are not really saying, "the school system is failing;" you are saying, "the people that run the school system are failing, and, therefore, the Mormons are failing."[82]

The question is not who to blame, but how to stress the benefits that immigrants offer to the state. Latino immigrants, both documented and undocumented, have consistently bolstered the state's economy. The buying power of consumers in Utah has increased 117 percent since 1990, a trend that a University of Georgia study attributes in part to the increase in migration. After spending $753,337 in Utah in 1990, Latinos spent more than $3 million in 2002 and are expected to spend almost $6 million by 2007.

More importantly, Latino immigrants have diversified Utah's economy. Latino consumers spend more than any other group on groceries, telephone services, and furniture, according to the Georgia Business and Economic Conditions Report. In Utah, one has only to look at the Latino grocery stores and supermarkets, the competition for long-distance telephone services to Latin America, and the Spanish-language advertisements for electronics and furniture stores. However, the same report establishes that when compared with other ethnic and racial populations, Latinos nationwide "spent substantially smaller proportions of total outlays (and substantially less money) on health care, education, life and other personal insurance."[83] While there are no statistics that corroborate this situation for Utah, the state's Latino immigrants are no better adapted to U.S. institutions than their counterparts elsewhere in the country.

Mormonism remains a powerful magnet that attracts Latinos to the state. As both a religious organization and a powerful economic enterprise, it has attracted Latino Mormons and non-Mormon Latinos pursuing job opportunities. But regardless of their reason for coming, immigrants have experienced the close interrelationship between religion and industry for more than a hundred years. At the start of the twentieth century, some Hispanic miners shifted their religious identification because their churches disappeared. Priests and ministers vacated when the mining economy took a downturn, leaving congregations to their own devices. In one example, Joseph Gallegos and his family who lived in Carbon County were members of the Mormon Church, the Assembly of God, the Catholic Church, and Pentecostal Churches. As Gallegos stated, it was not a specific religion that interested him, but the need to satisfy his spirituality and leave a religious inheritance to his children.

I don't think you have to be a member of the Assembly of God to get to heaven, and I don't think you have to be Catholic, or Mormon, or whatever. I think it is really the relationship that you have with God. [In my family] there was a need for the formalization and the experience of going to church. But I don't think that it's the church in itself. I do have a need to go to church on Sunday. I have a need to teach my child about the importance of believing in God, about the importance of church attendance, about the importance of paying your tithing, about the importance of living like a Christian.[84]

Today, many Latino Mormons are attracted to Utah because it represents the Mecca of their beliefs and the place where they can fulfill their religious values. Such is the case of Bertha Alcazar who was born in Tamaulipas, Mexico. When she was asked why she came to Utah, she replied:

For religious reasons. I was single at the time I moved here. I am LDS. In my religion it is advised that you marry within your religion for many reasons. And I felt very strongly that I should marry an LDS person. But at the time I was twenty-nine years old there were no eligible men, my age, that were LDS. And I had the choice of either marrying outside the Church or remaining single. And I didn't feel I could be single. So, I prayed. And I felt I received the answer of coming to Salt Lake City. And that's mainly what brought me here.[85]

Following the teachings of the Book of Mormon and the description of the origin of indigenous people, some Latino Mormons said their emigration to Utah was an effort to return to the land of their ancestors. Juan Balderas put it in the following terms: "I am returning to what you might call the mother faith, to the place of our ancestors."[86] Many non-Mormon Mexicans and Chicanos who consider Utah part of Aztlán, the sacred land of the Aztec people, share this perception. But for other Chicanos, Aztlán is nothing but Zion, the city of God that Mormons need to recreate in Utah.

> Some Latinos are returning to Zion. You get an interesting return, whether they're from Mexico, whether they're from Colombia or Nicaragua, all the countries South of the United States. You get a certain number of Latter-Day Saints Mormons who are saying, "I'm coming back. I'm going back, this is where I want to be. I want to be close to the center of my religion." If you're Catholic you go back to Rome [to] be close to the Vatican and the Pope. If you are Muslim you want to be close to Mecca. And so it is with Mormons. They want to be close to the seed of the religious center, the religious head, which is the president of the LDS church or the prophet.[87]

The Latino population in Utah, shaped by immigration, is fragmented by social class, nationality, gender, and religion. It is estimated that by the year 2020 Latinos will represent more than 50 percent of the membership of the Mormon Church. Some Latin-American Mormons come to study at Brigham Young University, which is owned and operated by the LDS Church. But Latinos also represent at least 60 percent of the state's Catholic population, a community that has publicly celebrated its culture and faith. The tree of the Virgin Mary in downtown Salt Lake City has attracted thousands of Catholics from the mountain region, and symbols of the cross have begun appearing at accident sites on Utah's highways.

Latino immigration to Utah has created challenges with deep implications for the future of the state and the country. Just as African-American intellectuals at the beginning of the century saw the future in terms of the resolution of racial conflict, Utah's future might depend on the resolution of its religious conflicts. Reading the signs of the times, one wonders whether an LDS Revelation is in place, like the one in 1978 that allowed blacks to receive the priesthood and temple ordinances. This time, a Revelation within the LDS Church would dispel the long-maintained position about the Lamanites, the undocumented workers, the poor, and the less fortunate members of our society. Within this new Revelation a space for social justice and a preferential option for the disenfranchised would be reasons for celebration and unity. This Revelation would go against some of Utah's traditions but it would facilitate the accommodation of those still waiting at the gates of the Kingdom. In the analysis of Jessie L. Embry, "Like other religions [the LDS Church] has not been sure how to deal with ethnic groups who are not a part of that middle-class upwardly mobile image."[88] A new Revelation, however, would bring the Church to transcend issues of social class and immigration status.

Latino immigrants in Utah have posed not an economic or legal dilemma to the state, but an ontological one. Is religious *mestizaje* possible? Can people of different religions live in harmony? Virgilio Elizondo, a Chicano theologian, argues that racial relations are improving in the United States. But not much effort has been invested in interfaith understanding. He concluded: "Yet, it is precisely at this level that the greatest challenge for a united humanity presents itself."[89] The foundation for religious amalgamation and for a better understanding between Latino immigrants and members of the predominant religion in Utah was already suggested at the genesis of the Mormon experience. Brigham Young understood immigration as a symbolic act, as a rite of passage, a human action as old as history itself. The integration of Latino immigrants, as any other group of immigrants, should be considered as an important step in the fulfillment of our broken humanity.

NOTES

1. Leonard Arrington, *Great Basin Kingdom: An Economic History of the Latter-Day Saints, 1830–1900* (Cambridge, MA: Harvard University Press, 1958), vii.

2. In this chapter the broad term "Latinos" refers to people whose ancestry is traced to Spain, Mexico, and Central and/or South America. The term "Spanish" is used to describe people living in the United States whose ancestors came from Spain. Mexicans are people who came to the United States from Mexico, while Mexican Americans are people of Mexican ancestry born in the United States. The term "Hispanics" describes Spaniards who came to Utah from New Mexico or Colorado. "Chicanos" are the people of Mexican-American decent who are politically active, or identify themselves as such.

3. U.S. Census Bureau 2000.

4. B. H. Roberts, *A Comprehensive History of the Church of Jesus Christ of Latter-Day Saints: Century I* vol. III (Salt Lake City, UT: Church Deseret New Press, 1930).

5. Arrington, *Great Basin Kingdom*, 97.

6. Katherine Coman, *Economic Beginnings of the Far West*, vol. 2 (New York:

Macmillan, 1912), 184. See also Wilbur S. Shepperson, "The Place of the Mormons in the Religious Emigration of Britain, 1840–1860." *Utah Historical Quarterly* 20 (1952): 218.

7. Dean L. May, "A Demographic Portrait of the Mormons, 1830–1980," in *After 150 Years: The Latter-Day Saints in Sesquicentennial Perspective*, ed. Thomas G. Alexander and Jessie L. Embry (Provo, UT: Charles Redd Center for Western Studies, 1983), 39–69. Also see Arrington, *Great Basin Kingdom*, 354.

8. The Constitution of the State of Deseret. *Millennial Star* 12: 19–25.

9. May, "Demographic Portrait of the Mormons," 67.

10. F. LaMond Tullis, *Mormons in Mexico: The Dynamics of Faith and Culture* (Logan: Utah State University Press, 1987), 6.

11. Arrington, *Great Basin Kingdom*, 380.

12. William Mulder, "Immigration and the 'Mormon Question': An International Episode." *Western Political Quarterly* 9 (1956): 416–23.

13. Robert S. McPherson, *A History of San Juan County: In the Pal of Time*, Utah Centennial County History Series (Salt Lake City: Utah State Historical Society, 1995), 112.

14. McPherson, *History of San Juan County*, 176.

15. McPherson, *History of San Juan County*, 176.

16. Arrington, *Great Basin Kingdom*, 410.

17. McPherson, *History of San Juan County*, 176.

18. William H. González and Genaro M. Padilla, "Monticello, the Hispanic Cultural Gateway to Utah." *Utah Historical Quarterly* (Winter 1984): 9–28.

19. Leonard J. Arrington and Gary B. Hansen, *"The Richest Hole on Earth": A History of the Bingham Copper Mine*, Monograph Series 11, no. 1 (October 1963) (Logan: Utah State University Press, 1963), 1–102.

20. Armando Solórzano and Jorge Iber, "Digging the Richest Hole on Earth: The Hispanic Miners of Utah, 1912–1945," in *Perspectives in Mexican American Studies*, vol. 7 (Tucson: Mexican American Studies & Research Center, The University of Arizona, 2000), 1–27.

21. Edith Melendez, "Spanish-Speaking Oral Interview." MS # 96. Interview 74. Marriott Library. Special Collections (Salt Lake City: University of Utah, 1973).

22. Milton R. Hunter and Thomas S. Ferguson, *Ancient America and the Book of Mormon* (Oakland: California Kolob Book Company, 1950).

23. Mario Barrera, *Race and Class in the Southwest: A Theory of Racial Inequality* (Notre Dame, IN: University of Notre Dame Press, 1979).

24. Jesus Amador, Interview 002 (Salt Lake City, UT, 1973).

25. Miriam B. Murphy, "Mexican Families and the Sugar Industry in Garland." *Utah History to Go* (November 1995).

26. "Mexican Labor to Be Admitted in Utah," *Salt Lake Tribune*, April 15, 1920, 18.

27. P. Morgan and V. Mayer, "The Spanish-Speaking Population on Utah: From 1900 to 1935," in *Towards a History of the Spanish-Speaking People of Utah* (A Report of Research of the Mexican-American Documentation Project. Occasional Paper No. 3, American West Center, University of Utah, 1973), 36.

28. P. Morgan and V. Mayer, "Mexican Labor to Be Admitted in Utah," 39–42.

29. John E. Christiansen, "The Impact of World War II." In *Utah's History*, ed. R. D. Poll, G. A. Thomas, E. E. Campbell, and D. E. Miller (Provo, UT: Brigham Young University Press, 1978), 497–514.

30. William C. Blair, "An Ethnological Survey of Mexicans and Puerto Ricans in Bingham Canyon, Utah." Master's thesis, University of Utah, Salt Lake City, 1948.

31. Joseph E. Allen, "A Sociological Study of Mexican Assimilation in Salt Lake City." Master's thesis, University of Utah, Salt Lake City, 1947.

32. Jessie L. Embry, *In His Own Language: Mormon Spanish-Speaking Congregations in the United States* (Provo, UT: The Charles Redd Center for Western Studies, Brigham Young University, 1997), 24.

33. "Praise Given Women for Mission Work." *Church News* (October 4, 1952); cited in Embry, *In His Own Language*, 24.

34. Solórzano and Iber, "Digging the Richest Hole on Earth," 1–27.

35. Philip Martin and David Martin, *The Endless Quest: Helping America's Farm Workers* (Boulder, CO: Westview Press, 1994).

36. Manuel G. Gonzalez, *Mexicanos: A History of Mexicans in the United States* (Bloomington: Indiana University Press, 2000), 193.

37. Embry, *In His Own Language*, 42.

38. John Deloy Glassett, "South American Immigration to Utah." Master's thesis, Department of Geography, Marriott Library, University of Utah, Salt Lake City, 1972.

39. *Economic Report to the Governor* (Salt Lake City, UT: Governor's Office of Planning and Budget, January 1996), 12–13.

40. U.S. Census Bureau, "Region and County or Area of Birth of the Foreign-Born Population." Utah. Summary File 3. 2000.

41. "Race and Ethnicity: Understanding the Issues. Meeting the Demand in Utah" (Salt Lake City, UT: Governor's Office of Planning and Budget, May 1996), 23.

42. "A Graphic Look at Utah's Ethnicity," U.S. Census Bureau, 1990.

43. Annual Report, State Office of Ethnic Affairs. Department of Community and Economic Development. Salt Lake City, UT, June 19, 1999.

44. Governor's Office of Hispanic Affairs. 1995. Annual Report. 4.

45. Shinika A. Sykes, "SLC District Leaving Kids Behind?" *The Salt Lake Tribune*, August 5, 2002, p. D-3.

46. Kirsten Stewart, "Education Slippage among Latinos, Asians Is Puzzling." *The Salt Lake Tribune*, August 13, 2002, p. A-1.

47. Cecilia Romero and Andrea Martinez, "A Comparative Analysis on Ethnic Identity between Latino High School Students in School and Latino High School Dropouts in the Salt Lake City Area." Paper presented at the National Association for Chicana and Chicano Studies, Mexico City, June 24–27, 1998.

48. Health Status Indicators by Race and Ethnicity. 2000. Utah Department of Health, Salt Lake City.

49. Tim Sullivan, "Diablos de Salt Lake, Sport Links Utah Players." *The Salt Lake Tribune*, October 22, 2002.

50. State Office of Ethnic Affairs, Annual Report. June 1999.

51. Neil Ashdown, quoted in *The Salt Lake Tribune*. "Census Panel Member Calls for Changes." August 20, 2002.

52. Peter Jennings and Todd Brewster, *In Search of America* (New York: Hyperion, 2002), 238.

53. "Minority Population in Utah Grew 37% in the Past Decade." *Deseret News* (Salt Lake City, UT), March 6–7, 1991.

54. Mike Martinez. 2002. Interview by author.

55. Utah Office of Hispanic Affairs. Park City Assessment. October 2, 1997.

56. John Medina, cited in "Utah Police May Receive INS Powers: Opponents Fear Officer Will Target Minorities: Police May Receive INS Powers." Kimberly Murphy. *Salt Lake Tribune*, July 5, 1997, p. D-1.

57. House Bill 387. Utah State Legislature. 1997. General Session.

58. Utah Code Ann. Vol. 63-13-1.5 (1) and (2).

59. Utah Code Ann. Vol. 63-13-1.5 (5)(a). My gratitude goes to Laura Nava for collecting the official documents for these Bills and Initiatives.

60. "English-Only Challenge Is Turned Back." *Salt Lake Tribune*, March 6, 2001, p. A-1.

61. Orrin Hatch, cited in "Anti-Immigrant Groups Oppose Tuition Break." *Salt Lake Tribune*, June 28, 2002, p. B-3.

62. David C. Knowlton, *Mormonism in Latin America*. Book manuscript. Department of Anthropology, University of Utah.

63. Embry, *In His Own Language*, 70–71.

64. Embry, *In His Own Language*, 121.

65. Mike Martinez. 2002. Interview with author.

66. Cited in the LDS Employment website. See also Dan Harrie and Peggy Fletcher Stack, "Glimpse at LDS Church Workers: The State No. 1 Employer Is Cutting Back Some Jobs." *The Salt Lake Tribune*, December 22, 2002, p. A-1.

67. Kristen Moulton and Jesus Lopez Jr., "Vital and Vulnerable." *The Salt Lake Tribune*, January 27, 2002, p. A-1.

68. Moulton and Lopez, "Vital and Vulnerable."

69. Fr. Jim Flynn. Homily. 30th Sunday Ordinary Time # 2. October 27, 2002. St. Mary's Church, Park City, Utah.

70. Cited in Moulton and Lopez, "Vital and Vulnerable."

71. Tim Sullivan, "Business May Leave Provo for Mexico." *The Salt Lake Tribune*, May 6, 2003.

72. Dawn House, "Social Security Called 'Silent Raid' on Illegals." *The Salt Lake Tribune*, July 7, 2002, p. A-1.

73. Ron Morgan, president of Utah Restaurant Association, quoted in "INS Target Utah restaurants, Leaves Farms Alone." *The Salt Lake Tribune*, December 30, 1991, p. D-6.

74. Mike Martinez, interview with author, 2002.

75. Quoted in Tim Sullivan, "Utah Government Latino Agencies Face Identity Issues, Budget Woes." *Salt Lake Tribune*, January 23, 2003, p. A-1.

76. David Montejano, ed., *Chicano Politics and Society in the Late Twentieth Century* (Austin: University of Texas Press, 1999).

77. Quoted in "Utah Government Latino Agencies Face Identity Issues." *Salt Lake Tribune*, January 23, 2003, p. A-1.

78. Oscar Handlin, *The Uprooted*, 2nd ed. (Philadelphia: University of Pennsylvania Press, 2002).

79. Interview with Mike Martinez, October 3, 2002, Salt Lake City, Utah. Elżbieta M. Goździak, Micah Bump, and Armando Solórzano.

80. Dale F. Pearson, "The Gang Scare as a Bureaucratic Propaganda: Utah's Response to Structural Changes in Cities Affected by Hispanic Immigration." *Encyclia: The Journal of the Utah Academy of Sciences, Arts, and Letters* 71 (1994): 69.

81. Mike Martinez, interview, 2002.

82. Mike Martinez, interview, 2002.

83. Jeffrey M. Humphreys, "The Multicultural Economy 2002: Minority Buying Power in the New Century." *Georgia Business and Economic Conditions* 62, no. 2 (2002).

84. Joseph Gallegos, Oral history interview. October 6–13, 2000 (Salt Lake City, UT).

85. Bertha Alcazar, Oral history interview. December 14, 2000 (Murray, UT).

86. Juan Balderas, Oral history interview.

87. Louis Barraza, Oral history interview. November 22, 2000–January 25, 2001 (Ogden, UT).

88. Jessie L. Embry, *Black Saints in a White Church: Contemporary African American Mormons* (Salt Lake City, UT: Signature Books, 1994), 35.

89. Virgilio Elizondo, *The Future Is Mestizo: Life Where Cultures Meet*, rev. ed. (Boulder: University Press of Colorado, 2000), 107.

8

Newcomers in Rural America: Hispanic Immigrants in Rogers, Arkansas

Andrew I. Schoenholtz

In 1990, very few Hispanics resided in Rogers, Arkansas. However, by 2000, Hispanics constituted almost 20 percent of the local population. Not surprisingly, the host community reacted in complex and mixed ways to the influx of newcomers. Of course, the newcomers, too, faced major challenges in becoming part of the changing Rogers community.

This chapter analyzes one of the most extraordinary achievements that occurred in Rogers in the 1990s—the integration of these new immigrants into the U.S. banking and credit system, especially home-ownership. Confronted by significant population change, this community struggled to find ways to bridge divides between newcomers and established residents. That struggle continues.

BACKGROUND

The Newly Arrived Immigrant Population

A part of the Fayetteville-Springdale-Rogers, Arkansas, metropolitan statistical area (MSA), Rogers is a small town of 39,000, located in Northwest Arkansas. In 2000, the foreign-born population was estimated at almost 20 percent.[1] Nearly all of these immigrants came to

213

Rogers since 1993, attracted by the availability of work in the poultry processing industry as well as the quality of life in the community.

Poultry processing plants in the MSA experienced a tremendous upswing in turnover rates in the early 1990s. One poultry processor conservatively estimated turnover costs in these plants at $3,000 to $4,000 per worker, which includes both the costs of new worker training and productivity losses. This problem so severely hurt production that certain plants were within two to three months of shutting down. The largest of these processors reported 700 unfilled job openings at any one time in all of their area plants. Furthermore, the training period at the plants can take two weeks, which caused production lines to be constantly bogged down with the training and inconsistent skills of new workers.

In 1993, large numbers of immigrants started to move to the area to work in the poultry plants. The first wave of workers consisted largely of married males of Mexican origin, mostly in their twenties and thirties, primarily from rural California where they worked in the agriculture industry. The typical scenario involved these young men moving into the community without their spouses and children. Families often stayed behind in the workers' home country, and a large portion of the workers' wages were sent home to support the families. This created a situation where workers employed innovative means to live as economically as possible on wages ranging from $8 to $9 per hour. Poultry processing is a twenty-four-hour operation that relies on two or three daily shifts, and it was not uncommon for four or more workers to share rent on a two-bedroom housing unit. In such an arrangement, workers assigned to different shifts could maintain privacy even though sleeping quarters were shared, as each worker occupied a bed when another one was at work.

The Community of Rogers, Arkansas

Rogers is located in an MSA where the three major employers are leading players in sizable industries: Wal-Mart Corporation General Offices (retailing), Tyson Foods Corporate Headquarters (poultry processing), and J. B. Hunt Transport (trucking-motor freight). The population of Rogers grew from twenty-five thousand in 1990 to thirty-nine thousand in 2000. Up until 1990 there was very little ethnic diversity, with nonwhites making up less than 5 percent of the population, and only a handful of Spanish speakers.[2]

As more foreign-language speakers came to work in the area, Rogers' community leaders quickly realized that they had no effective infrastructure to provide information to the newly arrived immigrants. Local ministers, social work organizations, law enforcement, and the school system came together to initiate a dialogue, that is, to identify community leaders and to entice them to come forward and help find ways to address any potential friction created by the integration of the immigrant community into the daily lives of established citizens.

Much of this initiative was spearheaded by John Sampier Jr., who was at that time the mayor of Rogers. Sampier first sought locals who could speak both English and Spanish, and used these individuals to assist in identifying and solving potential hot spots in the school system and neighborhoods. His initial search yielded only two people. One was hired by the school system to bridge the two communities and to counsel children of immigrants and their parents. The other was the community development officer at an important local bank, First National.

Local institutions worked to acclimate newly arrived immigrants to the community by providing access to resources such as language training, life skills, financial training, and citizenship programs. In addition, the newcomers were also offered cultural venues, and their participation in the community soccer league was both solicited and encouraged. By the end of the 1990s, institutions routinely employed bilingual staff. First National expected its employees to use very basic conversational Spanish to make customers feel welcome. In addition, bilingual newspapers and radio stations developed, and the local cable system offered two Spanish-language channels. Movements within the community to encourage voter registration among newly naturalized citizens also emerged.

Despite progress, significant tensions arose in certain quarters of the community. Some members of the host community resented the influx of Spanish speakers and felt their culture was being challenged by the newcomers. These residents ultimately voiced their concerns regarding population shifts by forming a local chapter of an organization that called for a moratorium on immigration to the United States. They were particularly disturbed that some of the newcomers were undocumented because they believed foreign-born workers depressed wages. This vocal group played an important role in both political and law enforcement changes that Rogers experienced.

First National Bank and Trust Company, Rogers

Founded in 1915, First National is the largest and oldest bank currently operating in Rogers. The bank was purchased by Sam Walton, founder of Wal-Mart Corporation, in 1975 and is now part of the Arvest Bank Group, of which the Walton family is primary shareholder. Other Arvest-owned sister banks are operated in adjacent communities; the holding company operates banks in northwest Arkansas, southwest Missouri, and central Oklahoma.

First National has a long history of providing support to the local school system, the chamber of commerce, and the local United Way chapter. Its senior management set an example by actively participating in charitable, service, and community organizations and encouraging similar involvement by all bank associates. The bank also established itself as an industry leader by offering new and innovative products. In 1976 First National was the first bank in Benton County to operate an automated teller machine and in 1998 it was among the first banks in the state to offer Internet banking. According to Federal Deposit Insurance Corporation (FDIC) report data, First National's market share in Rogers ranged from 48.94 to 52.53 percent between 1994 and 1999. This market share has remained constant despite the appearance of several new financial institutions during the same period.

Member banks in the Arvest Bank Group subscribed to common principles of focusing on the customers' needs. Exploiting customers so that the banks can realize short-term returns was specifically addressed in associate orientation materials, and this practice was clearly and emphatically forbidden. As leaders in several communities, Arvest's banks strove more diligently than many other financial institutions to offer services that appealed to all market segments. Because of this, First National was in a unique position; its product line contained services suited to and priced in a way to appeal to low-to moderate-income consumers, and the bank's associates underwent a minimum of forty hours of training in recognizing customer needs and providing a high level of service to a diverse customer base. This combination made the bank appealing to consumers, especially those with limited language skills and financial resources.

At the time that First National made a commitment to reach the population of newly arrived immigrants, the bank's senior management team was comprised of six members, all of whom were white and all but one was male. For a bank of this size, this senior management team was unusual in that all members were originally from other communities (four were actually from other states), and all had worked in banks in other communities. They had an exposure to and a comfort level with an ethnically diverse customer base. By 2000, this same senior management team continued to exist with the addition of two new members, both of whom were women. While it still lacked nonwhite members in senior management, the bank had two Hispanic associates in middle-management positions.

In 1994 the bank's senior management team recognized not only the problems and needs of the immigrant population, but a potential emerging market as well. At the same time, Arvest Bank Group's chairman encouraged the bank's management to study active and aggressive entry into the immigrant market. One member of senior management, Marilyn Barnes, actively championed the initiative, largely because of her admitted identification with the immigrant population's struggles and hardships, having experienced personal challenges in the 1970s as a single parent and rising bank officer.

With this high-level support, senior management approached the community development officer, Roland Goicoechea, who immigrated to the United States in 1962 when he and his young siblings fled their native Cuba to escape the regime of Fidel Castro. Senior management recognized Goicoechea as an ideal candidate for this challenge, not merely because of his Spanish-speaking skills and his informal appointment by the mayor as a liaison with the growing population of Spanish-speaking immigrants. The bank's senior management realized that the success of any attempt to reach the immigrant market lay in the ability to work in cooperation with major employers of newly arrived immigrants, in this case poultry processors. Prior to working at First National, Goicoechea spent twenty years selling employee benefit services to large employers, and it was predicted that this experience would play an instrumental role in the bank's success, once a task force developed a product to pitch to area employers of newly arrived immigrants.

Goicoechea envisioned a way to improve the lives of Rogers' newly arrived immigrants while at the same time addressing the turnover problems at local poultry processing plants. According to Goicoechea, "Our community saw the growth of industries that were targeting low-income immigrant workers by using overpriced credit to sell goods that were often equally overpriced, or of poor quality. The bank saw a way to educate these consumers and to make a conscious long-term commitment to this market segment." A task force was assembled within the bank to identify the needs of the emerging market, and determined that most problems of newly arrived immigrants were rooted in a single issue: lack of hope. Many of the newcomers were moving from areas with living conditions that the average native-born

U.S. citizen could not comprehend, with a social structure that often included barriers to improving one's quality of life. Perhaps, the task force surmised, the problem was not a lack of opportunities available to the immigrants now that they were in the United States, but the immigrants' ability to believe that these opportunities *actually existed*. This led to the development of a financial seminar series titled "Creating Hope in the Work Place," taught in Spanish.

Employers

The state of Arkansas has long been a leading grower of poultry, and only recently did Georgia surpass the state as having the nation's largest population of chickens. The perishable nature of poultry products dictates that processing must be performed near major growers. For this reason Arkansas is home to businesses that support the complete cycle of poultry processing, from farming, slaughtering, cleaning, cutting the carcasses to specifications, and down to preparation and precooking of microwavable entrées. Information provided by the Rogers Area Chamber of Commerce indicated that the industry employed 2,000 workers in Rogers alone, with an annual payroll in excess of $25 million. It is estimated that every dollar paid to workers turns over six to seven times in the local economy. In addition, the industry occupied physical plants, which represented a $200 million investment.

Like many communities and industries across the nation, Rogers' poultry industry experienced an ongoing labor shortage, where there was a need to find a pool of labor that could quickly fill available jobs. Throughout the 1990s, many communities found themselves facing an ultimatum: either open doors in the community to immigrant workers or risk the loss of a major employer. Jobs in the poultry processing industry were often attractive to low-skilled immigrant workers because these jobs are not seasonal, and they offer a climate-controlled environment, relatively attractive wages, and a comprehensive benefits package. In addition, most plants were located in smaller communities, and many workers originally from rural areas preferred this location to one in a larger city.

As the nation's largest poultry processor, Tyson Foods employed more than seventy thousand people in twenty states. Nationwide by the end of the 1990s, Hispanic workers comprised more than 20 percent of Tyson's workforce; however, depending on the region, this percentage ranged from a high of 65 percent to a low of zero. During the early

1990s, the company experienced a nationwide turnover rate of 70 percent, with an estimated annual cost per lost worker of $3,000 to $4,000.

Tyson employed more than eleven thousand workers in the four-county area including and surrounding Rogers, Arkansas. Each Tyson plant is evaluated as an autonomous operation, which means that each location's continued operation is dependent on its bottom line. Rogers is home to three Tyson plants, with several other plants located within a fifty-mile radius. The growth of the poultry industry in Northwest Arkansas led to the creation of many employment opportunities; however, this growth also led to widespread job vacancies as the pool of available workers diminished due to a strong economy. This labor shortage reached a critical stage in the early 1990s, at which time Tyson had seven hundred unfilled job openings in Northwest Arkansas alone. The plants sought and attracted workers from areas outside of both the region and the United States. From a staffing standpoint, this influx of immigrant workers resulted in a dramatic reduction of average job vacancies at Tyson's Northwest Arkansas plants to some twenty-five openings in a given week by 2000. This success is a reflection of both Tyson's attractiveness to certain low-skilled immigrants as an employer and the good quality of life that families can have in northwest Arkansas.

One of the First National Bank's most active business partners is North Arkansas Poultry, a Tyson subcontractor. With three hundred employees working two daily shifts, the plant employs approximately six hundred employees and has a $10 million annual payroll. Between 1990 and 1993, management of the plant reported a turnover rate of 200 percent; in the words of one manager, "we were two months away from closing our doors." The bank's partnership with the plant started in 1994, at which time the bank began a series of financial information classes for workers. By 1995 this turnover rate had stabilized to between 15 and 20 percent, and plant management attributes much of this improvement in turnover to the bank's classes. With Hispanic workers making up approximately 95 percent of the plant's workforce by 2000, management was satisfied that they had and could maintain a pool of hardworking, dependable employees.

LINGUISTIC, CULTURAL, AND SOCIAL ISSUES

Among the important challenges Rogers residents faced as the new immigrant populations increased were linguistic and cultural behavior changes. In some ways, these lay at the heart of the concerns of those residents who felt that their way of life was changing too much in an undesirable direction.

The use of a foreign language by relatively sizable numbers of people troubled some Rogers residents:

> I've gone to the grocery store and other places on more than one occasion and had 'em get in line behind me and speak, you know, rattle off just, you know, gobs and gobs of Spanish, and I've just felt like I was in a completely different country, and they were making fun of me for not being like them. And it really is uncomfortable. And I don't want my kids to have to feel like that in their own town.[3]

> "All of a sudden I looked around and everything had changed overnight," said Joy Johns, who owns a lawn and garden shop. "I go out to the Wal-Mart and there were piñatas on the shelves and the babbling of Spanish everywhere. I felt like I was in Mexico."[4]

Like most communities, Rogers also had to reconcile social differences between native Rogers residents and Latino immigrants. Some native residents complained about Latinos slaughtering goats in their yards for barbecues, loud music, and the differences in driving styles. The initial population of mostly single males frightened some of the elderly population when these newcomers shopped in groups in the grocery stores. According to Roland Goicoechea:

> The community was feeling culture shock. For the first time ever there were different faces, a different culture. There were myths and misconceptions. There were cultural differences. There were complaints that there were too many people living in one place, that the music was too loud.
>   Some of those customs that are totally acceptable in rural Mexico are not acceptable here.[5]

To help address these social differences, Mayor John Sampier hired Al Lopez as a special community liaison for the city.[6] An English and Spanish speaker from Puerto Rico, Lopez worked on the community and individual level to allay tension and resolve conflict. To bridge cultural gaps, he designed public service announcements that ran on local television stations.[7] When a resident called City Hall to complain that her Mexican neighbors were slaughtering a goat in the yard, Lopez would meet with those involved and try to deal with significant cultural differences between rural norms in Mexico and the United States.[8]

According to Roland Goicoechea, the mayor sets the tone for a town, and the tone that John Sampier set for Rogers was one of hospitality and welcome.[9] He worked with other leaders in the community to establish dialogue and promote integration of the newcomers. A former Peace Corps volunteer who served in Panama organized a Multicultural Forum that met quarterly to enable community leaders to discuss ethnic frictions.[10] In 1994, civic leaders at the Rogers Chamber of Commerce developed a plan that "placed high priority on 'the integration of the Hispanic community . . . in all neighborhoods, locations and areas." Avoiding the segregation of Hispanics, the report added, "is paramount to our ability to keep Rogers a desirable place to live and work."[11]

EDUCATION

One of the primary concerns of native Rogers residents was the effect of immigration on the school system. Not long after the male heads of households settled in Rogers, they brought their families. In 2000, Latinos made up 15 percent of the student body in Rogers' public school system.[12] By 2004, that percentage had increased to an estimated 30 percent.[13] Many of these students entered the school system with little or no prior knowledge of English. The school system worked to both increase its capacity to teach English to Spanish-speaking students and to reduce tensions between Latino and Anglo students.

First, the school system recognized the immediate need to teach English to its new Latino students. The district added twenty English-language teachers[14] and began sending teachers to Mexico during summer vacation to learn about the culture from which many of their students came.[15] The schools began to offer "Spanish for Spanish speakers" classes to help Spanish-speaking students learn proper grammar. Teachers claim that such classes not only helped students learn correct Spanish, but also improved their understanding of English.[16] The local high school also introduced an Advanced Placement Spanish Literature class.[17] In response to claims that such expansions of the curriculum would drain the schools' resources, the Rogers deputy superintendent of schools said that the state provides most of the funds for teaching English as a second language and that the school district would not have received the funds otherwise.[18]

The school district also needed to address tensions between Anglo students and their new Latino peers. The district hired Al Lopez, who had been working in the larger community of Rogers as a special adviser to then mayor John Sampier. Lopez worked to bring students together by organizing various activities that promoted ethnic harmony. For example, he founded a multicultural club at the local high school. He also produced rap videos with themes of ethnic accord and showed them on local television stations and at civic association meetings.[19] Perhaps one indicator that the district made progress introducing tolerance and acceptance into its schools was the selection of the 2001 Miss Rogers High School: Jessica Diaz, part Puerto Rican, part black, and raised in Mexico.[20]

CRIME AND LAW ENFORCEMENT

Another issue that the town addressed was crime. Although there was an increase in nonviolent gang activity, police data indicated that the arrest rate of Latinos was low. Between June 1996 and June 1997, of the 5,549 arrests made in Rogers, Latinos accounted for 456, most of which were for traffic infractions.[21] Some crimes reportedly involved drugs and violence.[22]

Some members of the community believed that the influx of Latinos had increased crime, and the community tried to bring all groups together to address these concerns and make the area safer. For example, the town organized open community meetings about crime, particularly gang prevention. Both Anglos and Latinos attended these meetings, and in fact, it was Latino parents who supported strict controls on youth, such as curfews and school uniforms.[23] Some of these newcomers had left areas of California where they felt gang violence made the community unsafe for their children.[24]

Newcomer cooperation with the police, however, faced two different types of challenges. According to the Rogers chief of police, immigrants did not trust the police because they came from corrupt societies where the police could not be trusted.[25] In addition, after a political change described below, the police allegedly began to improperly stop and investigate Latinos based on their ethnicity and perceived immigrant status. In 2001, the Rogers police department faced a lawsuit in which Latino residents, represented by the Mexican American Legal Defense and Educational Fund (MALDEF), claimed that police officers were using racial profiling and attempting to enforce federal immigration laws. Although local police were prohibited from enforcing immigration laws, Rogers' police officers had been pulling over Latinos and those who appeared Latino and asking for immigration status verification. This created a distrust of the police department within the Latino community. The city ultimately settled with the residents, agreeing to prohibit racial profiling and local police enforcement of immigration laws.[26]

While these police activities exacerbated ethnic tension in Rogers, the settlement also indicated the ability of the town's leadership to find a way to enforce the law in a way that respected the constitutional rights of the newcomers. According to MALDEF:

> This is a win-win situation for the community, city and police, and a model for other police departments that builds better ties with the community and makes sense from a policing perspective. . . . This settlement includes measures to address the issue of racial profiling through clear policy and zero tolerance, documentation and an accessible and transparent complaint process. Perhaps most importantly, the measures will help ensure confidence with the immigrant and Latino community in the local police by not confusing their roles with immigration enforcement.[27]

POLITICAL CHANGE

The attempt by police to address illegal immigration in Rogers developed following the 1998 election of a new mayor, Steve Womack, a change that many considered evidence of ethnic tension and anti-immigrant sentiment in the area. Whereas the former mayor, seventeen-year incumbent John Sampier, was known for his hospitable and accepting attitude toward immigrants, Womack ran "on a platform of 'zero tolerance' toward illegal immigrants and insistence that legal newcomers 'speak the language' and immigrants conform to community norms."[28]

Whether or not his victory was due to his position on immigration, many say that it did exacerbate tensions. Anti-immigrant organizations, such as Americans for an Immigration Moratorium (IAM), felt empowered, and Latinos became more reticent to participate in larger community activities.[29] In late 1999, two Immigration and Naturalization Service (INS) agents began to work out of the Rogers Police Department while their office in a nearby town was being completed:

> Almost immediately after INS agents moved into the police department early last year, complaints from Latinos began streaming in—stories of traffic stops that became fishing expeditions as cops sought proof of legal residency.

One driver the police might have wished to avoid: Donna Hutchinson, who's part Native American and the former sister-in-law of Asa Hutchinson. 'The only reason for stopping me was to check my license and make sure I'm supposed to be here,' she told the *Arkansas Democrat-Gazette*. By last summer the pastors at St. Vincent de Paul Church noticed that formerly overcrowded services now had rows of empty pews. Hispanic churchgoers, they heard, were afraid to leave their homes.[30]

There is some evidence that the anti-immigration sentiment has calmed down since the election and police activities targeting Hispanics. When Mayor Womack came into office, he also hired a community liaison, Cesar Aguilar, and created a task force of Latinos and native residents.[31] Further, the town provided cultural outlets for Latinos by, for example, forming a Latino soccer league.[32] The Latino community itself organized, forming a Northwest Arkansas chapter of the League of United Latin American Citizens.[33] The city opened a Community Support Center in April 2000 that helps immigrants with housing, job, and government issues. Mayor Womack has tried to portray Rogers as a tolerant community.[34] In addition, "Critical letters show up in the local newspapers from time to time, but the immigration moratorium groups have gone into hibernation."[35] Although ethnic tensions remain in Rogers, the city has made some progress bridging the different cultures.

IMMIGRANT HOMEOWNERSHIP

Not long after the arrival of significant numbers of Hispanic workers, Sam Walton inquired with First National's president as to what the bank was doing for the newcomers. This catalyzed activity at the bank. Research conducted by the bank's community development officer revealed that the newcomers did not understand the U.S. credit system, basic banking, or how to get a traditional loan. This research also pointed to potential abuses of the immigrant population, due to a lack of a credit history, limited knowledge of the United States financial system, and limited proficiency in the English language. These factors often forced new immigrants to seek sources of high-cost financial services, such as nontraditional car loans.

In addition to finding the effects of predatory consumer lending in the immigrant community, the bank research uncovered a housing problem. When the first wave of immigrants arrived, Rogers lacked a supply of affordable rental property for these newcomers. The male population often lived in overcrowded conditions, particularly before family members arrived. Home ownership became a key opportunity to creating better housing conditions for both immigrants and their families.

Financial Literacy Seminars

With this information, a bank task force decided to develop a financial seminar series titled "Creating Hope in the Work Place," to be taught in Spanish. Most of the newcomers had little formal education and no knowledge of the credit system in the United States. As more than one manager at First National pointed out, most bankers are too close to their profession and incorrectly assume that all consumers know how to do such basic transactions as writing a check, understand how bank accounts work, and have a basic trust in the banking system. Unfortunately, this is often not the case for newly arrived immigrants. Realizing that a lack of basic banking knowledge would frustrate both immigrant customers and bank associates, the bank developed a curriculum that provided a foundation of financial knowledge, including how to write a check, establish a credit history, buy a house, and plan for retirement.

First National purposely designed the seminars using simple concepts. The first seminar, covering basic banking services, introduced financial services and gave a brief overview of future seminars. Attendees were taught the very basics: the advantages of keeping money in the bank instead of at home, and the fact that no consumer has ever lost money on a U.S. government-insured deposit. The seminar on how to write a check included a pocket card that translated the parts of the check ("Pay to the order of," "Memo," "Dollars") into Spanish, and gave examples of writing the date and the check amount in English. The size of this class was typically limited to no more than ten workers, to ensure that the instructor was able to give adequate instruction to students as they learned to write out checks, fill out deposit slips, and use the automated teller machine.

Seminar instructors from the bank gradually introduced more complex financial topics as workers attended subsequent seminars. Topics such as buying a house offered the bank instructor an opportunity to extend an invitation to those interested in specific bank services to see him at the bank. While the seminars gradually covered more complex subject matter, the seminar materials still broke down the topics into basic, understandable terms. Probably the most effective example of this occurred in the retirement planning seminar, where the instructor illustrated how a worker can immediately realize a return of fifty cents for every dollar invested. How? The answer was not a highly speculative stock or mutual fund, but the employee's 401(k) plan, which offered a 50 percent employer match on contributions. The instructor knew that most of these workers were not participating in their plans because they did not understand them.

To gain the trust of the newly arrived immigrant audience, the bank determined that the seminar instructor needed to able to communicate in the workers' native language and be familiar with the audience's cultural and educational backgrounds. This helped the instructor to better explain the concepts included in the seminars, and enabled the audience to learn better. This strategy ultimately benefited the bank and the newcomers.

Bank-Employer Partnership

Making this financial literacy information accessible to newcomers was not a small task. The greatest challenge was finding a time and place when the newcomers were most open to learning. The bank offered sessions in various locales, including churches, but ultimately put its most concentrated efforts in developing a partnership with a local employer of large numbers of immigrants.

The bank believed that the workplace provided the best time and place to ensure an attentive and interested audience. After a shift, workers were often too tired to learn, and on weekends they attended to family matters. Accordingly, the bank tried to convince employers why providing such seminars at the workplace would benefit them.

Aware of the high turnover costs for the chicken processing plants, the bank explained to employers that the workers would settle more permanently in Rogers if they understood and utilized the U.S. credit system, particularly to buy homes. That stable workforce would save the employer significant turnover costs, estimated at $3,000 to $4,000 per turnover. If the bank conducted the seminars at the workplace, employees would clearly see that the employer was trying to provide a direct form of help to them and their families.

The major employer that accepted the bank's offer to partner was North Arkansas Poultry. Starting in 1994, the employer provided classroom space for one-hour seminars scheduled during the workday. Management closed down the production line one section at a time to allow all workers to attend the seminars. To minimize effects of these shutdowns on monthly production, management tried to schedule seminars in production months containing five weeks (versus four weeks in most production months). To show their serious commitment to the value of the seminars and to encourage worker loyalty, the plant continued to pay the immigrant workers while they attended the seminars.

Preparing the Bank for the Immigrant Market

The bank recognized that educating the newcomers about the U.S. credit system was not the only obstacle that had to be overcome before the immigrants could start banking: the bank itself needed to be prepared to receive these new customers. First National prepared by training and hiring new staff as well as by developing new procedures to address the immigrants' financial experiences—or lack thereof:

Cultural Training

Most bank employees had no previous experience with the Hispanic population. The bank wanted not only to provide services to the newcomers, but to also do so in a friendly manner. A community college professor was brought in to teach bank employees about the people they would be serving. His instruction addressed several fundamental questions about the newcomers: Where did the immigrants come from? What was rural Mexico like? Why were they in Rogers? How did they value family, church, and work? Why didn't they speak English?

Hiring Bilingual Staff

To provide quality services, the bank wanted to make the newcomers feel welcome. In addition to providing staff with training in survival Spanish, the bank hired bilingual tellers and loan officers. That was not an easy task in Northwest Arkansas, as the newcomers represented the first major group of Spanish speakers in the area. Initially, the bank hired the U.S.-born wife of a Mexican immigrant. Ultimately, the bank tapped various networks to find bilingual staff. The immigrant community itself included young adults who learned English as children in California schools. Their parents came to Rogers, and they completed high school there. The bank also hired bilingual high school students as interns. They started as part-time employees and were hired full-time when they graduated. Finally, the bank tapped the network of multicultural leadership throughout the region for recommendations about potential loan officers and tellers. Since the bank played an important role in community life, the bank was able to rely on its good relationships with such leaders to identify existing talent. For example, the bank approached the director of the multicultural center, the church, the community college, and various business owners for referrals.

One lesson the bank learned was that it is important to quickly and aggressively build a pool of potential bilingual candidates. This enabled the bank to select the very best from the beginning. By starting off with the very best, the non-Spanish speaking employees would hopefully understand that individuals were not hired for their language ability alone. In addition, any ethnic stereotypes would be quickly dispelled.

Essentially the bank found it more effective to train a bilingual person to be a banker than to teach a banker to speak Spanish. The majority of their bilingual staff began as tellers and learned the business from the ground up. Those who showed promise were then promoted to new accounts officers. Some later advanced to loan assistants, and three eventually became loan officers. Since the bank needed bilingual employees at a variety of levels somewhat quickly, promising staff were moved rapidly to higher levels of work. This at times brought complaints from the monolingual employees. The bank had required Spanish for the initial hire and believed that the language skills were like other talents individuals brought to the customer service tasks demanded of them. If they performed them well, the bank put them in more demanding positions that required those skills.

As other banks in Rogers also developed an immigrant clientele, the demand for bilingual bank employees resulted in a very competitive market for such individuals. Tellers and loan officers trained by First National found a very good market for their skills at area banks. These banks clearly recognized their own need to prepare for providing services to the newcomers. To do so, they enticed away several officers trained by First National. The lesson the bank learned here was that good talent should never be neglected.

Developing Alternative Underwriting Guidelines

The customary credit report did not fit the experience of many newcomers, who simply had no traditional credit history. To address this issue, the bank examined alternatives to traditional credit histories, which allowed loan officers to make loans decisions and anticipate what underwriters needed to know. For example, the payment histories for rent, utilities, water, and cable were used to supplement the traditional credit report. In addition, the bank used payment reports from used car agencies that typically accept installment payments only in cash, and do not report to the three major credit agencies in the United States.

Of the mortgage loans that First National made to recent immigrants, 90 percent were Federal Housing Administration (FHA) or similar types, such as U.S. Department of Agriculture Rural Development, Arkansas Development Finance Authority's Home Buyers Assistance Program, or Fannie Mae's Community Lending Program. Under FHA guidelines, a borrower cannot be turned down for having no credit history; instead, the guidelines emphasized employment stability and qualifying ratios (the ability to make payments based on income). In lieu of balances in bank accounts, cash on hand was also acceptable for payment of closing costs under FHA guidelines. In these instances, the bank asked the borrower to deposit the cash, and the borrower provided a letter explaining the cash and how it was saved.

While a credit history was not necessary, one full year of employment history was required to qualify for an FHA loan. This was easily achievable for many of the recent immigrants who applied for mortgage loans, since most were seminar participants with a stable work history in a local processing plant. However, the bank's underwriters noticed a number of circumstances where applicants were showing gaps in employment during the December holiday season. Lenders quickly realized the existence of a cultural practice where workers would quit jobs to go back to their native countries for the Christmas holidays, and then return to readily available jobs in the early part of the year. The bank's underwriters responded by annualizing income from the months in which the applicant worked. Employers also assisted with this dilemma by encouraging employees to take a leave of absence during the holidays instead of quitting. This emphasis on establishing a full year of employment history in the United States was of great importance, because in many instances, previous employment in other countries could not be verified.

Helping Immigrants Establish a Credit History

As mentioned earlier, one of the seminars taught consumers how to create a credit history. During the early stages of implementing this training, associates of First National quickly realized that many immigrants entering the local economy desired a way to establish credit. Naturally, First National hoped to attract new business from this hardworking population that generally had no previous credit experience. Among native-born citizens of the United States, young adults often establish credit by having a parent cosign for a first loan, or by dealing with a banker with whom the family has established a relationship. However, in most cases neither of these options were available to the newly arrived immigrants served by First National.

Associates of the bank worked together to devise a creative, low-cost way for these consumers to develop a credit history, in a manner that carried almost no risk for the bank. At the end of the credit history seminar, the instructor explained that the bank offered a way to help consumers establish credit:

1. the borrower applies for a one-year, $1,000 term loan with monthly payments of approximately $85;
2. funds from the loan ($1,000) are invested in a certificate of deposit (CD); and
3. the bank holds the funds in the certificate of deposit as collateral for the loan.

Note that this loan/CD arrangement did not require the bank to create a special product; rather, this arrangement was structured using existing, "off the shelf" banking services that First National already offered. Most bankers are averse to risk when dealing with unknown borrowers; however, the bank realized almost no credit risk on these loans since the CD was used as collateral. Because the CD earned interest, the net interest cost to the borrower was less than $15. By repeating this process twice, borrowers gained confidence in the lending process and in the banker, as well as met certain regulatory requirements for the FHA-type of home loans offered by the bank.

As it turned out, the major challenge in teaching the immigrants how to establish credit was correcting their desire to pay off the loan immediately. Unused to lending, many came to the bank in month two of the loan ready to pay off the entire loan. Bank officers ultimately convinced them of the value of the credit experience to their future financial activities.

Leadership at the Bank

Both the bank and the community faced several obstacles, including unfamiliarity with the conditions of an emerging immigrant community, a language barrier between immigrants and members of the larger community, and little understanding of the culture from which the immigrant populations came. All of these conditions created special circumstances that required the right persons to understand and overcome.

An important part of the success of First National's immigrant program was the commitment of "champions"—individuals with exceptional commitment. In this instance, both the bank's sales manager and the community development officer convinced bank management to support these activities and to commit other bank personnel to a range of tasks. This included the following:

- bringing in experts to teach bank employees about Mexican culture,
- designing the seminars,
- convincing employers of the utility of the seminars,
- teaching the seminars,
- hiring and training bilingual staff to service immigrant customers, and
- adjusting the bank's traditional ways of processing mortgage loans.

As these activities required considerable bank time and effort, these "champions" needed to initially convince management of the value of the seminars, and keep management behind this program at different points when the practice was being reexamined and refined. The commitment of bank management was essential. First, the program changed both key aspects of the bank's culture and its way of doing business. Second, significant resources were needed to carry out these services. Third, particularly in the context of a smaller community, long-held prejudices caused some valuable customers to resist the idea of the bank serving the financial needs of immigrants, particularly when the immigrants did not speak English or were minorities. This commitment was long term and required vision on the part of management.

Rob Brothers, president and CEO of First National Bank and Trust Company, Rogers, made it clear that while the bank saw an opportunity to benefit financially from the immigrant market, there was also a commitment to do the right thing. He gave several tests of what an institution must be willing to do to achieve the needed level of development:

1. a commitment of resources, particularly in terms of staff,
2. a willingness to reckon with cultural issues by sensitizing current staff to the customs and mores of the immigrant population,
3. the development of the staff's bilingual capacity as the market grows through the institution's push for expansion, developing staff with bilingual capacity, and
4. a long-term approach to profitability.

Early on, First National jumped enthusiastically into marketing to immigrants by conducting on-site survival Spanish lessons for bank employees (e.g., greetings, "deposit slip," "we need your signature on the back of the check"), and by launching an aggressive direct mail program. First National did some initial research and consultation with Hispanic market resources, and knew to avoid such common pitfalls as simply translating English-language advertisements into Spanish. However, the bank did indeed make mistakes, but quickly learned from them. For example, it was soon discovered that the key to communicating with Spanish-speaking customers was not to teach a new language to native speakers of English, as proficiency in a second language is difficult for many adults. Instead, the bank focused on hiring native speakers of Spanish with some knowledge of English as tellers and as loan staff. Attempts at identifying Spanish-speaking customers for direct mail lists proved to be mildly embarrassing to the bank's management, as some surnames assumed to be of Hispanic origin turned out to be Italian, while some Hispanic surnames belonged to families that had been in the United States for several generations. However, it is important to note that these setbacks did not cause bank management to abandon the effort; instead, they strengthened the resolve to refine the process into one that worked even better.

Employment and Housing Availability

While Rogers did not have an adequate supply of affordable rental housing for the newcomers, its homeownership costs were relatively low, particularly when measured against the annual income of immigrant workers. In the 1990s, most entry-level jobs in poultry plants earned between $8 and $9 per hour, not including overtime, shift differential pay for night work, or other additional wages. Families followed the first wave of immigrant workers into the Rogers community, and in a good number of these families both adults worked in the same plant, taking different shifts to accommodate childcare needs. With dual incomes, these families often earned an annual income of $32,000.

Fortunately, the housing market in Rogers included an ample supply of small three bedroom houses, including new houses, with prices in the $70,000 to $85,000 price range. While still below the national average, real estate prices in Rogers have steadily crept upward as the area experienced tremendous population growth during the last twenty years. In some areas, land prices have doubled in the last decade. Most new houses built in the Rogers area were listed with real estate agents at prices well above $100,000, and it appeared that builders had little trouble finding buyers for these houses, given the average time that new houses stayed on the market. Builders might have ignored the needs of buyers wanting houses in a lower price range, given the healthy demand for more expensive houses.

But some builders in Rogers carved a niche in this lower end of the housing market, with excellent results. On the southern end of Rogers, for example, there was a small housing development containing perhaps one hundred houses constructed in 1998 and 1999. Located along wide, winding streets and cul-de-sacs were quarter-acre lots with neat, well-maintained three bedroom homes covered in vinyl siding. The average house price in this neighborhood was approximately $75,000, which included land costs ranging between $8,000 and $10,000. Houses in this neighborhood proved popular with recent Hispanic immigrants not only due to their price, but also because the neighborhood's location was convenient to both schools and poultry processing plants. However, this neighborhood is far from being an ethnic enclave located "on the wrong side of the tracks." These houses also attracted a fair number of non-Hispanic buyers. Developers were quick to note the popularity of this area with recent Hispanic immigrants, and worked with real estate agents to modify their standard package to include features popular with this market segment:

1. Houses often had a master bedroom suite on a separate end of the living area from the other two bedrooms and bath, allowing more privacy for extended families.
2. Kitchens were equipped with gas ranges, which are more familiar to Hispanic buyers.
3. Paint and carpet colors were darker and brighter than in most homes of this price range, which usually feature "safe" neutrals.
4. Interior walls were finished in a stucco texture reminiscent of finishes often seen in Latin America. And

5. houses were marketed by real estate agents who were culturally sensitive and familiar with loan programs tailored to low- to moderate-income buyers.

The experience of builders in Rogers proved that there was a viable, profitable market for houses tailored to newly arrived immigrant buyers, provided that builders were willing to adapt their product to the needs, desires, and price requirements of immigrant buyers. Again, the bank managed to offer financing without creating special loan programs or products, and instead used existing resources to serve low- to moderate-income buyers.

RESULTS

Sustainable homeownership

From 1994 to 2000, more than 700 immigrant families purchased houses for the first time through mortgages from the Arvest Bank Group (which includes First National). Many of these families bought their houses prior to 1997. In a pool of loans of this size, one expects a percentage of defaults approximating the community's average of around 4 percent; however, as of August 2004, none of these loans were in default.

Approximately half of the newly arrived immigrant buyers purchased newly constructed houses. As mentioned earlier, several new housing developments have been anchored and expanded by the infusion of investment from the immigrant community. In total, about 50 percent of the newcomers have become first-time homebuyers.

Capturing a New Market and Increased New Business

First National began its seminar series in September 1994. Based on information covering North Arkansas Poultry's 650-member workforce, only 8 percent of the poultry processor's employees were First National customers prior to the first seminar. Results were rapid and dramatic: after eight months and two seminars, 37 percent of the plant's employees were customers; and after two years, 60 percent were customers.

At the end of this two-year period, employees of North Arkansas Poultry had total deposits at First National in excess of $1 million, and it was not uncommon for immigrant workers to open accounts with initial cash deposits of $5,000 to $7,000. In addition, 7.4 percent of the employees had purchased houses with mortgage loans from First National with an average mortgage balance of $60,000, and 26.9 percent had consumer loans with the bank, with an average loan balance of $2,400. This growth and success is in spite of the fact that almost all of the immigrant customers of First National had not previously been customers of a bank.

While a certain percentage of any population either cannot or will not use banks, as of April 30, 1999, approximately 52 percent of the immigrants in Rogers were customers of First National, representing a total of $26.5 million in business:

- $5 million in deposit accounts,
- $1.2 million in consumer loans,
- $20 million in mortgage loans, and
- $341,000 in commercial loans.

Trends have indicated that the average deposit account balance has increased, and the immigrant customers have moved into new investment alternatives offered by the bank's investment and brokerage subsidiary, such as mutual funds, annuities, and stocks.

First National's share of the immigrant homeownership business was directly related to the lender's seminars and preparation of the bank's associates to serve immigrant customers. Underlying the bank's success was the bridge of trust built between these new customers and the bank through the use of bank associates to both conduct seminars and assist immigrant customers with loan applications when they came into the bank.

During this period, First National's high satisfactory Community Reinvestment Act (CRA) rating for lending and service was due in part to the bank's work with the newcomer community. The regulators not only examined the bank's record at attracting low- and moderate-income business, but gave the bank additional credit for servicing the needs of underserved populations. In assigning the CRA rating, the regulators took into account the effort expended, the creativity required, and the results obtained from the effort. To ensure that the regulators understood the bank's efforts, First National took the examiner to the poultry plant in order to observe the seminar. The bank also took the examiner to visit the actual homes that newcomers purchased.

The bank made sure that newspaper articles and other outside reports about the financial seminars and the bank's work with the new population came to the attention of the examiner.

While First National reaped considerable benefits from its approach to the new immigrant population of Rogers, the seven other banks in the city also benefited from the seminars. While these banks did not participate in the seminars, they gained a significant volume of new customers and issued hundreds of mortgages to the immigrants. The very fact that some hired bilingual staff away from First National (paying higher salaries to provide them with incentives to switch bank employers) demonstrates that other banks also saw a benefit to attracting immigrant customers.

Stable Workforce

The turnover rate in the chicken processing plants throughout the Rogers area dramatically decreased. At North Arkansas Poultry, for example, the turnover rate in 1992 was 200 percent. As of September 1999, the workforce there had only 15 percent to 20 percent turnover; the employees were 96 percent Hispanic by that point. North Arkansas Poultry saw improvement in the turnover rate after the seminars began. Management there claimed that the new immigrant employees have been more loyal to the company because the employer helped them with both their banking and homeownership interests.

CONCLUSION

Rogers resident and newcomer populations faced significant challenges in developing a new community that for the first time in over a century included significant numbers of foreign-born people. For some residents, linguistic and cultural differences meant an undesirable change. Conflicts at the schools, on the road, and in the residential housing developments needed to be addressed. Ethnic tensions erupted socially and politically.

Through various forms of leadership, the Rogers community tried to address many of these issues. Political, business, and civic leaders organized community meetings to confront actual and perceived problems. Bilingual liaisons worked at the schools and in the community. Through research, institutional change, and creative planning, banking and other business leaders enabled many newcomers to become first-time sustainable homeowners and thus develop deeper roots in the community. According to one newcomer who left California for Rogers:

"Our life is much better now," Santillan said through an interpreter at his modest one-story house. "We are fulfilling our American dream. We want our children to grow up here, to have a nice place to study, to learn English and to become independent. Here I have a life."[36]

NOTES

Dr. Schoenholtz, deputy director of the Institute of the Study of International Migration (ISIM), and Kristin Stanton, a financial institution and community-based organization consultant, conducted interviews on-site in Rogers during the summer of 1999. They met with senior management of First National, the bank's community development officer, senior management of Tyson Foods and North Arkansas Poultry, and community leaders, including the current and previous mayors. The research team also conducted site visits to local poultry processing plants and to new housing developments that have predominant Hispanic ownership, where they met with a number of immigrant families. This field research and other site visits around the United States formed the basis for a best-practices study published by the Fannie Mae Foundation and Georgetown University in 2001, *Reaching the Immigrant Market: Creating Homeownership Opportunities for New Americans*, www.fanniemaefoundation.org/programs/pdf/rep_immigrant.pdf. Dr. Schoenholtz thanks Tracey King, ISIM research assistant, for her very helpful research on news reports about Rogers.

1. Daryl Kelley and Carlos Chavez, "California Dreaming No More; The Carranza family, like many Latino immigrants, found its way into the American middle class by leaving the Golden State," *Los Angeles Times*, February 16, 2004, p. A-1.

2. Andrew Green, "Immigration in Arkansas: Harmony Here, Tension There; Arrival of large numbers of Hispanics changes face of U.S., two small towns," *The Baltimore Sun*, April 17, 2002, p. 1-A.

3. Tom Bearden interviewing Mandy Riggins, *The NewsHour with Jim Lehrer*, February 16, 1998.

4. Lois Romano, "A Community Adapts to Newcomers; Accommodation, Anxiety Follow Influx of Hispanic Workers," *Washington Post*, March 24, 1998, p. A-2.

5. Arthur Brice, "Special Report: 1998 Southern Economic Survey: Waves of new workers; Cuban banker builds success in Arkansas town," *The Atlanta Journal-Constitution*, April 19, 1998, p. 2-P.

6. Arian Campo-Flores, "Struggling with the Pain of Change, Rogers, Arkansas—Yes, Arkansas—Is a Testing Ground for Hispanic Growth in America," *Newsweek* (June 4, 2001): 34.

7. Bearden, *The NewsHour*.

8. Campo-Flores, "Struggling with the Pain of Change."

9. Editorial, *The Arkansas Democrat-Gazette*, March 18, 2000, p. B-8.

10. Dirk Kirschten, "A Melting Pot Chills in Arkansas," *The National Journal* 30, no. 46 (November 14, 1998): 2728.

11. Kirschten, "A Melting Pot Chills in Arkansas."

12. Erin Hayes, "Latino Growth in Rogers, Arkansas, Causes Strain," *ABC News, World News Tonight* (January 21, 2000).

13. Melinda Rogers, "Springdale Courses Fill Spanish Language Void; District Broadens Curriculum to Aid Hispanic Students," *Arkansas Democrat-Gazette* (April 19, 2004).

14. Romano, "A Community Adapts to Newcomers."

15. Jon Meachem et al., "The New Face of Race," *Newsweek* (September 18, 2000): 38.

16. Rogers, "Springdale Courses"; *supra* n2.

17. Rogers, "Springdale Courses."

18. Romano, "A Community Adapts to Newcomers"; *supra* n3.

19. Kirschten, "A Melting Pot Chills in Arkansas."

20. Campo-Flores, "Struggling with the Pain of Change."

21. Romano, "A Community Adapts to Newcomers"; *supra* n3.

22. Campo-Flores, "Struggling with the Pain of Change."

23. Romano, "A Community Adapts to Newcomers"; *supra* n3.

24. Bearden, *The NewsHour*.

25. Hayes, "Latino Population Growth in Rogers, Arkansas, Causes Strain."

26. MALDEF Press Release, November 14, 2003.

27. MALDEF Press Release.

28. Kirschten, "A Melting Pot Chills in Arkansas."

29. Green, "Immigration in Arkansas."

30. Campo-Flores, "Struggling with the Pain of Change."

31. Hayes, "Latino Population Growth in Rogers, Arkansas, Causes Strain."

32. Campo-Flores, "Struggling with the Pain of Change."

33. Kirstan Conley, "Rogers *Newsweek* Article on Immigration One Sided, Leaders Say," *The Arkansas Democrat-Gazette*, May 31, 2001, p. B-1.

34. Conley, "Rogers *Newsweek* Article on Immigration One Sided, Leaders Say."

35. Green, "Immigration in Arkansas."

36. Romano, "A Community Adapts to Newcomers."

BEST PRACTICES

9

Promising Practices for Immigrant Integration

Elżbieta M. Goździak and Michael J. Melia

An objective of the research for this volume was to identify practices adopted in new settlement areas that might prove useful elsewhere, whether by easing the integration of newcomers or mitigating the negative impacts of migration on receiving communities. In the course of our fieldwork, several best practices became apparent. These included programs facilitating English-language acquisition, access to culturally sensitive and linguistically appropriate health care services, vocational training, and community development. Support for these programs has varied from public funding to private money to purely volunteer efforts. The programs also varied in focus. While some catered to multiethnic clientele, others served a single ethnic group or even a particular gender or age group. In some of the more innovative programs, the beneficiaries were many. While facilitating access to public and private service organizations for immigrants, for example, some have enriched the host community by fostering multicultural programming, entrepreneurship, and cooperation between the immigrant and host communities.

This chapter provides a review of promising practices and innovative strategies facilitating immigrant integration.[1] It includes brief descriptions of model programs and an analysis of programmatic challenges and opportunities. The discussion is organized thematically around general areas in which improvements have the greatest potential to enhance integration: English-language training, access to higher

241

education, health care service, community development, law enforcement, and commerce.

ADULT ENGLISH-LANGUAGE TRAINING PROGRAMS

Knowledge of the English language is an important, if not the most important, measure of integration. While it is possible to find work without English-language ability, language skills affect newcomers' capacity to earn sufficient wages to raise household income above poverty level. Participation in U.S. institutions and meaningful interaction with the mainstream community also rely greatly on language skills. Fluency in English correlates with upward mobility and attainment of economic, social, and cultural capital.[2] Immigrants who are not able to communicate in English cannot represent themselves or benefit from a dialogue without the help of an interpreter. Communication barriers, in turn, often lead to tensions between newcomers and established residents. As Portes and Rumbaut write:

> In the United States, in particular, the pressure toward linguistic assimilation is all the greater because the country has few other elements on which to ground the sense of national identity. Made up of people coming from many different lands, lacking the unifying symbols of crown or millennial history, the common use of American English has come to acquire a singular importance as a binding tie across such a vast territory.[3]

Addressing language-training needs of newcomers is therefore instrumental in fostering integration in all spheres of life. Immigration critics and community advocates alike cite lack of English skills as a leading concern in many immigrant communities. According to the 2000 Census, more than four out of every five foreign born speak a language other than English at home. Of this subgroup, 52.3 percent speak Spanish, 21.9 percent speak Indo-European languages, 21.6 percent speak Asian and Pacific Islander languages, and 4.2 percent speak other languages. Among the foreign born who speak a language other than English at home, only 39.5 percent reported speaking English "very well," 26.3 percent "well," 22.9 percent "not well," and 12.2 percent "not at all."[4]

Research suggests that limited English skills cost businesses more than $175 million annually because of work-related miscommunication.[5] Poor English skills also keep many immigrants in low-wage jobs.[6] Yet under existing immigration policies, there is no formal incentive for immigrants to learn English. The naturalization process requires applicants for U.S. citizenship to understand and speak a sample of short sentences. Critics point out that standards for passing the required English test seem arbitrary and do not reward those who actually learn the language.[7] In 2002 more than one out of three foreign born were naturalized, but rates of naturalization seem to be decreasing. Among those who arrived before 1970, 80.5 percent had obtained citizenship by 2002. Of those who entered the United States between 1970 and 1979, 66.6 percent had obtained citizenship by 2002, compared with 45 percent of those who entered from 1980 to 1989, and 12.7 percent of those who entered in 1990 or later.[8] Those that choose to maintain their permanent residency status and never naturalize face no English-language requirement. And those immigrants who are undocumented and see no possibility of having their immigration status adjusted have even fewer incentives and opportunities to learn English.

Despite these deterrents, most immigrants recognize the value of learning English.[9] In 1998 alone, 1,927,210 adults were enrolled in federally funded ESL programs, according to the U.S. Department of Education. This figure represents 48 percent of the overall enrollment in national adult education programs.[10] English-language skills open avenues to better paying jobs, increase opportunities to build social networks, and help ensure that immigrants will not be victimized by unscrupulous translators or others who might prey on their dependence.[11] Many newcomers and ethnic community leaders interviewed in the course of this study expressed interest in English-language courses and advocated for improvement of the English as a Second Language (ESL) training programs. But they also pointed out the many challenges that newcomers face in acquiring English-language competency.

Learning a new language is a challenge that most adults in the United States would find overwhelming. It can be even more difficult for adults with limited or no formal education in their native language. Immigrants who must work two or three jobs to make ends meet and immigrant women who work outside the home and care for small children face additional obstacles, particularly when language classes are held during the day or do not offer childcare. Nevertheless, learning English is essential to accelerate economic self-sufficiency and social integration. Research has shown that participation in formal English-language courses is important and more effective in the early stages of integration.[12]

English-language training is now widely available to many immigrants. Almost every community has ESL training programs, but classes are frequently overcrowded with long waiting lists. In Seattle, a recent report counted three thousand adults on one program's waiting list, and more than one thousand immigrants were awaiting an opening in a New York public library program. In Dallas, there were reports of six thousand people on a one-year waiting list.[13] The quality of these programs also varies widely. Nevertheless, our fieldwork has identified shining examples of programs that have enhanced the English competency of adults. There is no one formula. The model programs utilized a variety of funding strategies, involved different actors, followed different curricula, and were implemented at different venues.

Public School-Based Adult Education Programs

The Adult ESL Program in Winchester, Virginia, is an excellent example of a public school-based program. Latino Connection spearheaded the effort, which was facilitated by the TESOL director at the Shenandoah University and an ad hoc coalition of service providers and community advocates. Using data from a needs assessment as a point of departure, administrators improved on an existing program by establishing regular meeting places for classes and developing a competency-based curriculum. ESL instruction was divided into four levels, including an advanced stage that incorporated a civic education component. Students' progress was regularly assessed and childcare was provided to students with families.

As a result of these initiatives, student enrollment in adult ESL classes increased significantly. The level-based curriculum and block enrollment also lowered dropout rates. One of the most recent initiatives sought to organize a daytime adult ESL class that mirrored the evening program. All these efforts were supported by a 21st Century Grant, a three-year federal grant from the U.S. Department of Education.

Alternative High Schools

At some alternative adult high schools, immigrants and refugees can complete their high school education and receive vocational training. One example is the Horizonte Instruction and Training Center in Salt Lake City, Utah, whose programs are designed to help students intellectually, culturally, and vocationally. The primary focus of the ESL program is to provide intense, survival, and preemployment English training. It includes ten levels of instruction, ranging from preliterate, basic survival skills to postsecondary academic preparation and TOEFL (Teaching of English to Foreign Learners) training.

In 2003, Horizonte served 2,100 students in the day program and an additional 1,800 in the evening program. Students ranged in age from eighteen to eighty-seven and represented sixty-nine countries. Support from the federal Office of Refugee Resettlement (ORR) allowed refugees to attend the school free of charge. Other students paid a nominal tuition fee. Recognizing the needs of students who are young parents or pregnant teens, Horizonte staffed an on-site childcare center with aides, volunteers, and peer parents. The program runs year-round and includes five sessions, lasting approximately thirty-six days each during the regular school year. There is also a summer term, lasting approximately twenty days from early June through early August.

Public Library-Based Programs

The Glenwood Library in Greensboro, North Carolina, responded to the area's new ethnic diversity by offering a wide range of English language, literacy, and citizenship programs for immigrants and refugees. The library also offers training for tutors and publishes a quarterly ESOL newsletter, *Speak Out!* Opportunities for students include one-on-one and small-group tutoring for adults learning to read and write English, a conversation club, an ESOL computer lab, a women's literacy program, and a special class that prepares newcomers for the Test of English as a Foreign Language (TOEFL). All of these programs are housed in the Multicultural Resource Center, which hosts other citywide projects including the Hispanic Outreach and the Foreign Language Collection.

Family literacy programs

Two programs in Salt Lake City have chosen to focus on family literacy as the key to enhancing English-language proficiency and literacy in both English and Spanish for Latino immigrant families. *Centro de la Familia de Utah* receives public funds through the Migrant Head Start Program and is able to serve migrant families who receive most of their income from agricultural work. Its economic survival, however, will depend on its ability to nurture other sources of funding. The Even Start Family Literacy program, hosted by Salt Lake City's Western Hills Elementary School, has more financial stability. It is a need-based program with participant eligibility established under the Head Start Act by reference to the official poverty line. The family literacy program developed by *Centro de la Familia,* which aims to help newcomers achieve self-sufficiency, fosters language skills in both Spanish and English. It is based on the premise that parents—who are full of stories, regardless of their language skills—play a key role in nurturing a love of stories and books in their children. Instructors from the center help parents record and share their own stories as a starting point for cultivating literacy. As parents share their stories, they also share their culture, validating the knowledge already possessed by immigrant families. Building on their Spanish-language skills, Latino parents learn to read and write in English more quickly and retain literacy in both languages. A key resource for participants is the Americas Award Reference and Resource Library, a collection of fiction, poetry, folklore, and nonfiction for children and young adults, published in Spanish and English. As immigrant families enrolled in the program share stories found in this collection, they develop their reading skills and enhance their cross-cultural communication skills.

VOCATIONAL TRAINING, RECREDENTIALING, AND ACCESS TO HIGHER EDUCATION

English-language competency is not the only factor that facilitates immigrant integration. Many newcomers, even those who speak English, benefit from access to educational programs including GED (General Equivalency Diploma) and vocational training, recredentialing, or university studies. According to the U.S. Census Bureau, immigrants aged twenty-five or older were less likely to have graduated from high school than natives the same age: 67.2 percent and 86.9 percent, respectively. More than one-fifth of the foreign born had less than a ninth-grade education (21.9 percent), compared with one-twentieth of the native born (4.4 percent).

The highest percentages of high school graduates among the foreign born were from Asia (86.8 percent) and Europe (84.0 percent). In contrast, the percentage of high school graduates from Latin America was much lower (49.1 percent), and Central Americans were the least likely to have high school diplomas (37.3 percent). The proportion of those with a bachelor's degree ranged from 48.9 percent for Asians to 6.0 percent for Central Americans.

Mentorship Programs

The Lutheran Ministries of Georgia has launched the Refugee Health-care and Medical Mentorship Project (RHEMP), designed to assist refugee and immigrant professionals with training and experience in the medical field to reenter their profession upon arrival in the United States. By providing referrals for participants, the program functions as an engine for integration into the U.S. health care system. The goal is to prepare professionals for health care jobs through on-site work experience, professional development training workshops, and certification assistance or training. One impetus was the decision by the nearby DeKalb Medical Center, a project partner, to build a $67 million hospital. The medical center foresees a need for a multicultural, multilingual staff to attend to the increasingly diverse community in the Atlanta area. At the time of our research, twenty-six clients were enrolled in the program.

Utah's Dream Act

The state of Utah took a landmark step by allowing undocumented immigrant students to pay in-state tuition while attending public universities and colleges. The legislation was approved under the provision that undocumented students must be enrolled in a public high school for at least three years before attending college. Utah is one of seven states that have passed similar legislation and Senator Orrin Hatch has proposed Utah's version as a model for the act to take effect on the national level. The bill advanced in part through the efforts of Silvia Salguero, an undocumented high school student in Park City who dropped out of the University of Utah to work as a housekeeper. Salguero was in no position to pay $8,800 in tuition while the resident students were paying $2,900. Working with teachers, legislators, members of Congress, and presidents of Utah's universities, Salguero and other immigrant students established a precedent in the nation.

ACCESS TO APPROPRIATE, CULTURALLY SENSITIVE HEALTH CARE

Access to regular and comprehensive health care is essential to effective settlement and integration of immigrants. Investment in health care services for newcomers early in the settlement process increases immigrants' ability to integrate and minimizes costly public interventions at later stages. Health programs that increase accessibility and continuity of care constitute good public policy because they save public money and strengthen a valuable human resource. Yet under current law, immigrants who arrived in the United States after August 1996 are barred for five years from receiving health benefits under Medicaid or State Children's Health Insurance Programs (SCHIP). Even taxpaying families with pregnant women and children are affected. These restrictions, enacted as part of the Personal Responsibility and Work Opportunity Reconciliation Act of 1996 (PRWORA), have left a large hole in the social safety net for new Americans. Since permanent residents and other legal immigrants lost their eligibility for many benefits, Medicaid for low-income noncitizens decreased from 19 percent in 1995 to 15 percent in 1999.[14]

Two key factors affecting immigrants' access to health care are lack of insurance and insufficient capacity of safety net providers. According to Census Bureau data, the foreign born are more than twice as likely as U.S.-born individuals to lack health insurance. The Census Bureau's Current Population Survey (CPS) data for March 2002 indicate that, nationally, 33 percent of foreign-born residents have neither private nor public health insurance coverage, compared to 13 percent of U.S.-born residents. Of those living in poverty, 26 percent of U.S.-born residents do not have health insurance, compared to 55 percent of the foreign born.

The 2000 Medical Expenditure Panel Survey indicates that high rates of unstable medical coverage are especially likely to affect Hispanic children in low-income families. Forty-four percent of Hispanic children were uninsured in 2000, compared with one-third of U.S. children in low-income families. According to a Children's Defense Fund analysis, the percentage of immigrant (noncitizen) children without health insurance increased from 39.2 percent in 2000, to 41.6 percent in 2001, and 42.1 percent in 2002. By contrast, the percentage of all children who are uninsured did not change between 2001 and 2002, remaining at 11.6 percent.[15]

Immigrant women of child bearing age and older immigrants are also at risk for insufficient health care coverage. More than 50 percent of foreign-born women are of child bearing age.[16] Although publicly funded health care programs such as Medicaid cover the costs of delivery, most uninsured immigrant women have no access to prenatal care. Sixty-one percent of Hispanics age fifty to sixty-four were uninsured in 2000, compared with 41 percent of their peers in the general population. One-quarter of Hispanics age fifty to sixty-four went without necessary care in the same year, either skipping medical tests or failing to fill prescriptions. The uninsured tend to neglect preventive care, use the emergency room for primary care, and delay seeking treatment until problems become acute and care is much more costly. As Bump indicates in his case study of Winchester, Virginia, in this volume, the barriers to health care for immigrants can lead to disaster and death.

Language and cultural differences also impede immigrants' access to health care services. Many non-English-speaking immigrants, including those with insurance, struggle to negotiate the complex terrain of the American health care system. Many studies have shown that a lack of language skills is a significant barrier to receiving adequate care. In one survey, Latino children had much less access to medical care than Caucasian children, but the gap was negligible when their parents' English proficiency was comparable to that of white parents.[17] Too often immigrants with limited English language proficiency are forced to rely on untrained interpreters. Miscommunication and poor translations of medical terms can lead to an onset of otherwise preventable diseases and even death. Young family members are frequently called on to serve as interpreters, which can lead to violations of privacy and embarrassment.

Federal and state laws crafted to remedy this situation have not always produced the intended results. Title VI of the Civil Rights Act of 1964, which prohibits discrimination based on national origin, has been interpreted to mean that federally funded service programs (including health care) must ensure that individuals with limited English proficiency have access to linguistically appropriate services. Unfortunately, the provisions are not always enforced, impeding immigrants' utilization of available health care services. Language barriers lead newcomers to postpone seeking care and limit comprehension, thereby reducing compliance with prescribed treatment regiments. Language barriers have also been associated with increased hospital admissions and lower patient satisfaction.

Research indicates that language barriers also have a number of indirect effects on immigrant patients and the health care system itself. Ethnic minorities who are not proficient in English are underrepresented in both clinical and health service research. This exclusion means that study results cannot be generalized to the entire population and that less is known about specific risk factors, the prevalence of certain diseases, and the response to treatment among newcomer groups. Language barriers also affect provider effectiveness and satisfaction. Some evidence indicates that language barriers may increase health care costs through their impact on services and health outcomes.

Immigrants' use of health care services is also affected by cultural issues such as a lack of sensitivity on the part of health care providers and newcomers' attitudes about disease and illness. Unfamiliarity among many health care professionals with the backgrounds and experiences of their patients makes it difficult for them to diagnose and develop appropriate treatment plans. In many immigrant cultures there is a great stigma attached to certain diseases, particularly mental health problems, which makes it difficult to seek help from American health care providers.

Policymakers, service providers, and community leaders interviewed in the course of this study were quite aware of what often seemed like insurmountable obstacles to health care access and utilization. Nevertheless, many communities succeeded in designing and implementing very creative strategies. Some created international clinics or established direct service programs for low-income, uninsured immigrants; others focused on advocacy and health promotion. Still others focused on training refugee and immigrant health care workers.

International Clinics

Localities with a large number of newcomers and an established tradition of providing health care services to refugees and immigrants have been well positioned to establish comprehensive international clinics at local hospitals. The Center for International Health at Regions Hospital in St. Paul, Minnesota, is an excellent example of a health care facility for ambulatory patients who come from all corners of the world. Patricia Walker, a medical director at the center, offered insights on how health care providers can start their own international clinics or refine their care of immigrant patients. To prepare to serve new Americans, Dr. Walker said, ambulatory facilities must hire medically trained professional interpreters; pay attention to the layout and equipment (including multilingual telephone lines) of the clinic to make it accessible and culturally sensitive; hire bilingual and bicultural staff from the front desk all the way to the doctors; share expertise as a way of expanding horizons among health care providers; take a multidisciplinary approach to ambulatory health care, including internists, psychologists, psychiatrists, pediatricians, nurse practitioners, and nurse midwives; promote cultural competency; and recognize that community involvement is a cornerstone of international care.

Specialized Health Services

Other programs followed a strategy of developing specialized health care services for different groups of low-income immigrants. These include Partners in Perinatal Care, a program developed in Winchester, Virginia, for uninsured women, and Healthy Families of Northern Shenandoah Valley, designed to work with first-time families to support positive parenting and provide infant care. In Clarkston, Georgia, a Senior Citizen Center provides gerontological and nutritional services for elderly refugees and immigrants.

Partners in Perinatal Care (PIPC)

The Partners in Perinatal Care program targets pregnant, uninsured women who are Medicaid ineligible, uninsured, and unable to afford proper care out of pocket. Through a community-based effort initiated by a bilingual nurse from the Winchester Health Department, Valley Health System obtained a grant from the Health Resources and Services Administration (HRSA). PIPC was implemented in November 2002. A full-time bilingual nurse and part-time administrator were hired along with an interpreter, a transport aide, and three *doulas*, or midwives. The program provides transportation to the health care facilities and interpretation during prenatal visits, delivery, and postpartum as well as newborn care. It also provides assistance with Medicaid and birth certificate applications. The goal is to provide a continuum of quality prenatal care as well as an opportunity for information sharing between health care providers, community advocates, and client groups.

Healthy Families of Northern Shenandoah Valley

A private, community-based collaborative with about twenty sites in Virginia, Healthy Families works with young families on a voluntary basis to support positive parenting through information, referral, and home-visiting services. Family support workers are available to work with qualified new parents before the child is born and stay with the family until the child is ready to enter school. The Winchester site has ten staff members, but only one Spanish-speaking bilingual and bicultural worker. Given the time demands of working with foreign-born, monolingual mothers, the Spanish-speaking worker had her caseload reduced considerably and was recently working with eight Mexican single mothers. Services provided by Healthy Families include a six-week postpartum checkup, support groups for new mothers, CPR training, and recreational activities.

Facilitating Access to Healthcare Services

There were several examples of programs facilitating or enhancing access to health care services. Their strategies included utilization of lay health promoters recruited from among target refugee and immigrant populations, and provision of interpretation and translation services to the foreign born seeking medical assistance. In many instances the health advocates played both roles.

Immigrant Health ACCESS Project (IHAP)

The IHAP program, based in Greensboro, North Carolina, helps newcomer communities create stronger relationships with local health care providers. Building on an immigrant network developed in Guilford County by an AmeriCorps project, IHAP hired and trained several bilingual and bicultural Lay Health Advisers (LHAs) from targeted communities. The advisers facilitate integration into the local health care system by providing interpretation and transportation as necessary, conducting health education activities, and advising providers on immigrant health and cultural traditions. The advisers initially included Latino, Somali, Sudanese, Montagnard, and Laotian representatives, but are now expanding to include representatives of other newcomer groups. A project of the social work department at the University of North Carolina at Greensboro, IHAP is funded by the Moses Cone-Wesley Long Community Health Foundation.

Promotoras de Salud (Lay Health Promoters)

As a community, Winchester has been challenged for years to dispel fears regarding the American health care system and foster immigrant trust. A program directed by a Salvadoran member of the Latino Connection has begun to address this issue. Through a federal grant and a four-way partnership among Valley Health System, James Madison University, Shenandoah University, and the Lord Fairfax Health District, members of the local Winchester/Frederick County Hispanic community have been trained as *promotoras de salud* (or health educators). This program, which began in 1999 in Harrisonburg, is viewed by the community as a positive step in educating the newcomer community on pertinent health-related issues and making the sometimes daunting local health care system more accessible. According to the program director, the nine recent graduates of the program have already made contact with 400 members of the Latino community in an effort to improve "access to health care and health education for all Hispanics in [their] locality."

Medical Interpretation Training

Even in cases where monetary costs are not prohibitive, language barriers have obstructed access to adequate healthcare. Traditionally, many health care facilities have relied on a limited number of bilingual personnel, family members, or a list of paid but untrained interpreters to assist their non-English-speaking patients. As newcomer populations have grown, however, health care providers have sought permanent solutions to medical interpretation challenges. Two of the groups interviewed in this study, Valley Health System in the Shenandoah Valley and the Center for International Health at Regions Hospital in St. Paul, Minnesota, used the Bridging the Gap Medical Interpreter Training Program. Offered through the Seattle-based nonprofit Cross-Cultural Health Care Program, the forty-hour course trains interpreters on issues including communication styles, medical terminology, professionalism, ethics, confidentiality, health care, and insurance. To qualify for the course, bilingual speakers must pass oral and written comprehension tests in two languages and possess basic knowledge of medical terms and common diseases.

Effective Use of Medical Interpreters

As much as trained interpreters improve communication, medical professionals need to know how to use them effectively. The Latino Connection in Winchester, Virginia, addressed this need by developing a companion program, "Effective Use of Interpreters," which teaches English-only speakers to make the best use of interpreters and judge the quality of interpreted communication. This training has been provided to local schools and several hospital departments and was scheduled for social services and other community agencies.

Alternative Modes of Service Delivery

Across the country some service providers and community leaders have developed creative ways of delivering health services. The People's Health Clinic in Park City, Utah, uses a medical van staffed with volunteer physicians, nurses, and translators to provide both primary and specialized care, while the Cambodian community in Greensboro, North Carolina, offers mental health and psychosocial services out of a Buddhist temple for Cambodian refugees.

The People's Health Clinic (PHC)

The mobile clinic was created to provide health care for the residents of Summit and Wasatch Counties in Utah after a one-time health fair drew nearly seven hundred people, highlighting the need for affordable health care. Following its inception in 2000, the clinic logged more than 3,500 patient visits in its first three years. Ninety-one percent of the patients are Hispanic and 89 percent live in Park City. The clinic offers general care on Monday nights and prenatal care on Wednesday nights. In 2003, it launched a "Partners in Caring" program, inviting local businesses to contribute to the clinic and become health care partners for a day, a week, a month, or longer. At the launching ceremony, six companies pledged $600 each for one-week partnerships.

The Greensboro Buddhist Center

In 1985, the Khmer Aid Group of the North Carolina Triad established a Buddhist Temple in Greensboro to provide culturally appropriate mental health services to the many traumatized Cambodians. The temple, assisted by Lutheran Family Services and supported by a grant from the Z. Smith Reynolds Foundation, has become an invaluable resource for community organizing and heritage preservation. It has also anchored a support network for more than five hundred Buddhist refugee and immigrant families in the Carolinas and Virginia.

Training Bilingual and Bicultural Health Care Providers

A well-trained bilingual and bicultural staff is essential to facilitating newcomers' access to culturally sensitive and linguistically appropriate health care services. Several localities have developed creative medical training and recertification programs to accomplish this goal. Faced with the shortage of nurses, the International Institute of Minnesota has developed career training programs funded by the United Way, the State Refugee Coordinator's office, the federal Office of Refugee Resettlement (ORR), and the McKnight Foundation. They include:

Nursing Assistant Training Program

The program follows state-approved curriculum for training nursing assistants with language instruction, but its lengthy duration (eight to eleven weeks) gives students time to master other skills including conflict resolution and résumé preparation. From its inception in 1990 through 2002, the program enrolled 739 students. Of those, 674 have completed the training and 657 have been certified as nursing assistants and were employed by sixty different health care facilities in the Twin Cities metropolitan area.

Academic Skills for Medical Careers Program

The preparatory course for medical training programs at technical colleges caters to motivated students already employed as nursing assistants. It allows them to spend twelve hours a week studying academic writing, reading, and advanced grammar. Students also receive instruction in word processing and Internet search procedures.

COMMUNITY DEVELOPMENT

Ethnic community development is a complicated measure of immigrant integration. Many researchers, policymakers, service providers, and community leaders focus on the importance of ethnic community development and community-based organizations (CBOs), which can be effective vehicles for serving immigrants. They are based within the newcomer communities and have the linguistic and cultural competency to reach many needy immigrants. Ethnic self-help groups and mutual assistance associations serve as intermediaries between newcomers and the host society, introducing immigrants to mainstream expectations and communicating ethnic interests to decision makers outside the community. Ethnic communities "cushion the impact of cultural change and protect immigrants against outside prejudice and initial economic difficulties."[18]

An overemphasis on ethnic community development, however, may be at odds with expectations and aspirations about social integration of immigrants into the broader U.S. society. Members of ethnic enclaves may integrate economically but not socially, supporting themselves without public assistance but remaining culturally isolated from mainstream society. The capacity and inclination to communicate with native-born U.S. residents and work alongside them to solve social issues are important marks of cultural and social integration. Reliance on ethnic communities, in other words, may not be conducive to social integration and civic engagement with the wider society.

Since the founding of the United States, ethnic communities have nevertheless played an important political and economic role in supporting the aspirations of their members. Confronted with the unknown, many newcomers seek out the familiar. They tend to live in close vicinity with other newcomers and shop at grocery stores that carry products from their home countries. Newcomer neighborhoods and businesses anchor a social support network that is vital to newcomers' well-being and the achievement of early economic self-sufficiency. Most immigrants find employment, particularly the first job, through relatives and friends. Tightly knit ethnic enclaves are manifestations of immigrant entrepreneurship: "employment within an ethnic enclave is often the best route for promotion into supervisory and managerial positions and for business ownership."[19]

Indeed, behavioral science theory suggests that individuals who adopt a bicultural modus operandi in the face of change—that is, retain their own cultural identity while incorporating elements of the new culture—are more likely to succeed than people who choose to assimilate completely, retreat to the familiar, or reject both the old and the new.[20] Our research indicates that integration involves a balancing of tendencies to retain the values, practices, and skills immigrants bring versus the pressures to adopt the norms and behaviors of the new society. Many successful integration initiatives identified by the research team blended the old and the new.

Every locality visited in the course of this project displayed examples of CBOs, mutual assistance associations (MAAs), or community development initiatives. The motifs for working together to facilitate integration of newcomers were quite diverse. So were the organizing principles. Most CBOs and MAAs were organized on the basis of common ethnic identity (e.g., the Khmer Aid Group of the Triad and the Montagnard Dega Association, both in North Carolina) or shared language (e.g., the Latin American Association in Atlanta). Most immigrants in the studied communities came from Mexico or Latin

America and shared a common native language: Spanish. But the refugee communities, even those originating in the same continent or region, did not have the benefit of a lingua franca. Most refugee-led organizations were established instead on the basis of shared ethnic or tribal identity. In some instances, members of the same ethnic group with opposing political persuasions established competing organizations, which created further divisions within the community. The Somali Bantu in Atlanta, for example, appeared to have been establishing at least two different community organizations.

Umbrella Coalitions

Practices developed by umbrella groups or coalitions catering to diversified newcomer communities are promising engines of integration. Not only do they facilitate integration of newcomers into the native U.S. society, they also foster linkages with other immigrant groups. In these instances, the linear integration process takes on new dimensions. Umbrella groups are organized on the basis of several different principles, including shared interest in a particular issue (e.g., domestic violence) or gender (e.g., refugee women). Two Atlanta-based examples are TAPESTRI, Inc., a coalition of community organizations serving domestic violence victims, and the Refugee Women's Network (RWN).

Immigrant and Refugee Coalition Challenging Gender-Based Oppression

TAPESTRI, a statewide coalition of ethnic community-based organizations, aims to end violence against women, children, and the elderly in immigrant and refugee communities. The coalition was formed in 1994 by five ethnic agencies: the Center for Pan-Asian Community Services; Shalom Bayit/Jewish Family and Career Services; Raksha, Inc. for South Asians in Distress; the Refugee Family Violence Prevention Project; and Mercy Mobile's Latino Families at Risk. Three other agencies have since joined the coalition, whose name symbolizes the different threads of society coming together to cover and protect its many communities. TAPESTRI's activities include multicultural training on domestic violence issues, services for victims of human trafficking, and a family violence intervention program for immigrant batterers.

The Refugee Women's Network, Inc. (RWN)

A national organization devoted to the needs of refugee women, the Atlanta-based RWN represents diverse ethnic communities. Two refugee women, Xuan Nguyen Sutter from Vietnam and Darija Pichanic from Bosnia, created the network in 1995 with a small grant from the Office of Refugee Resettlement (ORR). Eight years later, the organization had an annual operating budget of $800,000, including funds from ORR, the Ford Foundation, the Annie E. Casey Foundation, the Community Foundation for Greater Atlanta, the Atlanta Women Foundation, and many other private donors.

The network draws its strength, however, from the untapped human capital of refugee women resettled in the United States. Its programs include training in community organizing, technical assistance to refugee women's groups, and microenterprise. The training encourages refugee women to find strength in their united voices, participate at all levels of society, and bring about changes that will benefit themselves and their communities. The network has trained more than one thousand refugee women living in twenty-seven states. Each year, some five hundred refugee and immigrant women also attend a leadership conference held by RWN to share experiences and build alliances. More than fifteen organizations nationwide have taken advantage of the network's technical assistance. In Dallas, an organization has raised funds to train refugee women in computer skills and childcare business. In San Diego and Sioux Falls, women are planning community centers, and in Arizona women are starting a family violence prevention program.

Toward a Broader Sense of Community

Despite the propensity to focus on one's ethnic community, newcomers interact with established residents in many different social arenas. Community boundaries are created through the exchanges between these groups in schools, workplaces, government offices, law enforcement, and health care facilities. It is this social space that fosters integration and change, on one hand, or isolation and conflict on the other. Successful integration often requires both newcomers and established residents to expand their notions of community.

Even among long-standing residents, establishing a sense of community is often a challenge. "Community" refers both to where people live and how they feel and act. In one sense, it evokes a feeling of collectivity that is linked to a specific geographic area or physical space such as a city, a town, a school, a place of worship, or a city block. In another sense, it transcends geographic limitations to unite a group of people sharing common behavioral patterns, values, and social ties related to traits such as ethnicity, religion, and nationality. It often takes time to feel comfortable when moving to a new city or town, entering a new school, or changing jobs. This challenge is heightened for both newcomers and established community members when the newcomer's cultural and linguistic background is different from that of the majority.

Many localities create action plans to promote positive social interaction between newcomers and established residents and ensure that all residents receive quality service. These plans often emerge from the grassroots level as concerned residents, businesses, and public officials join forces to respond to rapid population change. In other instances, community governments take it upon themselves to create committees or task forces dedicated to incorporating all residents into community life. One approach is bottom up; the other is top down. The two often work in unison and can both be effective in solving challenges posed by rapid new settlement of foreign-born populations.

Winchester, Virginia: A Grassroots Approach

In Winchester, Virginia, a grassroots organization has effectively addressed the needs of the new Hispanic population vis-à-vis community institutions. The Latino Connection, founded in 1999 by a coalition of outreach workers, evolved into a networking and advocacy group that works on quality-of-life issues affecting the local Hispanic community. The group's mission is twofold: (1) to coordinate efforts to provide culturally and linguistically appropriate services to Hispanic newcomers in Winchester and Frederick County, and (2) to uphold the power of diversity in decision making by providing a forum to spread accurate, meaningful information among the newcomers, established residents, and community mediating institutions.

The Latino Connection is made up of thirty-five representatives from various community organizations, most of them involved in education and health care. These members, approximately half of them Hispanic, have permission from their employers to meet during regular working hours on a monthly basis for special events targeting the Latino population. Valley Health System, a nonprofit organization of health care providers, allows the group to use its facilities for meetings free of charge. That members of the Latino Connection are employed independently of the advocacy group allows it to remain informal—it has no paid staff and is not incorporated as a nonprofit entity. This structure frees the group from worrying about its own economic preservation, allowing it to concentrate all its energy on issues related to the newcomer Hispanic population. By not seeking outside funds, the group also avoids stipulations that government regulations or private philanthropists might impose.

The Latino Connection's outreach and information initiatives focus on closing the gap between institutions unprepared for serving newcomers and immigrants unprepared for life in their new communities. In this sense their work is both "bottom up" and "top down" because it targets individual newcomers and the community institutions at their service. The group capitalizes on its members' standing employment with traditional mediating institutions such as schools, hospitals, and different sectors of local government. The arrangement allows members of the Latino Connection to provide information and resources directly to members of the newcomer community while simultaneously strengthening institutional capacity to meet newcomer needs through the education of colleagues.

Chamblee, Georgia: A Community-Consensus Approach

The experience of Chamblee, Georgia, a small Atlanta suburb in DeKalb County, exemplifies the benefits and hardships that rapid population growth can bring. A widely publicized case in 1992 illustrated the challenges that can emerge as a result of newcomer settlement.[21] Residents complained about Hispanic men who gathered on a street corner to be picked up for day labor, accusing them of stirring trouble, and using private property as a dump. At a city council meeting, officials suggested using bear traps in residents' yards to discourage the men from trespassing. These comments came in the wake of the remarks by Chamblee's police chief that the "problem will continue until these [foreigners] go back where they came from."

The council meeting sparked a tense community-wide debate that was eventually settled by a conflict resolution team from the U.S. Department of Justice. Chamblee changed course and began to actively seek newcomer settlement and investment, attracting immigrant businesses that have revitalized the economy. In 1999, Chamblee's community development director put it clearly: "If the immigrants hadn't come, Chamblee would look like a bombed-out,

1950s American dream, complete with empty strip malls and abandoned buildings." Today Chamblee has higher tax revenues and a vibrant economy that capitalizes on its international flavor.

The engine for this growth has been the city's International Village District. A home to more than five thousand immigrants representing at least twenty-five different ethnic groups, the International Village is one of the most diverse areas in the country. A partnership among the city of Chamblee, DeKalb County, and the DeKalb Chamber of Commerce, the Village is an ongoing redevelopment of four hundred acres immediately north of the DeKalb Peachtree Airport. The commerce chamber formalized the concept in 1992, calling for a "village" that would become a nucleus for a growing international community within the greater metropolitan area. The village was to be a home, workplace, learning center, tourist center, retail center, and recreation area for individuals and businesses with a variety of cultures. Chamblee developed a long-range master plan in 1994, formalizing plans for a pedestrian-friendly area with mixed-used opportunities, retail, and related developments. At a three-day public workshop, city residents stressed a desire to maintain the residential land use component within the village, the importance of public open spaces, and the appeal of a self-sustaining community that, on its own, would attract businesses, residents, and tourists.

Over the next five years, the city witnessed significant redevelopment of properties, including preparations for the International Village Cultural and Community Center (IVCCC). The plan for the IVCCC consisted of development of a community daycare center in a first phase and a cultural center in a second phase. The city renovated a condemned apartment complex with funds from a federal block grant and essentially donated it to the nonprofit group in charge of developing the community center, leasing it for $10 a year.

In early 1999, ground was broken for a $3 million, seventeen thousand-square-foot childcare center in the International Village area. The facility, which was constructed in less than a year, is a testament to the prioritization of the needs of the area's diverse population. Affordable childcare had long been a major need in Chamblee. The new facility, known as the Sheltering Arms Center, offers childcare for low- to moderate-income families who pay based on their earnings. Anonymous donations paid for $2 million of the construction costs. The completion of the first phase of the project has permitted the facility to serve 140 children from approximately thirty-six countries, speaking more than thirteen languages.

The plans for a recreation and cultural center call for office space for nonprofit social service agencies and a performing arts center. This second phase of the project was still being designed, but Chamblee officials passed special zoning rules to control development and drive the International Village Project forward. Officials razed several run-down apartment complexes and renovated others, and they were trying to persuade entrepreneurs to set up shop in the district. Plans for the district include shops, restaurants and a cultural and community center. While the primary goal remains assisting the local multicultural population, village boosters hope their development will draw tourists and locals who aren't aware of the diversity in the international corridor. They estimate it could draw more than three hundred thousand tourists a year, with annual retail sales of $160 million.

In another example of community development, Guilford College, founded by Quakers, is one of five colleges in Greensboro, North Carolina, that provide opportunities for students to work with immigrants and refugees. The college describes the emphasis on hands-on work as "community learning," the accomplishment of tasks that meet human needs while fostering educational growth. Students involve themselves through courses with service components, service-oriented internships, and alternative projects during school vacations.

Guilford students have worked directly with the immigrant population through placements with community-based organizations such as the Montagnard Dega Association, the Center for New North Carolinians at the University of North Carolina Greensboro, the Buddhist Center, and the Glenwood Library. The Montagnard Dega Association is a nonprofit organization established not only to help the Montagnards resettled in Greensboro, but also to advocate for the freedom of the Montagnard population that remains in Vietnam. Students help with after-school programs, tutoring programs, grant writing, elderly outreach, and youth programs. Other organizations enlist students for similar service projects that engage the immigrant population.

CULTURAL HERITAGE PRESERVATION

Cultural traditions and histories provide an important touchstone for ethnic immigrant communities to preserve their sense of self for the next generation. For some communities, sharing their rich histories and celebrating native heroes have also represented key strategies for teaching mainstream society about their backgrounds. One way of accomplishing this goal is the promotion of cultural heritage preservation activities.

"We Remember, We Celebrate, We Believe: A Photo History of Latinos in Utah"

Since 2000, Armando Solórzano, an associate professor of ethnic studies at the University of Utah, has been gathering oral histories among Latinos from different socioeconomic, religious, occupational, and national backgrounds. More than two hundred interviews touch on family structure, social attitudes, work history, cultural practices, and gender roles. In a companion photo exhibit, Solórzano chronicles Latinos' past and current involvement in the state. The exhibit, titled "We Remember, We Celebrate, We Believe: A Photo History of Latinos in Utah," is comprised of fifty-two large photographs organized around themes with commentary in Spanish and English. It opened with a ceremony at the Utah State Capitol Rotunda in 2002 and has traveled to other Utah universities, to California, and abroad.

Solórzano hopes the exhibit will promote diversity, increase Latino's visibility, and humanize their experiences. "Latinos are an integral part of Utah," Solórzano says. "We were here even before the pioneers. We need to be seen. We just want to be treated as equals and as humans." The photographic images, collected from individuals, organizations, families, friends, archives, and the Utah State Historical Society, each depict a story about Latinos' contributions to Utah. The frames capture Latinos' contributions to the surging sheep industry in Monticello, their influence in the establishment and growth of the Catholic Church and the Church of Jesus Christ of Latter-Day Saints, and their work in Utah mines and railroads. The final frames depict more recent activities, including Utah Latinos' successful campaign to name a Salt Lake City street after Cesar Chavez, leader of the first successful U.S. farm workers' union.

When asked to discuss her history, one elderly Latina told Solórzano, "I have none—only photographs." So precious were these pictures, many of their owners, rather than loaning them to Solórzano, insisted on accompanying him to the copy store to reproduce the images. "For some Latinos, the photos were the only remaining memories they have of their family and of their people. When I touched these photos I felt like I was touching something sacred," he said.

Tou Ger Xiong: Multicultural, Multilingual, Multicool

Tou Ger Xiong bills himself as the world's first Hmong storyteller and rap artist. He was born in Laos in 1973, but his family left after the communist takeover in 1975, seeking refuge in a Thai refugee camp. His family immigrated to the United States as refugees of war four years later and Xiong began his childhood in America in the public housing projects of St. Paul. The valedictorian of his high school, he enrolled at Carleton College in Northfield, Minnesota, where he developed a passion for the performing arts. He created Project Respectism, an educational service project that uses comedy, storytelling, and rap music to bridge cultures, which he presented to schools, churches, colleges, and community groups throughout the Midwest while writing his thesis.

Since Xiong graduated from college with a degree in political science, Project Respectism has evolved into a program that provides cultural entertainment, or "preservation education," for people of all professions and backgrounds. Xiong has taken his message of respect to thirty-five states in the past six years. He has given over eight hundred presentations nationwide to audiences of all ages and ethnic backgrounds, sometimes reaching as many as eight thousand people in a week.

RELIGION AS A FORM OF SOCIAL CAPITAL

In his book *What It Means to Be an American*, Michael Walzer reminds us that Americans first acquire political competence within their ethnic, cultural, and religious associations.[22] In their religious associations, newcomers not only negotiate differences with one another, they also inevitably encounter people of different religious backgrounds, including representatives of the host society. Places of worship have had a long history of facilitating integration of newcomers into the host society. Churches, synagogues, temples, and mosques can be especially effective organizers of inter- and intragroup accommodation. Places of worship typify the institutional combination of resources and shared values around which newcomers and members of the host society meet for common projects.

Yet despite the diversity of religious and spiritual beliefs and practices that sustains many migrants amid their displacement and integration into the host society, policymakers tend to neglect the role of religion and spirituality as a source of emotional and cognitive support. Religion offers a form of social and political expression and mobilization as well as a vehicle for community building and group identity.

Ethnic Spiritual Centers

In Greensboro, North Carolina, the Buddhist temple described above has become an invaluable resource not only for community organization but also for cultural heritage preservation. The temple, which provides culturally appropriate mental health services for traumatized refugees, helped forge a viable ethnic and religious enclave that attracted other Buddhists. The Triad area is now home to about fifteen hundred Cambodian refugees and more than one thousand Laotians with multiple small businesses and communities of faith.

One key to the success of the region's ethnic spiritual centers was a gifted community organizer. A Thai Buddhist monk who spoke Khmer, Lao, Thai, and English came to serve at the Greensboro Buddhist Center in 1989. The monk served as a well-spoken representative of the refugees for the general population and was well-liked within the community.

Mainstream Churches Accommodating Newcomers

While many refugee and immigrant communities establish their own places of worship to preserve their culture and religious traditions, several mainstream religious organizations have taken an integrated approach to worship. Beyond merely sharing worship space, as religious institutions have done across the country, these efforts have incorporated newcomers into standing practices. In Greensboro, North Carolina, St. Mary's Catholic Church, a historically black church, has services in multiple languages and a multicultural pastoral staff. Its congregation includes immigrants from Southeast Asia, Latin America, and Africa. Our Lady of Grace Catholic Church, also in Greensboro, recently acquired a Spanish-speaking priest and initiated a mass in Spanish.

LAW ENFORCEMENT

As newcomer populations grow, challenges arise from diverging expectations about appropriate social behavior. A lack of familiarity with local laws and cultural barriers can generate misunderstandings between established residents and newcomers that lead to the involvement of the law enforcement community. For example, in some countries, large groups of people commonly gather on weekends to drink beer, socialize, and play soccer. But established residents in some communities find these gatherings inappropriate or threatening, even if no laws are being broken. In a society with different behavioral norms, newcomers find themselves treading unfamiliar water. Language barriers only aggravate the frustration of both newcomers and law enforcement.

Crime and victimization concern everyone, but they have an especially devastating impact on newcomers. Many immigrants fear and mistrust the police because of traumatic experiences with uniformed officials in their native countries. Newcomers and police departments alike must work together to overcome mutual feelings of mistrust. Two programs, one in Atlanta, Georgia, and the other in Park City, Utah, have improved relations between newcomers and the law enforcement community.

Bridging the Gap

The Atlanta-based Bridging the Gap (BTG) Project is based on the idea that the biggest integration challenge for immigrants stems not from racial barriers but from misunderstandings related to cultural diversity. The project uses three primary strategies to reduce those misunderstandings: a crisis intervention program; an education initiative for immigrants, landlords, and law enforcement officials; and a youth program. It began in 1994 with the sponsorship of the U.S. Department of Health and Human Services' Office of Refugee Resettlement, the U.S. Department of Justice's Community-Oriented Policing Services, and the Governor of Georgia's Children and Youth Coordinating Council.

New American Services Program

Under the New American Services Program (NASP), BTG was working to facilitate some of the technical stages of integration. A one-stop center developed by the program would distribute immigration forms, take immigration photographs, issue money orders, register newly naturalized Americans to vote, provide passport applications, and refer customers to legal counsel for assistance. The NASP operated in conjunction with offices of the U.S. Immigration and Naturalization Service in Atlanta, Georgia, and Charlotte, North Carolina.

Crisis Intervention and Police Program

The crisis intervention program was initiated to respond to 911 calls from non-English-speaking callers. BTG employed more than twenty staff members, speaking fifteen different languages, to take calls on a special hotline and notify emergency responders. The program aimed in part to reduce a perception among immigrants that police were hesitant to enter their communities. As part of the project, BTG worked with law enforcement agencies to recruit personnel from diverse cultural populations.

Mediation Project

Mediation between landlords and immigrants has been another focus of the project. The community outreach division convened meetings to educate ethnic communities about life in the United States and helped them build relationships with mainstream social service providers. The project also provided employment referrals for immigrants and implemented translation services so that immigrants could better interact with government institutions.

The Youth Program

The project has developed a program to target immigrant youth because they were involved in many of the crimes reported to the hotline. The youth program featured support groups, a newsletter, and a truancy prevention program. An annual "Youth Challenge Day" brought ethnic youth together with law enforcement officers to participate in sports activities and educational workshops. Another initiative provided conflict resolution and diversity training to young leaders at a high school plagued by hate crimes.

The Community Outreach Program of the Park City Police Department

In Park City, Utah, an upscale resort community an hour from Salt Lake City, the demand for low-wage service workers skyrocketed in the late 1990s amid a booming economy and preparations for the 2002 Winter Olympics. An influx of Latinos, mostly Mexicans, met the demand, but posed new challenges for the police department. An inability to engage the newcomers because of language and cultural barriers strained officer morale. Some local business and residents began to express fears about the new population. Confusion over their relationship with INS (now Immigration and Customs Enforcement) also complicated matters.

Realizing that the newcomers were there to stay, police Chief Lloyd Evans concentrated on proper service provision instead of fruitless deportation efforts. Considering they could be victims, complainants, or witnesses, he wanted newcomers to have access to basic services. Frustration over an inability to communicate pervaded the police ranks and required immediate attention. A series of public forums helped Evans identify key problems confronting local law enforcement and the needs of newcomers. Recognizing a need for a liaison between the newcomers and the police, the department created a community advocate position. The idea was for a figure to encourage newcomer trust and use of police department resources, teach newcomers how law enforcement operates in Park City, implement a newcomer community crime prevention program and act as a point person for the community at large.

With the community outreach program, the Park City police stressed that immigration status was not their main concern. Racial profiling was denounced and a police accountability program was set into motion. The community liaison has access to the police chief and all police reports dealing with the newcomer population. Another series of public forums on concerns regarding the police ensured the participation of the wider community. While language barriers and funding still pose a challenge, the program has successfully addressed community needs. Newcomer communities now have the strongest neighborhood watch programs in Park City. The outreach program enjoys the support of local elected officials, has assuaged concerns from the established community vis-à-vis newcomers, and has added its voice to those advocating state and federal legislation to improve relations between newcomers and law enforcement.

COMMERCE

Immigrant involvement in commerce has obvious advantages for newcomers, who can develop economic self-sufficiency and confidence through participation in the larger economy. Less noted are the benefits for mainstream society. Beyond the cultural contributions of ethnic businesses, they also breathe new life into neglected urban neighbor-hoods or towns and provide a sustainable base for community improvement. With both objectives in mind, several projects in Minne-sota and Georgia have taken creative approaches to boosting immi-grants' economic integration.

Mercado Central

Until recently, Lake Street in central Minneapolis was an example of urban decay, an inner-city area with several dilapidated buildings. Today more than thirty small Spanish-speaking businesses have set up shop in the area through the Mercado Central, a project coordinated by several public and private organizations. Businesses include a tortilla factory, a retail outlet, a bakery, and a place to mail packages and make money transfers.

The Mercado is a model of cooperation among immigrant churchgo-ers, the broad faith community, nonprofit urban institutions, city neighborhoods, federal and local government, lenders, and philan-thropic donors. Comprised of numerous small retail ventures under one roof, it reflects the growth of Minneapolis' Hispanic population over the last decade. The project began when a survey of the Hispanic congregation at a local church identified three concerns among immi-grants: starting small businesses, access to education, and immigration policies and practices. Almost simultaneously, the Neighborhood Development Center (NDC), a St. Paul-based, nonprofit community development agency, graduated its first Latino class. With training in business and technical assistance to help inner-city residents revitalize their neighborhoods, the trainees generated the idea for the Mercado in partnership with other groups.

The groups that nurtured the growth of the Mercado Central include the Whittier Community Development Corp (WCDC), a nonprofit community development organization that helps inner-city residents revitalize small businesses; Interfaith Action, a thirty-church ecumeni-cal organization; Project for Pride in Living (PPL), a not-for-profit organization assisting low- and moderate-income people achieve self-sufficient by addressing their job, affordable housing, and neighbor-hood needs; and Neighborhood Development Center (NDC), a bank-sponsored provider of entrepreneurial training for low-income resi-dents in the twin cities.

The main building for the Mercado was acquired as a gift to PPL, which was allowed to redevelop the site if a tenant filled the space.

Once it became clear the Mercado Central could become that tenant, grants and loans from dozens of sources paid for a $2.5 million overhaul of the twenty-six thousand square feet of space. The thirty or so merchants are graduates of NDC training. They have business plans and necessary financing, which is typically modest.

The University of Minnesota's New Immigrant Farming Project

The University of Minnesota's Extension Service works on issues such as community development, the environment, and youth development in all parts of the state. It has developed two programs to specifically target new immigrant farmers.

The New Immigrant Farm Program

This program seeks to increase the productivity and profitability of fields worked by new immigrant farmers residing in the Twin Cities metropolitan area. These farmers, who usually own less than twenty acres of land, are located with the help of University partners from the various immigrant communities. At the time of the research about 140 farmers participated in the program, most of them Hmong or Hispanic. Most participants sell what they harvest at local farmers' markets.

The Farming Incubator Program

A second program targets immigrants who would like to be farmers but do not own or lease land. To help them develop sustainable small-scale farming operations, it leases parcels of land for up to four years at the University's Rosemount Research and Outreach Center. The program also provides instruction both in the classroom and the fields. "Even though they have agrarian backgrounds, they're not familiar with how food is farmed in this country," said Nigatu Tadesse, the director of both programs. "We're trying to improve their marketing techniques and production for them to be profitable in their businesses."

Plaza de Sol

An adaptive-use development opened in Chamblee, Georgia, in 2003. The retail plaza, known as Plaza de Sol, occupies a former industrial facility and caters to both Hispanic and Asian communities. The business agreements underwriting the shopping center are an indication of the cooperation that exists between the established ethnic business communities and ethnic consumers. Chang Bin Yim, a Korean-American businessman who bought the property in the mid-1990s, said he knew the project was a good idea after noting that the majority of the customers in Chamblee's Asian markets were Latinos. The local business community's embrace of the entire gamut of ethnicities has set the stage for the International Village to serve a multi-ethnic clientele.

The Plaza del Sol Limited Partnership includes some of the most prominent Latinos in Atlanta, demonstrating the ethnic community's capacity to take on significant development projects. It was put together by Norberto Sanchez, president of Norsan Group, one of Georgia's largest Hispanic-owned companies; Chuck Schmandt, the project's architect; and Yim. Diaz-Verson Ventures, an investment company, is also involved in the project. Sam Zamarripa, a founder and managing partner of Diaz-Verson Ventures, told the *Atlanta Journal and Constitution*, "[It shows that Latino] business leaders can get together and go outside ordinary boundaries. It demonstrates the capacity is there, the expertise is there, the understanding of the market is there" (July 17, 2002).

HOMEOWNERSHIP

Many immigrants to the United States have a strong desire to become citizens and sink permanent roots in their new country. Homeownership, in this sense, represents an important milestone on the road to permanent settlement and integration into American society. Since 1995, the foreign born have represented fully a third of household growth in the United States. The influx of immigrants, together with losses of older white households, has driven minority household growth ahead of white household growth both in absolute and relative terms. Immigrants represented more than 50 percent of Hispanic and over 80 percent of Asian household growth between 1996 and 2000.

To own their own homes, however, immigrants must navigate the mortgage loan process, a challenge for anyone, native or foreign born. The U.S. credit system represents a further barrier to immigrant homeownership. Unfortunately, this information is not taught in schools. Many community-based organizations, often with the backing of financial institutions, have begun to fill this education gap for economically and culturally diverse populations. The Salt Lake Neighborhood

Housing Services is an example of a community-based organization that improves homeownership opportunities for the foreign born.

Salt Lake Neighborhood Housing Services

Established in 1977, Salt Lake Neighborhood Housing Services (NHS) is a private, nonprofit corporation governed by residents, local businesses, and Salt Lake City officials. The organization unites youth, residents, businesses, and community leaders in an effort to provide affordable housing, community building, and a positive image of target neighborhoods.

The first-time homebuyer program at NHS assists families who may not qualify for a home loan with a traditional lender. Their one-on-one counseling program guides customers through the home-buying process. To ensure that families become successful homeowners, NHS requires potential homebuyers to participate for the entire length of the counseling program. Buyers participate in eight hours of homebuyer education and learn the basics of purchasing and financing a home.

Latin American Association

Based in Atlanta, Georgia, the Latin American Association is a non-profit organization that provides comprehensive transitional services for Latinos working toward self-sufficiency and an enhanced quality of life. Their mission is to respond to the Hispanic community's basic needs and help members gain the skills to fully participate in the larger community. Homeownership is a principal focus. The housing department assists families through seminars in Spanish on the home-buying process; an annual housing fair; and counseling on landlord relations, banking, and mortgages. In 2001, more than seven hundred people attended the association's housing fair, gathering information from local lenders, real estate agents, financial counseling groups, and government agencies. Since 1999, the Housing Services program has helped more than thirty people buy their first home.

CONCLUSION

While this chapter discusses a wide array of practices facilitating immigrant integration, it is not intended as an exhaustive list of existing programs. The programs and strategies described here offer only a glimpse into the wide array of innovative approaches developed in settlement areas around the country. Indeed, the diversity of practices found in this localized study of five states suggests a range of approaches beyond the scope of any one study.

The volume as a whole also should not be considered a cookbook of integration strategies with individual cases as transferable as recipes. The strategies identified in this chapter are not based on a formal evaluation of "best practices." They worked in the places where they were implemented and they certainly hold promise of being replicable elsewhere, but there is no guarantee that they will work everywhere. Even the most promising strategies must be adapted to local circumstances including the political climate, the availability of financial and human resources, and the cohesion of the newcomer community. Thumbnail sketches are provided here in the hope that they will save communities from reinventing the wheel. But local community organizers, policymakers, and administrators must take inspiration where they can to develop unique solutions for local problems and challenges.

A few identifiable elements are common to the most successful integration practices described in this volume. They are based on partnerships among groups including social organizations, churches, and businesses that may or may not channel their efforts through a formal organization. They assume that integration is a two-way street and encourage interaction among different groups of stakeholders and the host society, recognizing the agency of even the most recent immigrants. The lead actors show less interest in who gets credit for a particular initiative than the promotion of their wider goals. And finally, they depend on hard work. As practitioners affirm, even the most brilliant ideas require serious effort to become successful programs.

NOTES

1. For a more detailed description of these promising practices as well as contact information for the programs visited as part of this project, see a companion volume to these case studies: Elżbieta M. Goździak and Micah N. Bump, *Facilitating Immigrant Integration: Handbook of Best Practices*.

2. P. Bourdieu, *Raison practiques: Sur la théorie de l'action* (Paris: Editions du Seuil, 1994).

3. Alejandro Portes and Rubén G. Rumbaut, "Legacies," *The Story of the Immigrant Second Generation* (Berkeley: University of California Press, 2001), 114.

4. Elizabeth Grieco, "Characteristics of the Foreign Born in the United States: Results from Census 2000." *Migration Information Source* (December 2002).

5. Little Hoover Commission, *We the People: Helping Newcomers Become Californians* (Sacramento, CA: Little Hoover Commission, June 2002).

6. National Center for Policy Analysis, "Immigration: Language Barrier Problems." www.ncpa.org/pd/immigrat/pdimm/pidimm6.htlm.

7. Jane Eisner, "Discretion Can Be Better Part of Citizenship." *The Holland Sentinel*, January 25, 2001.

8. Dianne Schmidley, "The Foreign-Born Population in the United States: March 2002." *Current Population Reports*, P20-539 (Washington, DC: U.S. Census Bureau, 2003). Generally, at least five years of residence is required for U.S. citizenship, so rates for more recently arrived foreign born will always be lower.

9. Patrick J. McConnell, "Immigrants Americanizing, Study Finds." *Los Angeles Times*, July 7, 1999.

10. The American Immigration Law Foundation, ESL Education Helps Immigrants Integrate, www.ailf.org/ipc/policy_reports_2002_ESL.asp.

11. See, for example, Public Agenda, "A Lot to Be Thankful For: What Parents Want Children to Learn About America," www.publicagenda.org.

12. N. V. Hanh, "Southeast Asian Refugee Resettlement in the United States: A Socioeconomic Analysis." In *American Mosaic: Selected Readings on America's Multicultural Heritage*, ed. Y. I. Song and E. C. Kim (Englewood Cliffs, NJ: Prentice Hall, 1993).

13. The American Immigration Law Foundation, ESL Education Helps Immigrants Integrate, www.ailf.org/ipc/policy_reports_2002_ESL.asp.

14. Grantmakers in Health Resource Center. 2000. *A Different World: Immigrant Access to Culturally Appropriate Health Care.* Available online www.gih.org.

15. U.S. Census Bureau press release. September 30, 2003.

16. Dianne Schmidley, "The Foreign-Born Population in the United States: March 2002." *Current Population Reports*, P20-539 (Washington, DC: U.S. Census Bureau, 2003).

17. Robin M. Weinick and Nancy A. Krauss, "Racial and Ethnic Differences in Children's Access to Care." *American Journal of Public Health* 90 (November 2000): 1771–74.

18. Alejandro Portes and Rubén G. Rumbaut, *Immigrant America: A Portrait* (Berkeley: University of California Press, 1990), 88.

19. Weinick and Krauss, "Racial and Ethnic Differences in Children's Access to Care," 89.

20. John W. Berry, "Cultural Relations in Plural Societies: Alternatives to Segregation and Their Sociopsychological Implications." In N. Miller and M. Brewer, eds., *Groups in Contact* (New York: Academic Press, 1984). See also Dan A. Chekki, "Beyond Assimilation: The Immigrant Family and Community in a Canadian Metropolis." Paper presented at the Congress of the Humanities and Social Sciences, Canadian Sociology and Anthropology Meetings, Halifax, June 1–4, 2003.

21. The incident was reported in the New York *Village Voice* as well as in the local *Atlanta Journal-Constitution*.

22. Michael Walzer, *What It Means to Be an American: Essays on the American Experience* (New York: Marsilio, 1992).

IV

CONCLUSION

10

Challenges for the Future

Elżbieta M. Goździak and Susan F. Martin

In spite of being a country largely shaped by immigration, the United States does not have immigrant policies. No federal laws explicitly promote social, economic, or civic integration. The best practices identified in this volume emerged through trial and error, shaped by variables in each community including demographics and previous experiences with immigrants. While governments of other large receiving countries such as Canada and Australia have implemented policies designed to bring immigrants into the fold, newcomers are not necessarily worse off under the U.S. system.

Without officially endorsing multiculturalism, the U.S. government has developed a legal framework that nevertheless protects newcomers and guarantees a broad array of rights. Several policies protect both citizens and immigrants from discrimination on the basis of race, religion, nationality, and, in some cases, citizenship. Employers, for example, may be penalized for refusing to hire a foreign-sounding or foreign-looking person on suspicion that the applicant does not have appropriate documentation. These laws do not end prejudice, but they provide solid footing for immigrants to defend their rights.

The private sector has also taken a lead role in promoting integration in the United States. Family members and employers sponsor immigrants and take principal responsibility for ensuring their successful adaptation to their new country. A flexible labor market has facilitated the efforts of immigrant advocates by making employment easy to

277

find. Although many jobs do not pay well, it is possible for immigrants to improve their lot and even own their own businesses. Given their high levels of employment, immigrants are frequently characterized as hardworking contributors to the nation's economy, which also eases the integration process.

Integration is also aided indirectly by several broad and long-standing government policies. Among the most important is birthright citizenship, granted automatically to children of immigrants if they are born on U.S. territory. The provision applies even to the children of undocumented migrants. As a result only one generation carries the label of "foreigner," in contrast to many European countries where third and fourth generations are still considered outsiders. Such policies reflect a deep-rooted national conviction that immigration is good for the country and immigrants are its future. The basic framework for naturalization dates to the early nineteenth century and the ideas of the founding fathers, who generally saw immigrants as presumptive citizens who should enjoy the same rights and privileges as other Americans.

While children of immigrants may be considered Americans from the day they are born, economic, cultural and political integration takes place over the span of many generations. Like the children of immigrants who came decades ago, those who arrived in the most recent wave of migration see themselves as Americans and will almost certainly integrate more easily than their parents. But that is not to say they will achieve equal footing with their counterparts born to established residents. Integration does not happen overnight. The achievements described in this volume, which focuses on new settlement areas with limited previous exposure to migration, appear all the more successful in light of the social changes and paradigm shifts demanded of both newcomers and the host society.

Time and the overarching policy framework both indirectly favor integration, but neither is a substitute for action at the community level where the web of local relationships determines the immigrant experience. Indeed, one consequence of the federal government's hands-off approach to integration is an even greater reliance on communities and community leadership. Experiences at local levels shape not only immigrant attitudes toward their new country but also the cohesiveness of the neighborhoods, towns, and cities they adopt as their new homes. As the case studies in this volume have demonstrated, local actors including the newcomers themselves have found novel ways to assume this responsibility and foster the incorporation of newly arrived immigrants into broader society.

The dynamics of integration, of course, cannot be reduced to a negotiation between two groups. A categorization of two camps such as "established residents" and "newcomers" classifies individuals according only to when they arrived and does not account for infinite social divisions along ethnic, racial, and religious lines. The American host society itself is composed of different waves of newcomers, some more empathetic than others to the newest arrivals. Today's immigrant population is also comprised of several subcategories. Newcomers with refugee status benefit from generous U.S. assistance programs that can become a source of tension with other immigrants. In some cases, long-standing ethnic divisions are renewed in this country, as illustrated by tribal rivalries among Somali immigrants. This complexity means that immigrants arrive to find a country more diverse than the lands they leave behind. Integration becomes a multipronged process, with newcomers finding their way among the many segments of mainstream society and other immigrant communities.

A comparison of the five case studies in this volume nevertheless reveals many common obstacles to social, economic, and civic integration. While some of these challenges might be remedied with more effective policies, many of them also derive from cultural rifts that call for nothing less than changes in the perceptions that established residents, including earlier immigrants, and newcomers have of each other. Bridging the gaps that separate these different groups would strengthen communities, mitigate divisive social tensions, and, of course, position immigrants to participate more effectively in the wider society.

One obstacle that arises in several new settlement areas is a perception among some established residents that new immigrants will leave as quickly as they came, thereby making it unnecessary to include them in broad society. The history of migrant workers in agricultural areas, for example, frequently conditions business leaders and communities to view immigrants as temporary residents. Even as Hispanics and other immigrants gain permanent employment, stereotypes of poor, wayward laborers remain prevalent in the public eye. In Virginia's Shenandoah Valley, the perception that immigrants comprised a transient workforce was transformed in some cases into a denial of responsibility for Hispanic health care, education, housing, and retirement needs.

The exclusion of immigrants from conceptions of local communities, beyond contributing to their marginalization, can also lead to depictions of newcomers as liabilities. Particularly amid economic difficulties, immigrants perceived as lacking other links to a community are frequently seen to take advantage of support networks or, worse yet, take jobs that would otherwise go to established residents. In Faribault, Minnesota, working-class Caucasians expressed fears that declines in local industries could make immigrants dependent on public assistance. African, Asian, and Latino immigrants were seen not as full-fledged members of the community, but rather temporary residents without reason to stay once their labor was no longer needed.

Progress in changing these deep-rooted notions is hindered by skewed perceptions of newcomers' legal status. Indeed, much of the opposition to migration stems from the widespread belief that the majority of foreigners in the United States are here illegally, even though the opposite is the case. At a national level, even when policymakers seek to restrict benefits for undocumented immigrants, their decisions frequently affect family members who may be refugees or children who are U.S. citizens. At community levels, many programs and publications further complicate the issue by using definitions of immigrants that do not correspond with individuals' legal status. Examples include the designation of African-born children as "African Americans" in school data and counts of individuals who designate themselves "Latinos."

The news media significantly influence the popular perception of immigrants, reinforcing stereotypes in some cases while empathizing with the foreigner's experience in others. Particularly in new settlement areas with little previous ethnic diversity, the arrival of newcomers has attracted substantial news coverage, magnifying their presence. Newcomer status frequently influences the tone of the media's treatment. Compared to other immigrants arriving in Atlanta, for example, refugees have generally received more positive attention. Undocumented immigrants have been portrayed occasionally as criminal aliens, but they are more often described as an important source of labor. Regrettably, coverage of immigrant issues frequently concentrates on moments of conflict between natives and newcomers. And particularly in the aftermath of the attacks on September 11, 2001, carried out by nineteen foreign nationals, local media outlets have been more likely to cast newcomers in a menacing light. In Minnesota, media attention focused on the local Somali population and the arrests of individuals involved with Muslim charities.

A common challenge is to emphasize the contributions made by newcomers, encouraging their acceptance as full-fledged members of the community and promoting tolerance. Whether focused on economic or social aspects, successful integration programs have generally helped established residents to acknowledge that immigrants bring something of value. Beyond labor, immigrant contributions highlighted by advocates have included economic investment, cultural diversity, and the resuscitation of depopulated urban and rural areas. Responding to rising social tensions, the Atlanta suburb of Chamblee, Georgia, not only made public services more responsive to its newly diverse community but also took advantage of newcomers' economic and cultural activity to develop an "international village" with cross-cultural appeal. Elsewhere, however, the business community, while profiting from inexpensive labor, has been notably absent from the public dialogue on immigration. In cases where police, school, and health care representatives have depicted newcomers as a strain on community services, the business sector might stress that they also represent an irreplaceable resource.

By the same token, integration depends on the empowerment of immigrants for participation in the wider community. In both social and economic terms, it is important to stress opportunities and obligations as much as rights and entitlements. One of the largest obstacles to this goal is that mediating institutions such as schools, hospitals, and local governments often overlook the newcomer voice. This condition owes largely to immigrants' lack of familiarity with their new communities. Links of incorporation within newcomer groups and with broad society remedy this condition over time, but several smaller initiatives have potential to accelerate this orientation. Latino soccer tournaments organized in Salt Lake City, in one example, have encouraged players to identify with the communities represented by more than three hundred teams.

Much as the benefits of immigration must be realized, integration also requires an honest and clear assessment of the problems faced by newcomers. To ignore the costs of immigration—whether the fiscal costs to institutions unused to providing services to limited English proficient clients, or the social costs when immigrants knowingly or inadvertently break laws or violate community norms—is to jeopardize the future integration of immigrants. The programs described in this volume recognize such problems and seek solutions. Rather than hide domestic violence in immigrant families, TAPESTRI aims to stop such abuse. Rather than ignore the costs that a lack of interpreters can inflict on immigrants and health services, several programs provide training and deploy bilingual personnel. Patching over such pitfalls as they emerge helps communities to avoid larger problems in the future.

Economically, opportunities for upward mobility represent a crucial incentive for newcomers to integrate themselves. Investment and professional advancement beyond ethnic businesses not only promote linkages with the host society but also help newcomers build foundations for their children. Some authors have concluded that these opportunities are unlikely to be extended by the host community and depend on the organization of immigrants to demand fair treatment. Even when the established business community does seek to incorporate newcomers, language and cultural barriers make it difficult to connect. In Greensboro, North Carolina, the Chamber of Commerce tried to recruit members of the immigrant community to participate in a diversity committee on small business issues. But wary of mainstream events like immigrant groups elsewhere, the Latino business owners in North Carolina demurred because they did not appreciate the chamber as a resource.

Whatever the level of integration, one pivotal task for new settlement areas is to ensure that newcomers are not disenfranchised. Low graduation rates among immigrant high school students reflect a failure of integration efforts to date, given the lack of student engagement. By limiting the number of bilingual role models in public schools, the trend also promotes a vicious cycle and increases the likelihood of greater challenges in the future. Initiatives such as the Dream Act, proposed by Senator Orrin Hatch of Utah to make higher education more accessible to immigrants, represent promising top-down responses to such challenges.

In the context of the "war on terror," warnings against disenfranchisement of newcomers have taken on new resonance. Detentions of foreign-born residents are a high-profile example of what many have called a widespread erosion of immigrants' civil liberties. Raids targeting undocumented workers at transportation hubs and other workplaces, for example, have elicited protests and heightened social tensions. Although most newcomers are not suspected of criminal intentions, federal officials have argued that immigrants without the proper documents could become victims of extortion by international terrorists. Perceptions of antagonism nevertheless might make newcomers more reluctant to embrace and participate in their new communities.

At the most basic level, a culture of exchange among newcomers and established communities depends on establishing a baseline level of trust. Ideally, newcomers would receive a thorough orientation to the social mores, laws, and legal systems of their new country. For better or worse, law enforcement authorities become one of the most visible points of contact, setting a tone for wider community relations in their interactions with immigrants. Too often, police lack the resources to communicate with non-English-speaking newcomers, who frequently distrust law enforcement because of experiences in their homelands. A focus on immigration status, rather than a holistic approach that also views newcomers as potential victims and witnesses, can further antagonize relations. In this sense, attempts by several states to give local officers the authority to arrest residents for lacking appropriate documentation set a troubling precedent.

For all the efforts by host communities to facilitate integration, newcomers take charge of their own lives in this country soon after their arrival. As they negotiate their own transition from newcomers to established residents, their success depends in part on the degree to which they coordinate their efforts with one another. Just as immigrants maximize their power vis-à-vis broader society by articulating common political and economic interests, they improve their own prospects in integration by asserting themselves with one voice. A united front is most crucial in states such as Utah where cultural or religious homogeneity marginalizes outsiders, but all newcomer communities benefit from coordinating the efforts of internal subgroups and advocates. Such efforts allow newcomer groups to pursue their objectives more effectively, improve communication with the host society, and create political space that will benefit future generations.

Index

acculturation, immigrant, 6, 7
African American(s), 63–64, 85n10,
114; in Georgia, 87, 88, 89, 91; in
North Carolina, 83; percent of total
population, *88;* population growth
of, 42
African immigrants and refugees, 100,
108n14; in Georgia, 87, 98, *99,* 100;
in Minnesota, 113, 114, 115, *116,*
118, 119, 120, 121, *121,* 124, 125,
126, 127, 130; in North Carolina, 58,
60, 63–65, 81, 83; in Virginia, 139,
142, 143, *143*
African Services Coalition, 60, 84n3
age characteristics: foreign born, 20,
34, *36–37,* 42; native born, 20, 34,
36–37
agriculture: immigrant worker recruitment by, 4; Latinization of, 138
Aid to Families with Dependent Children (AFDC), 119
Americas Award Reference and
Resource Library, 246
AmeriCorp, in Greensboro, NC, 14, 75,
81, 252
amnesty: 1986 immigrant worker, 4;
immigrant family reunions and, 4
Asian(s): percent of total population,
88; population growth of, 44–49,

45, 46; socioeconomic characteristics of, 20; total population of, 20
Asian immigrants: in Georgia, 14, 87,
89, 90; history of, 3; migration patterns of, 34; in Minnesota, 113, 114,
116, 120, 121, 126; in new destination states, 4; new settlement patterns of, 138; population growth of,
19, 40–41; population percentages
of, 24, 27, *28–29,* 29, *50–51,*
52–53; predominance of, 3–4, 137;
settlement patterns of, 3, 4; in suburban cities, 4; in Virginia, 142, 143,
143
assimilation, immigrant, 6, 7; measures
of, 10; theories of, 7–9. *See also*
immigrant integration
Atlanta, GA, 91–93; 1990s immigrant
population growth in, 87, *92,* 101,
102; African Americans in, 87, 88,
91; Africans in, 87; Asians in, 87,
89; blacks in, 87; case study of, 12,
14, 42, 87–109; Europeans in, 87;
homeownership and immigrants in,
272; immigrant integration in, 89,
256, 258; immigration in, 91, 101–3,
108n10; integration in, 89, 91; Latinos in, 14, 87, 89, 102, 272; law
enforcement and immigrants in,

285

266–67; migrant labor in, 102; population changes in, *92;* race in, 88, 91; undocumented immigrants in, 101–3, 109n17; whites in, 87, 88, 91
Atlanta Metropolitan Area (AMA), 87, 91, 107n2, 108n3; immigration in, 93, 95–96; population growth and changes in, 93, *94,* 95–96, 102; undocumented immigrants in, 101–3, 109n17

birthright citizenship, 278
Bosnian refugees: in Georgia, 98, *99,* 100; integration of, 15n11; in North Carolina, 68
Boston immigrants, 3
Bracero Program of 1942, 184, 185
Bridging the Gap (BTG) Project: crisis intervention and police program of, 267; mediation project of, 267; New American Services Program of, 266–67; youth program of, 267–68
Buddhist Temple of Greensboro, NC, 265
Bush, George W., 190
business. *See* industries

California: immigrant resettlement programs and, 5; immigrant worker recruitment by, 4; immigrant workers in, 4; immigration in, 3
Cambodians: in Georgia, 98, *99,* 100; in North Carolina, 65–66, 72
Canadian immigrants, in Minnesota, 113–14
Caribbean immigrants, naturalization rates of, 10
Catholic Social Services, in North Carolina, 69, 70
Catholics: in North Carolina, 265; in Utah, 184, 185, 186, 187, 196, 198, 199, 201, 202, 205, 263
Census Bureau, 19; forecasts of, 42
census data, 19, 20, *22–23, 24, 25–26, 28–29, 30, 31, 33, 36–37, 38–39, 41, 88,* 90, *92,* 108n3, *112, 115, 116,* 143, *143,* 145, *145,* 193, 246, 248

Central America, U.S. worker recruitment from, 4
Centro Civico Mexicano, 197
Chamblee, GA: case study of, 12, 14, 103–7, 109n18; ethnic businesses in, 104, 105, 107; immigrant economic integration in, 270–71; immigrant integration in, 102–7, 260–62, 281; Latinos in, 103, 104, 270–71; law enforcement in, 106–7; Southeast Asians in, 103, 270–71
Chapel Hill, NC, in NC Triangle, *59,* 59
Chavez, Cesar, 151, 263
Chicago immigrants, 3
Children's Defense Fund, 248
Civil Rights Act of 1964, Title VI of, 76, 249
commerce access, immigrant, 242, 268; benefits to mainstream society of, 268–69; in Chamblee, GA, 270–71; in Minneapolis, MN, 269–70
communities, ethnic, 255; political and economic role of, 256
community based organizations (CBOs), 255, 256
community development, ethnic, 255; cultural and social integration *vs.,* 256, 257, 258
community development, immigrant, 15, 42, 255, 281; bicultural integration in, 256; broad-based, 258–62; cultural heritage preservation in, 262–65; refugees and, 257; umbrella coalitions in, 257–58
Council of Great Cities Schools, 74
county-level demographic analysis, 44–49, *45, 46*
Cuban refugees, 62–63
cultural heritage preservation, immigrant, 262; Hmong, 264; Latino, 263; in North Carolina, 265; in Utah, 263

DeKalb County, GA, 93; demographics of, 96–97; immigrant integration in, 260–61; immigration in, 89, 96–97,

101, 108n15; population of, *94,* 108n9
Department of Health Resources and Services Administration, 251
Department of Homeland Security, 167, 197
destination states, new, 4, 19, 57
Displaced Persons Act of 1948, 118
Double Citizenship Program, 200
Dream Act of Utah, 74, 247, 282
dual nationality laws, 11
Durham, NC, *59, 59*

Eastern European immigrants and refugees, 3–4, 137; assimilation of, 10; in Georgia, 98, *99,* 100; in Minnesota, 118; in North Carolina, 68, 85n11
Eastern Europeans, in Georgia, 98, *99,* 100
Eastern seaboard immigration, 3
education characteristics: foreign born, 20, 35, 37, *38–39,* 246; native born, 20, 35, 37, *38–39,* 246
education, immigrant: GED and, 246; higher, 246, 247; mentorship and, 247; recredentialing and, 246
ELL. *See* English Language Learners
English as a Second Language (ESL), 156–61, 174n41, 243, 244, 245
English for Speakers of Other Languages (ESOL), 72, 73, 245
English language acquisition, 15, 72, 74, 156–58; difficulties of, 243; necessity of, 242–43
English Language Learners (ELL), 115, *116*
English-language abilities, immigrant, 20, 35, *36–37*
English-language training programs, adult, 242; alternative high schools and, 244–45; availability of, 244; components of, 245; family literacy, 245–46; public library-based, 245; public school-based, 244; quality of, 244; variety of, 244

ESOL. *See* English for Speakers of Other Languages
ethnic spiritual centers, 265
European immigrants, 3–4; in Atlanta, GA, 87; early, 137; Eastern, 3–4, 10, 68, 85n11, 98, *99,* 118, 137; history of, 3; in Minnesota, 112, *112,* 113, *116;* settlement patterns of, 3; Southern, 3–4, 10, 137; in Utah, 179, 180; in Virginia, 142, 143, *14*
European immigration, early 1900s, 7, 9

Fargo, ND, new immigrant communities in, 5
Faribault, MN: Africans in, 113, 125, 126, 127; Asians in, 113, 126; case study of, 12, 14, 42, 113; education in, *125;* food industry and immigrants in, 124–27; immigrant integration in, 127–30, 280; immigrant worker recruitment by, 4; Latinos in, 113, 125, 126; Southeast Asians in, 125, 127; whites in, 113, 127–28; xenophobia in, 14, 280
farming: economic changes in, 148; immigrant programs in, 270
Farming Incubator Program, 270
Favorable Alternative Sites Project (FASP), 65
Federal Housing Administration (FHA), 229
Federal Office of Civil Rights, 76
First National Bank and Trust Company, 215–18, 224–32, 234–36, 237
Florida, immigrant worker recruitment by, 4
foreign born: 1990s population growth, 20–23, *22–23, 24,* 40–41, 87; 1990s population percentage, *50–51, 52–53;* 2000 population by birth region, 24, 26, *50–51, 52–53;* 2000 population percentage, *25–26;* age characteristics, 20, 34, *36–37,* 42; education characteristics, 20, 35, 37, *38–39,* 246; gender characteristics,

20, 35, *36–37;* homeownership characteristics, 20, *38–39,* 39–40, 271; industry employment, 20, 40, *41;* labor force participation, 20, 37, *38–39,* 39; linguistic isolation, 20, 35, *36–37;* in Minnesota, 112, *112,* 113, 114, 120–21; poverty characteristics, 20, *38–39,* 40; settlement states population growth of, 19, 20–23; settlement states population percentage of, *25–26, 50–51, 52–53;* socioeconomic characteristics, 20, 34–35, *36–37, 37, 38–39,* 39–43, *41;* total population, 20, *22–23, 24, 50–51, 52–53;* in United States, 112, *112;* in Virginia, 142, 143, 143, 144, *144. See also* immigrants; native born
Frederick County, VA, 145; 1990s immigrant population growth in, 146; case study of, 140–52; employment in, 148, *149;* English language acquisition in, 156–58; farm workers in, 147–48; immigrant integration in, 152; industry and, 148, *149;* industry and immigrants in, 147–48; Latinos in, 146, 151
Frey, William, 19

gender characteristics, foreign born, 20, 35, *36–37*
General Equivalency Diploma (GED), 246
Georgetown, DE, 4
Georgetown University, 12–15
Georgia: 1990s immigrant population growth in, 89–90, 91, 101, 102; 2000 demographics of, 90–91; African Americans in, 89; Africans in, 98, *99,* 100; Asians in, 90; Eastern Europeans in, 98, 99, 100; health care and immigrants in, 247; immigrant integration in, 90; immigration in, 89, 90, 97–99, *99,* 100–103; Latinos in, 90, 102, 103, 104; mentorship programs in, 247; Middle Easterners in, 98, *99,* 100; as new settlement destination, 19; population changes in, 89–91; racial and ethnic composition of, *88;* refugees in, 97–101, *99,* 108n13, 108n15; Southeast Asians in, 98, *99,* 100, 103; undocumented immigrants in, 101–3, 109n16; urbanization in, 90; whites in, 89
globalization, 9
government: foreign worker recruitment by, 4, 57; immigrant resettlement programs by, 3–4, 5
government policies: immigrant integration and, 9, 10, 12, 20, 42, 43, 44, 69, 70, 128–30, 131, 195, 197–202, 273, 278; immigration and, 5, 15n11, 183, 184, 185
Greensboro Buddhist Center, 254
Greensboro, NC: Buddhist and Cambodian refugees in, 254, 265; case study of, 13–14, 42; education and immigrants in, 245; health care and immigrants in, 252, 254; immigrant integration in, 262, 282; Latinos in, 282; in NC Triad, 58–59, *59;* new immigrant communities in, 5
Guilford College, 262

H-2A guest workers, 146, 147, *147,* 148
"Harvest of Shame," 151
Hatch, Orrin, 187, 195, 247, 282
Head Start Act, 246
health care, immigrant, 15, 247: access enhancement programs to, 252–53; alternative modes of, 254; coverage of, 248, 249; cultural barriers to, 250, 254; international clinics and, 250–51; language barriers to, 249, 253, 254; Latinos and, 248, 249, 253, 254; public policy and, 248–50; specialized, 251–52; training providers for, 254–55
Healthy Families of Virginia, 251–52
Highpoint, NC: case study of, 42; in NC Triad, 58–59, *59*

Hispanic League of the Piedmont Triad (HLPT), 69
Hispanic Services Coalition, 70
Hispanics: Latino terminology *vs.*, 84n1, 171n1, 207n2. *See also* Latinos
Hmong refugees: cultural heritage preservation of, 264; government resettlement of, 5; in Minnesota, 114, 118, 119, 120, *121;* in North Carolina, 59, 66–67, 71
homeownership characteristics: foreign born, 20, *38–39,* 39–40, 271; native born, 20, *38–39,* 39–40, 271
homeownership, immigrant: access to, 271–72; in Atlanta, GA, 272; in Rogers, AK, 213, 224, 225, 229, 232–34, 235, 236, 237; in Salt Lake City, UT, 272
host communities, integration in, 5, 6, 10, 278, 283
host society, integration in, 9, 278, 279

illegal aliens: *vs.* legal aliens, 280. *See also* immigrants, undocumented
immigrant(s): community development and, 15; contributions of, 280–81; health care and, 15; legal status of, 280; media stereotypes of, 280; in north central states, 4, as perceived liabilities, 280; refugees *vs.*, 114, 118, *119,* 119, 279, 280; residence preferences of, 4; in south central states, 4; as temporary residents, 279; unions and, 4; vocational training and, 15. *See also* foreign born; *specific topics*
immigrant communities, new, 3, 4; 1986 amnesty and, 4; businesses and, 3, 4; case studies of, 12–15, 279; in Fargo, ND, 5; in Greensboro, NC, 5; integration in, 12, 278–79; in Lincoln, NE, 5. *See also* settlement areas, new
Immigrant Health ACCESS Project (IHAP), 252

immigrant integration, 3; in Atlanta, GA, 89, 256, 258; case studies of, 42, 279; challenges, 277–83; in Chamblee, GA, 102–7, 260–62, 281; in DeKalb County, GA, 260–61; economics and, 282; education and, 282; in Faribault, MN, 127–30, 280; in Frederick County, VA, 152; in Georgia, 90; global, 9, 11; government policies and, 9, 10, 12, 20, 42, 43, 44, 69, 70, 128–30, 131, 195, 197–202, 273, 278; in Greensboro, NC, 262, 282; in host communities, 5, 6, 10, 278, 283; in host society, 9, 278, 279; immigrant children and, 278; labor market and, 277–78; language barriers to, 282; Latino Connection and, 141, 150, 151, 169, 252, 253, 259–60; law enforcement and, 266–68; measures of, 9–12; mediating institutions and, 154; methodology of, 12–15; in Minnesota, 111, 113, 119, 124–33; in new immigrant communities, 12–15, 154; in North Carolina, 69–84, 256; in Park City, UT, 267–68; private sector and, 277; race and, 6, 8, 9, 11, 14, 277; religion and, 14, 64, 118, 264–65; in Rogers, AK, 213, 214, 215, 216, 221, 222; in Salt Lake City, UT, 191, *192,* 281; in Shenandoah Valley, 139, 142, 152, 279; spiritual centers and, 265; struggles for, 5, 6, 15, 127–31, 139; theories of, 7–9; umbrella coalitions and, 257; in United States, 127–32, 202; in Utah, 177–84, 186, 190–97, 200–204; "war on terror" and, 282; welfare policies and, 70, 128–29; in Winchester, VA, 139, 140, 152, 155, 156–71, 259–60
immigrant integration, promising practices for, 273, 281–82; commerce access as, 242, 268–71; community development as, 241, 242, 255–62; cultural heritage preservation as,

262–64; educational access as, 241, 242–47; English language training as, 241; funding of, 241; health care access as, 241, 242, 247–55; home-ownership access as, 271–72; law enforcement improvements as, 242, 265–68; religion and spirituality as, 264–65; vocational training as, 241, 246

immigrant networks, 6: worker recruitment through, 4

immigrant worker recruitment, 4, 218

immigrants, undocumented, 118; English acquisition and, 243; in Georgia, 101–3, 109n17; from Mexico, 185; in Minnesota, 129; negative perceptions of, 280; in North Carolina, 61; in United States, 199, 200; in Utah, 185, 193, 195, 197, 198, 199, 200, 202, 204; "war on terror" and, 282; in Winchester, VA, 167–68

immigration, 3, 4; in Atlanta, GA, 91, 101–3, 108n10; in Atlanta Metropolitan Area (AMA), 93, 95–96; costs of, 281; in DeKalb County, GA, 89, 96–97, 101, 108n15; European, 7, 9; in Georgia, 89, 90, 97–99, 99, 100–103; and government policies, 5, 15n11, 183, 184, 185; in Minnesota, 111–12, 119, 120, 124; in North Carolina Piedmont Triad, 58–60; public policy and, 5, 15n11; in rural towns, 4, 124–27

Immigration and Customs Enforcement. *See* Immigration and Naturalization Service

Immigration and Naturalization Service (INS), 61, 106, 107, 167, 193, 194, 199, 267, 268

Immigration Reform and Control Act (IRCA), 69, 168

Income Tax Identification Number, 77

industries: foreign worker recruitment by, 4, 57, 131; U.S. immigrant worker recruitment by, 4

industry employment: of foreign born, 20, 40, *41;* of native born, 20, 40, *41*

INS. *See* Immigration and Naturalization Service

integration. *See* immigrant integration

integration, cultural, 10

intermarriage, immigrant, 10

International Village Project, 261–62

Iraqi refugees, 15n11

Khmer Aid Group, 256

labor force participation: of foreign born, 20, 37, *38–39,* 39; of native born, 20, 37, *38–39,* 39

Laotian refugees: in Georgia, 98, *99,* 100; in Minnesota, 118, 120; in North Carolina, 66–67, 72

Latin American Association, 256, 272

Latino(s): cultural heritage preservation, 263; in Faribault, MN, 113, 125, 126; in Georgia, 90, 102, 103, 104; Hispanic terminology *vs.,* 84n1, 171n1, 207n2; percent of total population, *88;* population growth of, 40–41, 44–49, *45, 46;* in Shenandoah Valley, 150, 152; socioeconomic characteristics of, 20; in Southern cities, 4; total population of, 20; undocumented, 118; in Utah, 14, 177–87, 188, *188, 189,* 189–207, 190, *190,* 192, *192,* 193, 195, 196, 201, 207n2; in Virginia, 14, 140, 141, 142, 143, *143,* 145, *145,* 150–52, 155, 156, 162, 165–67, 169, 170

Latino Connection, 140; English language acquisition and, 156–58, 244; immigrant integration and, 141, 150, 151, 169, 252, 253, 259–60; mediating institutions and, 141, 155; origin, organization and operation of, 152–54

Latino immigrants: in Atlanta, GA, 14, 87, 89, 102; in Greensboro, NC, 13–14; history of, 3; in Minnesota,

113, 115, *116,* 117, 118, 121, 124, 131; naturalization rates of, 10; new settlement patterns of, 138; in North Carolina, 57, 59, 60–63, *61,* 69, 70, 72, 73, 80, 83; population growth of, 19, 40–41; population percentages of, 24, 27, *28–29,* 29, 30, *30, 50–51, 52–53;* predominance of, 3–4, 137; in Rocky Mountain states, 4; in Rogers, AK, 213, 214, 218, 221, 222, 224, 236; in rural areas, 4; settlement patterns of, 4

Latter-Day Saints (LDS), 178, 263

law enforcement: in Atlanta, GA, 266–67; in Chamblee, GA, 106–7; immigrant integration and, 242, 265–68; integration challenges for, 265–66, 267–68, 283; in Park City, UT, 267–68; in Rogers, AK, 222, 223, 224; in Utah, 192, 193, 194, 197, 198, 199, 200; in Winchester, VA, 165–67, 168

Lay Health Advisors (LHAs), 75, 252

Lay Health Promoters (Promotoras de Salud), 252–53

LDS. *See* Latter-Day Saints

legal permanent residents (LPRs), 63

Legally Authorized Workers and Special Agricultural Workers Programs, 168 69

LFS. *See* Lutheran Family Services

Limited English Proficient (LEP), 73, 74, 78, 190

Lincoln, NE, 5

linguistic isolation, foreign born, 20, 35, *36–37*

Los Angeles immigration, 3

Lutheran Family Services (LFS), 59–60, 65, 66, 67, 68, 69, 254

mediating institutions, 140, 154, 155: problems serving newcomers by, 141, 281

mediating structures, 140–41

Medicaid, 70, 248, 251

medical interpretation, 253

Mercado Central, 269

Metropolitan Atlanta Rapid Transit Authority (MARTA), 95, 101, 109n18

Mexican Consulate, 197, 200, 201, 202

Mexican immigrants: in Minnesota, 113–14, 117, 124, 131; in Utah, 179, 180, 182, 183, 184, 185, 186, 187, 188, *188,* 189, *189,* 198, 200, 201, 202

Mexico, 181; illegal immigrants from, 61, 63, 185; U.S. and, 179, 180, 184, 185; U.S. worker recruitment from, 4

Miami immigration, 3

Middle Eastern refugees, in Georgia, 98, *99,* 100

migrant farmworkers, plight of, 151

Migrant Head Start Program, 245

migrant labor: in Atlanta, GA, 102; in North Carolina, 61–62; in Shenandoah Valley, 150–51; in Virginia, 139–40, 146–48, 150–51; in Winchester, VA, 139, 140

migrants, economic, 118

migrants, primary, 114, 119

migrants, secondary, 32, 65, 72, 114, 119

migration, internal, 32–34, *33,* 41

migration, international, 32–34, *33,* 41

migration, secondary, 32–34

Minneapolis, MN: 1990s immigrant population growth in, *121,* 121; case study of, 42; Hmong refugees in, 270; immigrant economic integration in, 117, 269–70; Latinos in, 269, 270

Minnesota: 1990s immigrant population growth in, 113, 114, *115,* 115, *116,* 117; African immigrants and refugees in, 113, 114, 115, *116,* 118, 119, 120, 121, *121,* 124, 130; Asian immigrants in, 113, 114, *116,* 120, 121; Canadian immigrants in, 113–14; Eastern Europeans in, 118; economic factors in, 115, 117, 122,

123, 130–32; English Language
Learners in, *116;* European immigrants in, 112, *112,* 113, *116;* European-origin natives in, 124; foreign
born in, 112, *112,* 113, 114, 120–21;
health care and immigrants in,
254–55; Hmong refugees in, 114,
118, 119, 120, *121;* immigrant integration in, 111, 113, 119, 124–33;
immigrants *vs.* refugees in, 118, *119,*
119; immigration in, 111–12, 119,
120, 124; industry and immigrants
in, 121–23, *124,* 124–27, 131; Laotian refugees in, 118, 120; Latino
immigrants in, 113, 115, *116,* 117,
118, 121, 124, 131; Mexican immigrants in, 113–14, 117, 124, 131; as
new settlement destination, 19; non-
English speakers in, *122;* population
shifts within, *123,* 124; refugees in,
113, 114, 118, 119, *119,* 120; religious immigrant integration groups
in, 118; resettlement programs in,
118, 119; rural towns and immigrants in, 124–27; Russian refugees
in, 120, *121,* 121; Southeast Asians
in, 118, 120; undocumented immigrants in, 129; Vietnamese refugees
in, 118, 120, 124; whites in, 112,
112; xenophobia in, 128, 129, 130,
280
Montagnard Dega Association, 256,
262
Montagnards of North Carolina, 67–68,
71, 72, 78, 82, 262
Mormons, immigrants and, 14
Multicultural Advisory Council (MAC),
73
Murrow, Edward R., 151
mutual assistance associations (MAAs),
65, 255, 256

native born: 1990s population growth,
20, 40–41; 2000 census percentage,
25–26; age characteristics, 20, 34,
36–37; education characteristics,

20, 35, 37, *38–39,* 246; homeownership characteristics, 20, *38–39,* 39–
40, 271; industry employment, 20,
40, *41;* labor force participation, 20,
37, *38–39,* 39; poverty characteristics, 20, *38–39,* 40; socioeconomic
characteristics of, 20, 34–35, *36–37,*
37, 38–39, 39–43, *41;* total population, 20, *50–51, 52–53. See also* foreign born
naturalization: policy, 278; rates, 243
Neighborhood Development Center
(NDC), 269
Nevada, as new settlement destination,
19
New American Services Program
(NASP), 266–67
New England, immigrant worker
recruitment by, 4
New Immigrant Farm Program, 270
New York immigrants, 3
newcomer activism, 167–71
newcomers: established residents *vs.,*
279. *See also* immigrants
No Child Left Behind Act, 190
North Carolina: 1990s immigrant population growth in, 57; African immigrants and refugees in, 63–65, 81,
83; African slaves in, 58, 63; Bosnian refugees in, 68; causes of 1990s
immigrant influx in, 57; early immigrants to, 57–58, 62–63; Eastern
European refugees in, 68, 85n11;
illegal immigrants in, 61; immigrant
integration in, 69–84, 256; Latinos
in, 59, 60–63, 69, 70, 72, 73, 80, 83;
migrant labor in, 61–62; migrant
programs in, 62; as new settlement
destination, 19, 57; recent immigrants to, 58–60; religion and immigration in, 58, 64, 265; Southeast
Asian refugees in, 65–68, 71, 72, 80,
82; Soviet Union refugees in, 68;
undocumented immigrants in, 61
North Carolina Piedmont Triad, 84n2;
African immigrants and refugees in,

60, 64; case study of, 12, 42, 57–85; component cities of, 58–59, *59;* Hmong tribal peoples in, 59; Latino immigrants in, 59, 60–63, *61,* 70, 72, 73; migrant labor in, 62; recent immigration in, 58–60

North Carolina Triad immigrant integration: community relations and, 81–82; ethnic community and, 80–81; future prospects for, 82–84; health care and, 75–77, 85n15; labor market and, 71–72; legal systems and, 77–78, 85n16; public policy and, 69, 70; public schools and, 72–75, 85n12; religious groups and, 69–70, 78–80

North Carolina Triangle, 59

Office of Civil Rights, 73, 190
Office of Ethnic Affairs (OEA), 192, 193
Office of Hispanic Affairs (OHA), 193, 194, 201
Office of Refugee Resettlement (ORR), 4–5, 65, 119; community development and, 258, 266; education and, 245; immigrant heath care and, 255; sponsored conferences by, 15n11
"Operation Safe Travel," 197, 199

Park City, UT: case study of, 12, 42; health care and immigrants in, 254; immigrant integration in, 267–68; Latino immigrants in, 267–68; law enforcement and immigrants in, 267–68
Partners in Perinatal Care (PIPC), 251
People's Health Clinic (PHC), 254
Personal Responsibility and Work Opportunity Reconciliation Act of 1996 (PRWORA), 70, 248
Plaza de Sol, 270–71
population characteristics of immigrants, in new settlement states, 19
population growth: of 1990s native born, 20, 40–41; of 1990s United States immigrants, 115, *115;* of African Americans, 42; of Asian immigrants, 19, 40–41; of Asians, 44–49, *45, 46;* of Atlanta, GA immigrants, 87, *92,* 101, 102; in Atlanta Metropolitan Area, 93, *94,* 95–96, 102; of county level minorities, 44–49, *45, 46;* of Frederick County, VA immigrants, 146; of Georgia immigrants, 89–90, 91, 101, 102; of Latino immigrants, 19, 40–41; of Latinos, 40–41, 44–49, *45, 46;* of Minneapolis, MN immigrants, *121,* 121; of Minnesota immigrants, 113, 114, *115,* 115, *116,* 117; of North Carolina immigrants, 57; of Rogers, AK immigrants, 213, 214; of Shenandoah Valley immigrants, 145; of Utah immigrants, 187–97, *188, 189;* of Virginia immigrants, 142–45, *143, 144;* and whites, 19, 42; of Winchester, VA immigrants, 140, 145, *145,* 146
population growth, foreign born, 3, 42; in 1990s, 20–23, *22–23, 24,* 40–41, 87; in moderate-growth settlement states, 19, 20–23; in new settlement states, 19, 20–23; in traditional settlement states, 19, 20–23
population percentage(s): of African Americans, *88;* of Asians, *88;* of Latinos, *88;* of whites, *88*
population, total, *22–23;* of Asians, 20; forecasts for, 42; of foreign born, 20, *22–23, 24, 50–51, 52–53;* of Latinos, 20, *50–51, 52–53;* of native born, 20, *50–51, 52–53;* racial and ethnic composition of, *88*
poverty characteristics: foreign born, 20, *38–39,* 40; native born, 20, *38–39,* 40
processing companies, recruitment of immigrants by, 4
Project Respectism, 264
Promotoras de Salud (Lay Health Promoters), 252–53

race: in Atlanta, GA, 88, 91; immigrant integration and, 6, 8, 9, 11, 14, 277; in Utah, 192, 194

Raleigh, NC, *59, 59*

Refugee Act of 1980, 68, 97

Refugee Medical Assistance (RMA), 75

refugees: immigrants *vs.,* 114, 118, *119,* 119, 279, 280. *See also* immigrants; *specific topics*

refugee-service agencies and programs, 279; in Atlanta, GA, 258; in North Carolina, 59–60, 62–63, 65, 66, 67, 68, 75; religious, 59–60, 118; for women, 258

religious groups: immigrant integration and, 14, 64, 118, 264–65; refugee-service agencies and, 59–60

resettlement agencies and programs, 3–4, 59–60, 62–63, 64, 65, 101, 113, 118, 119

Rocky Mountain States, Latino immigrants in, 4

Rogers, AK: 1990s immigrant population growth in, 213, 214; banking and immigrants in, 215–18, 224–32, 234–36; economics and immigrants in, 213, 214; education and immigrants in, 221, 222, 236; homeownership and immigrants in, 213, 224, 225, 229, 232–34, 235, 236, 237; immigrant integration in, 213, 214, 215, 216, 221, 222; immigrant worker recruitment by, 4, 218; integration challenges in, 215, 219, 220, 221, 223, 224, 231, 236; language issues in, 214, 215, 220, 226, 227, 228, 231, 236; Latino immigrants in, 213, 214, 218, 221, 222, 224, 236; law enforcement and immigrants in, 222, 223, 224; poultry industry in, 214, 217, 218, 219, 226, 236, 237

rural areas: industry relocations to, 138; Latino immigrants in, 4, 138

rural towns: immigration in, 4, 124–27; as new settlement areas, 19, 124–27

Russian immigrants and refugees: in Minnesota, 120, *121,* 121; in Virginia, 142

Salt Lake City, UT: case study of, 12, 14, 42; education and immigrants in, 244, 245, 246; homeownership and immigrants in, 272; immigrant integration in, 191, *192,* 281; Latino activism in, 191, 192; Latino immigrants in, 14, 185, 191, 245; Latinos in, *192,* 281; religious barriers to immigration in, 14; whites in, *192*

seasonal farm workers, 146, 147, *147*

September 11, 2001 terrorist attacks: immigrants, refugees and, 119, 129, 130, 170, 178, 280, 282

settlement areas, new, 3, 4, 137–38; 1986 amnesty and, 4; agriculture and, 3, 4; case studies of, 12–15, 279; industries in, 138; integration challenges in, 282; internal *vs.* international migration in, 32–34, *33,* 41; processing companies and, 4; public policy and, 5, 42, 168; rural towns as, 19; small cities as, 19; suburbs as, 19. *See also* immigrant communities, new

settlement patterns: of Asians, 3, 4, 138; of European immigrants, 3; of Latinos, 4, 138; new immigrant, 137–38

settlement states, moderate-growth: 1990s immigrant population growth in, 19–23, *22–23, 24,* 40–41; Asian population in, *31,* 31–32; case studies of, 42; county-level demographic analysis of, 44–49, *45, 46;* internal *vs.* international migration in, 32–34, *33,* 41; Latino population in, 27, *28–29,* 29, 30; population percentage of foreign born in, *25–26, 50–51, 52–53;* socioeconomic characteristics of, 20, 34–35, *36–37, 37, 38–39,* 39–43, *41*

settlement states, new: 1990s immi-

grant population growth in, 19–23, 22–23, 24, 40–41, 42; Asian population in, 31, 31–32; case studies of, 12–15, 42; county-level demographic analysis of, 44–49, 45, 46; immigrant populations of, 19, 20; internal vs. international migration in, 32–34, 33, 41; Latino population in, 27, 28–29, 29, 30; population percentage of foreign born in, 25–26, 50–51, 52–53; socioeconomic characteristics of, 20, 34–35, 36–37, 37, 38–39, 39–43, 41
settlement states, traditional, 3, 4, 19; 1990s immigrant population growth in, 19–23, 22–23, 24, 40–41; Asian population in, 31, 31–32; internal vs. international migration in, 32–34, 33, 41; Latino population in, 27, 28–29, 29, 30; population percentage of foreign born in, 25–26, 50–51, 52–53; socioeconomic characteristics of, 20, 34–35, 36–37, 37, 38–39, 39–43, 41
Shenandoah University, 244
Shenandoah Valley: 1990s immigrant population growth in, 145; English language acquisition in, 156–58; farm workers in, 146–48, 147; immigrant health care in, 251–52, 253; immigrant integration in, 139, 142, 152, 279; industry and immigrants in, 146–48, 150–51; Latino Connection in, 150, 152; Latinos in, 150, 152; migrant workers in, 150–51; newcomers in, 139; poultry industry in, 148, 150
small towns, immigrant pressures on, 138–39
socioeconomic characteristics: of Asians, 20; of Latinos, 20
socioeconomic characteristics, foreign born, 20, 271; age as, 34, 36–37, 42; education as, 35, 37, 38–39; English-language ability as, 35, 36–37; gender as, 35, 36–37; home-

ownership as, 38–39, 39–40; industry employment as, 40, 41; labor force participation as, 37, 38–39, 39; linguistic isolation as, 35, 36–37; poverty as, 38–39, 40
socioeconomic characteristics, native born, 20, 271; age as, 34, 36–37; education as, 35, 37, 38–39; homeownership as, 38–39, 39–40; industry employment as, 40, 41; labor force participation as, 37, 38–39, 39; poverty as, 38–39, 40
Solórzano, Armando, 263
Somalian refugees, in Georgia, 64, 98, 99, 257
south central states, immigrants in, 4
Southeast Asians: in Chamblee, GA, 103; in Faribault, MN, 125, 127; in Georgia, 98, 99, 100, 103; in Minnesota, 118, 120; in North Carolina, 65–68
Southern cities, Latino immigrants in, 4
Southern European immigrants, 3–4, 137: assimilation of, 10
Soviet Union refugees, 120; in North Carolina, 68
Special Agricultural Workers (SAWs), 69
spiritual centers, immigration and, 265
St. Paul, MN: case study of, 42; economic integration in, 269; health care and immigrants in, 250, 253
State Children's Health Insurance Programs (SCHIP), 248
suburban cities, Asian immigrants in, 4
suburbs: immigration in, 4; as new settlement areas, 19
Sudanese "Lost Boys": government resettlement of, 5, 85n17; integration of, 15n11; in North Carolina, 64–65, 72, 78
Supplemental Security Income (SSI), 70

TAPESTRI, 257, 281
Teachers of English to Foreign Learners (TOEFL), 245

Temporary Assistance for Needy Families (TANF), 70, 119
Temporary Identification Number (ITIN), 193, 194
temporary protective status (TPS), 63
Test of English as a Foreign Language (TOEFL), 245
Texas immigrant workers, 4
transmigrants, 11
transnational communities, 10–11
transnational identities, 11
The Triad. *See* North Carolina Piedmont Triad
The Triangle. *See* North Carolina Triangle
21st Century Grant, 244

umbrella coalitions: gender-based, 257; immigrant integration and, 257; refugee women, 258
unions, immigrants and, 4
United States: 1990s immigrant population growth in, 115, *115;* Canadian immigrants in, 113–14; foreign born in, 112, *112;* immigrant integration in, 127–32, 202; immigrants *vs.* refugees in, 114, 118, *119,* 119; immigration agreements of, 185; lack of immigrant policies in, 273, 278; Mexican immigrants in, 113–14, 184–85; racial and ethnic composition of, *88;* resettlement programs in, 119; undocumented immigrants in, 199, 200
University of Minnesota: Farming Incubator Program of, 270; New Immigrant Farming Project of, 270
upper Midwest immigration, 3
urban factories, immigration in, 3
U.S. Department of Education, 190: ESL programs and, 243, 244
U.S. Department of Health and Human Services, 266
U.S. Department of Justice, 260; Community Oriented Policing Services of, 266

U.S. Labor Department, 183
Utah: 1990s immigrant population growth in, 187–97, *188, 189;* agriculture in, 183; Catholics in, 184, 185, 186, 187, 196, 198, 199, 201, 202, 205; cultural heritage preservation in, 263; economics and immigrants in, 178, 179, 182, 183, 184, 186, 187, 188, 189, *189, 190,* 195, 197, 198, 200, 204, 207; education in, 74, 189, *189,* 190, 191, 195, 247; European immigrants in, 179, 180; health care and immigrants in, 191; immigrant history of, 177–84, 202; immigrant integration in, 177–84, 186, 190–97, 200–204; industries in, 178, 180, 181, 182, 183, 184, 193, 195, 200; integration challenges in, 178–83, 185, 191–95, 197–204, 283; labor issues in, 178, 181, 182, 183, 184, 185, 188, 189, *189,* 197, 198, 199, 200; language barriers in, 192, 194, 195; Latino activism in, 191, 192, 194, 197, 198, 199, 200, 201, 204; Latino immigrants in, 14, 177–87, 188, *188, 189,* 189–207; Latinos in, 190, *190,* 192, 193, 195, 196, 201, 207n2; Latter-Day Saints church in, 178, 179, 180, 185, 186, 187, 196, 199, 201, 202, 203, 204, 206, 207; law enforcement and immigrants in, 192, 193, 194, 197, 198, 199, 200; Mexican immigrants in, 179, 180, 182, 183, 184, 185, 186, 187, 188, *188,* 189, *189,* 198, 200, 201, 202; mining industry in, 178, 180, 182, 183, 184, 185; Mormons in, 177, 178, 179, 180, 181, 183, 185, 186, 187, 196, 202, 203, 205, 206, 207; politics and religion in, 186, 187, 203, 204; public policy in, 190, 191, 193, 194, 195, 197, 199, 200, 201, 202, 207; race and, 192, 194; railroad industry in, 178, 180, 183, 185; religion and eco-

nomics in, 177, 178, 179, 180, 181, 183, 197, 198, 199, 205; religion and immigrants in, 177, 178, 179, 180, 181, 183, 184, 186, 195, 196, 199, 202, 203, 205, 206; September 11, 2001 impact on, 197–202; undocumented immigrants in, 185, 193, 195, 197, 198, 199, 200, 202, 204; U.S. government and, 179, 183, 184, 197, 198, 199, 200
Utah Task Force on Racial and Ethnic Fairness, 192

Valley Health System, 259–60
Vietnam War refugees, 98, *99,* 100, 118, 120
Vietnamese refugees: in Georgia, 98, *99,* 100; in Minnesota, 118, 120, 124; in North Carolina, 67–68, 71, 72, 80
Virginia: 1990s immigrant population growth in, 142–45, *143, 144;* African immigrants in, 142, 143, *143;* Asian immigrants in, 142, 143, *143;* attitudes towards immigrants in, 137; European immigrants in, 142, 143, *143;* foreign born in, 142, 143, *143,* 144, *144;* immigrant health care in, 251–52; Latino immigrants in, 142, 143, *143;* migrant workers in, 146–48, 150–51; Russian immigrants in, 142
vocational training, immigrant, 15, 246

Washington, immigrant worker recruitment by, 4
Washington, D.C., 145
welfare policies, immigrant integration and, 70, 128–29
western U.S. immigration, 3
whites: in Faribault, MN, 113, 127–28; in Georgia, 87, 88, 89, 91; in Minnesota, 112, *112;* percent of total population, *88;* population growth and, 19, 42; in Salt Lake City, UT, *192;* in Winchester, VA, 139
Winchester, VA: 1990s immigrant population growth in, 140, 145, *145,* 146; African Americans in, 139; case study of, 12, 14, 42, 139–71; economic challenges in, 168; education and immigrants in, 158–61, 168; employment in, 148, *149;* English language acquisition in, 156–61, *159,* 244; health care and immigrants in, 161–65, 168, 174n46, 249, 251, 252–53; immigrant growth in, 21; immigrant history of, 139; immigrant integration in, 139, 140, 152, 155, 156–71, 259–60; industry and immigrants in, 140, 142, 148, 151; industry in, 148, *149,* 151; integration challenges in, 139, 140, 141, 142, 167–71; language barriers in, 163–64, 166; Latino Connection and, 141, 142, 152, 155, 156, 157, 158, 161, 162, 163, 164, 165, 169, 170, 259–60; Latinos in, 14, 140, 141, 145, *145,* 151, 155, 156, 162, 165, 166, 167, 169, 170, 259–60; law enforcement and immigrants in, 165–67, 168; mediating institutions in, 140–42, 155; migrant laborers in, 139, 140; poultry industry in, 150; racial and ethnic relations in, 139–40; socio-demographic changes in, 140; undocumented immigrants in, 167–68; whites in, 139
Winston-Salem, NC: case study of, 42; in NC Triad, 58–59, *59*
Women, Infants and Children program (WIC), 70

xenophobia, in Minnesota, 128, 129, 130
Xiong, Tou Ger, 264

About the Contributors

Raleigh Bailey is the Director of the Center for New North Carolinians at the University of North Carolina, Greensboro (UNCG). He is also a Senior Research Scientist in the department of social work at UNCG. Dr. Bailey has over twenty years experience working with refugee and immigrant populations in the United States and abroad. He holds a Ph.D. in anthropology of religion from the Hartford Seminary Foundation and a master of divinity from the Boston University School of Theology.

Micah Bump is a Research Associate at the Institute for the Study of International Migration (ISIM) at Georgetown University. Since 2001 he has studied best practices for facilitating social, economic, and civic integration of immigrant newcomers in new settlement communities in the United States. He holds an M.A. in Latin American studies with a certificate in refugees and humanitarian emergencies from the Graduate School of Foreign Service at Georgetown University.

Katherine Fennelly is a Professor at the Hubert H. Humphrey Institute of Public Affairs at the University of Minnesota. Her research and outreach interests include leadership in the public sector, the human rights of immigrants and refugees in the United States, and the preparedness of communities and public institutions to adapt to demographic changes. She has been Dean of the University of Minnesota Extension Service, a faculty member and department head at the Pennsylvania State University, and a faculty member at Columbia University School of Public Health. She holds a certificate of studies from the University of Madrid, a master of philosophy, a master of health education, and a doctorate in adult education from Columbia University.

Elzbieta M. Gozdziak is the Director of Research at the Institute for the Study of International Migration (ISIM) at Georgetown University and Coeditor (with Charles B. Keely) of *International Migration*, a peer reviewed, scholarly journal devoted to research and policy analysis of contemporary issues affecting international migration. Dr. Gozdziak's recent publications include two edited volumes (with Dianna J. Shandy): *Rethinking Refuge and Migration*, published by the American Anthropological Association in 2000, and a thematic volume of the *Journal of Refugee Studies on Religion and Forced Migration*, published by Oxford University Press in 2002. She holds a Ph.D. in cultural anthropology from Adam Mickiewicz University in Poznan, Poland.

Art Hansen holds the position of Associate Professor of International Development and Social Change at Clark Atlanta University. His major research interests include participatory and community development, conflict resolution and management, forced migration and resettlement, post-war demobilization and reintegration, food security and famine, post-war social reconstruction, adult education and in-service training, and sustainable farming systems. He is a member of the Georgia State Advisory Council on Refugee Resettlement and is past president of the International Association for the Study of Forced Migration. He holds a Ph.D. in anthropology from Cornell University.

B. Lindsay Lowell is Director of Policy Studies at the Institute for the Study of International Migration at Georgetown University. Previously, he was Director of Research at the Pew Hispanic Center of the University of Southern California and the U.S. Commission on Immigration Reform, where he was also Assistant Director for the Mexico/U.S. Binational Study on Migration. He worked as a Labor Analyst at the U.S. Department of Labor, and has taught at Princeton University and the University of Texas, Austin. He recently coedited *Sending Money Home: Hispanic Remittances and Community Development*, and has published some 100 articles and reports on his research interests in the low- and high-skill labor force, integration, economic development, and policy. He received his Ph.D. in sociology as a Demographer from Brown University.

Michael Melia is a writer with the Associated Press. He has worked with the Associated Press in San Juan, Puerto Rico; Buenos Aires, Argentina; Raleigh, North Carolina; and New York, New York. He holds an M.A. in Latin American studies with a concentration in transnational influences and Latin American politics from the Graduate School of Foreign Service at Georgetown University.

Susan Martin serves as the Director of the Institute for the Study of International Migration in the School of Foreign Service at Georgetown University. Dr. Martin is also Director of the Certificate Program on Refugees and Humanitarian Emergencies and Adjunct Professor at the Georgetown University Law Center. Previously, Dr. Martin served as the Executive Director of the U.S. Commission on Immigration Reform, established by legislation to advise Congress and the President on U.S. immigration and refugee policy. She earned her doctorate in American Studies from the University of Pennsylvania. She is the Managing Editor of the *World Migration Report: 2000*, published by the United Nations and International Organization for Migration, and author of *Refugee Women* and numerous monographs and articles on immigration and refugee policy.

Silje Pettersen is a Demographer with Statistics Norway. She holds an M.A. in demography from Georgetown University. She also holds an M.A. in international policy studies with a focus on population and migration from the Monterey Institute of International Studies.

Andrew I. Schoenholtz is the Deputy Director of Georgetown University's Institute for the Study of International Migration (ISIM). He also co-directs the Certificate Program in Refugee and Humanitarian Emergencies, which is open to master's-level students at the University. Dr. Schoenholtz conducts studies on a range of international migration matters, including the causes and potential responses to population movements, immigration and refugee law and policy, comparative migration, the integration of immigrants into their host societies, and the effects of international migration on social relations, economics, demographics, foreign policy, and national security. Dr. Schoenholtz holds a J.D. from Harvard Law School and a Ph.D. from Brown University.

Armando Solórzano is an Associate Professor in the department of consumer and family studies at the University of Utah. His research interests include the Americanization of medicine in Latin America and more particularly in Mexico. Race relations and minority families constitute the second area of his interest. Although he studies the four traditional minority families in the United States (Mexican Americans, Afro-Americans, Native Americans, and Asian Americans) his scholarship concentrates on Chicano families. Currently he is engaged in a research project that looks at the process of family formation and ethnic identity of Mexican Americans in the state of Utah. He is a member of the National Association for Ethnic Studies, the National Association for Chicano Studies, and the Sigeriest Circle. He holds a Ph.D. in sociology from the University of Wisconsin, Madison.